The Yoga of Discipline

The Yoga of Discipline

Swami
Chidvilasananda

A Siddha Yoga Publication
Published by SYDA Foundation

From the standpoint of the spiritual path,
the term discipline is alive with the joyful expectancy
of divine fulfillment.

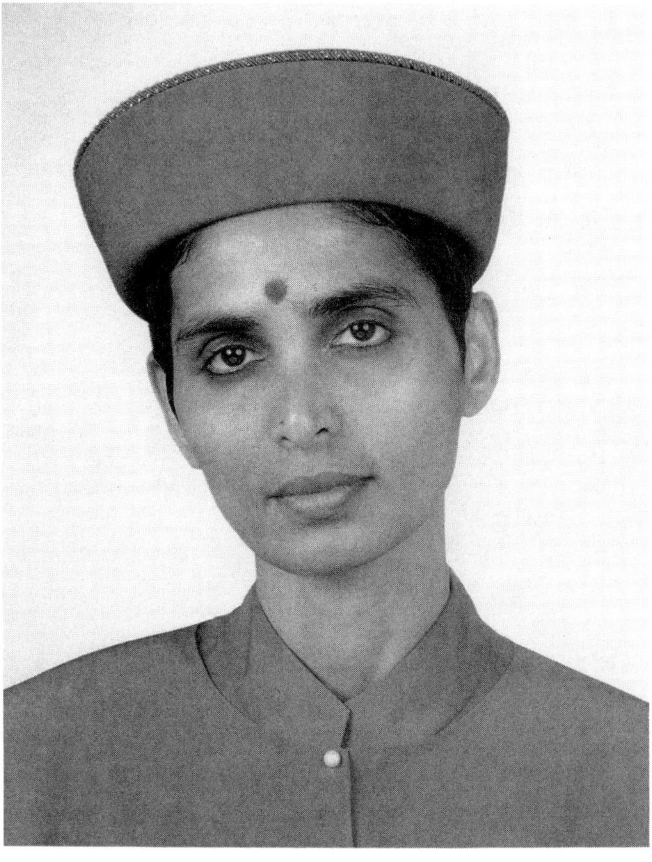

SWAMI CHIDVILASANANDA

Published by SYDA Foundation
371 Brickman Rd., South Fallsburg, New York 12779, USA

Acknowledgments

Many people helped prepare this book for publication. Invaluable editorial assistance was offered by Hemananda. Peggy Bendet was our energetic coordinating editor. Hans Turstig provided guidance with Sanskrit, Cheryl Crawford created the design, Diane Fast was the copy editor, and Stéphane Dehais the typesetter. Leesa Stanion compiled the index. Osnat Shurer, Sushila Traverse, and Valerie Sensabaugh oversaw production, and many others contributed their skills with willing hearts. We thank them all.

Sarah Scott and Jane Ferrar, editors

First published 1996
Printed in the United States of America
00 99 98 97 96 5 4 3 2 1

Permissions appear on page 205.

Library of Congress Cataloging-in-Publication Data
Chidvilasananda, Gurumayi.
The yoga of discipline / Swami Chidvilasananda.
p. cm.
Includes bibliographical references and index.
ISBN 0-911307-44-3 (pbk.)
1. Spiritual life—Hinduism. I. Title.
BL1237.36.C559 1996
294.5'44—dc20 96-19254
CIP

The paper used in this publication meets the minimum requirements of the American National Standard for Information Sciences — Permanence of Paper for Printed Library Materials, ANSI Z39.48-1984.

Contents

Introduction *ix*

I. The Sunrise of Supreme Bliss

1 The Foundation of Yoga 1

2 In Pursuit of a Great Goal 17

II. The Path of Discipline

3 The Road to Liberation 41

4 Teach Your Eyes How to See 51
Discipline in Seeing I

5 Who Is Looking Through Your Eyes? 63
Discipline in Seeing II

6 What Enters Your Ears Goes Straight to Your Heart 79
Discipline in Listening I

7 Hear Only What Is Worthwhile 95
Discipline in Listening II

8 Value Your Hunger 107
Discipline in Eating I

9 A Cause for Celebration 125
Discipline in Eating II

10 WITHIN THE WORD DWELLS THE RADIANT LORD 141
Discipline in Speaking

11 THE STATE OF SHIMMERING CONSCIOUSNESS 163
The Discipline of Silence

III. HOW DOES A TRUE SEEKER VIEW THE WORLD?

12 ACKNOWLEDGE YOUR OWN GOODNESS EVERY STEP OF THE WAY 181
Discipline in Thinking I

13 SWEEP THE PATH CLEAN EVERY DAY 193
Discipline in Thinking II

EPILOGUE 203

Note on Sources 205

Guide to Sanskrit Pronunciation 206

Notes 207

Glossary of Poets, Philosophers, and Sages 215

Glossary of Texts and Terms 219

Index 231

Introduction

"The truth is," says Siddha Master Swami Chidvilasananda, "you can cultivate anything you want in this body. You can let it go to waste, or you can use it as a vehicle that will carry you to God."

This teaching is the basis of the extraordinary series of talks that Gurumayi Chidvilasananda gave on discipline and the senses during the summer of 1995 at Shree Muktananda Ashram in New York State. She titled the series "The Yoga of Discipline," and I had the good fortune to hear one of these talks. It was about the discipline of eating. Listening to her words I suddenly realized that, while on one level Gurumayi was explaining how disciplining our sense of taste was beneficial for the body, she was at the same time describing a path by which our experience of the senses could become a vehicle for transformation. She said, "Discipline in eating fills you with spiritual radiance. The whole purpose of this, as of all yogic disciplines, is to know God, to become established in the awareness of God." How we use the senses, Gurumayi said, not only governs our experience of the world, but ultimately determines our experience of who we are.

As a neuroscientist, I found this view of the senses revolutionary. For nearly twenty years I have been doing research on sensory systems, and I also teach medical and graduate students about human sense perception. Although Western science has made enormous advances in understanding the mechanisms of sensory perception — from how the sense organs function to the processing of sensory information within the brain — this inner, transformative power of the senses has remained relatively unexplored. The traditional scientific view of the senses is that they are tools that enable us to navigate in the world. Our organs of perception provide us with a flow of information from which our brains select those elements that are relevant and necessary for us to live the life we choose.

Yet herein lies the crux of Gurumayi's message: to a degree unique among living creatures, we *choose* what our eyes will see, what our ears will hear, what our taste buds will taste, and so on. These acts of choice, of conscious discrimination, made every day and in the most ordinary of situations, are in fact precious opportunities for deepening our experience of ourselves.

Drawing on many of the classic texts of yoga, Gurumayi reveals the true marvel of the human senses: properly disciplined, they are gateways to the Divine. Quoting the poet-saint Kabir, she says, "Don't consider these senses of perception to be an obstacle. They are actually the means to know God, to know the Truth."

The foundation of this teaching is the Guru's extraordinary experience that every moment in time and every particle in the universe is full of sweetness — "divine sweetness," as Gurumayi describes it. To experience this sweetness, however, requires serenity; and to experience serenity, we need a quiet mind. The challenge, therefore, is to harness the senses so that, rather than intruding on the mind's serenity, they deepen it. By choosing a path of discrimination, in which we learn to distinguish between thoughts and actions that further ensnare us in the grip of the senses and those that liberate us, we cultivate inner freedom. Thus, the yoga of discipline is not about austerity for its own sake, nor is it a punishment for past wrongdoings. We discipline the senses, Gurumayi says, so that we can experience the sweetness of life and live fully in the awareness of God.

In 1842, the German physiologist Johannes Muller wrote, "The things we know are only the essences of our senses: of outer objects we only know their actions on us in terms of our own energies." This statement articulated two fundamental principles of sensory physiology that to this day remain central to the scientific understanding of perception. The first, almost axiomatic to the modern reader, is that the brain has no capacity to perceive the shape, sound, smell, or texture of outer objects independent of the information it receives from the sense organs. The second principle, even more profound in its implications, is that what Muller called the "energies" of the mind determine the content of sensory perception.

In the hundred and fifty years since Muller's work, sensory neurobiologists have made enormous progress in unraveling the mysteries of how the sense organs function. But the mind, as the yogis have told us for centuries, has a profound impact on what the senses perceive. In the words of the *Yoga Vāsishtha,* an ancient Indian scripture, "The world is as you see it." In other words, the content of perception is determined not only by the sense organs themselves but by the way their inputs to the brain interact with the field of consciousness, i.e., our state of mind. It is a common experience, for example, that if one is deathly afraid of being alone in the dark, then shadows, the creaking of a door, or the brush of a cobweb against one's face take on an emotional significance far beyond any real threat they pose. In other words, our inner state profoundly influences how we perceive the world.

Neuroscientists have identified numerous systems within the brain that mediate this interaction between perception and inner state. It is clear, for example, that areas of the brain that process sensory information are strongly interconnected with regions where we evaluate, either consciously or unconsciously, the emotional significance of events in our life. Given these linkages, we can begin to understand how our state of mind can actually delude our experience of life, as in the classic Vedantic story that Gurumayi tells about the man who mistook a piece of rope lying in the road for a poisonous snake. The man saw what he feared. It was as though his mind "retouched" the image his eyes saw so as to confirm his own expectation. Remarkably, recent studies have uncovered a neurologic mechanism that seems to correspond to this process. Investigations of the visual system indicate that certain cells in the cortex of the brain literally add information to or subtract information from what the eyes see, depending on internal biases imposed by the viewer.

Perhaps, then, when Gurumayi speaks of purifying the senses, we can understand this as a process of untangling sense perception from the needs and biases we have created through our past experience. In doing so, we remove the veil imposed on our senses and create the conditions for a more refined and subtle level of perception, a perception that is more accurate and truthful. And it is precisely this more subtle perception that the Guru encourages us to cultivate, because it is our gateway to the experience of the Divine. Properly refined, sharpened, and purified, the senses enable us to perceive not only the true glory of the world outside, but the light of Consciousness shimmering in our own heart as well.

Every action we perform provides an opportunity for this purification to take place. To take advantage of these opportunities, Gurumayi says, we need simply to take a moment before we act and ask, "What is my goal?" Before we take something to eat, we ask, "Why am I eating? Is it just to satisfy a craving, or to nourish my body in the best way possible?" Before we join in a gossipy conversation, we ask, "Is this really what I want my ears to hear?" Before turning on a violent movie, we ask, "Is this really what I want my eyes to see?" The instant we ask these questions, we short-circuit the impulsive attraction of the senses and establish ourselves in the perspective of our higher Self. This immediately attenuates the energy of our desires, allowing us to exercise judgment and control over them. In so doing, Gurumayi says, we continuously realign our actions with the will of God. We eat what is beneficial, not simply what seems good at the time. We choose to set aside some time in the evening for meditation, rather than simply filling our time with distractions until we fall asleep exhausted.

When we pursue this practice over time, we eventually move quite naturally from a reactive mode of living, driven principally by the activity of the senses, to a more reflective mode, in which we weigh our actions in the balance of higher goals we have set for ourselves. By refocusing just some of the energy of our desires onto the Self, we harness the power of the senses and use that energy to take us to a higher state. The inner freedom and sweetness we experience in that state provide the reinforcement we need to keep moving ahead.

When I first met Gurumayi in 1984, I had a tangible experience of what this higher state might be. I had gone to Shree Muktananda Ashram to attend a Siddha Yoga Meditation Intensive. At the time, I was doing my postdoctoral training in developmental neurobiology. The concept of meditation intrigued me — I'd even tried it on my own for a while when I was in college — but nothing had ever come of it. During the first day of the Intensive with Gurumayi, I found myself in a deep meditation, something I had never experienced before. For the first time in my life, I lost awareness of external sensations and became absorbed in an inner state of peace and calm. Later that evening, after the program had ended, I began to feel an energy rising up inside me, subtle at first,

SWAMI MUKTANANDA

then stronger and stronger. I didn't know what it was or where it was coming from, but I did sense that something important was about to happen.

That night, I was awakened from my sleep by an enormous jolt of energy shooting up my back, from the base of my spine to the top of my head. When it reached the top, this energy exploded with a loud "bang" and I saw a brilliant flash of light. This light, more beautiful than anything I had ever seen before, filled my body. I was consumed by an indescribable ecstasy, and waves of love flooded up inside of me. I no longer had any sense of individual existence. I felt as though I had entered the heart of God. And yet, in that very moment, I felt more "myself" than ever before.

The next day I learned that I had had a classic experience of *shaktipāt* initiation, the awakening of the inner spiritual energy, or *kundalinī*, that takes place through the grace of the Siddha Master. The yogic scriptures speak of two aspects of this energy: one that makes the outer senses function, and another that lies dormant until awakened, revealing the Consciousness hidden within our own being. *Shaktipāt*, which means "descent of grace," is the transmission of energy from Guru to disciple that makes this inner perception possible.

With *shaktipāt*, Gurumayi gave me the direct experience that right here and now, in this very body, it is possible to transcend ordinary perception and to experience a state of ecstatic freedom. That awakening opened a new dimension in my awareness, a dimension that has remained open ever since, allowing me to dive deeper and deeper inside, and enabling me to touch the source of love in my own heart.

The initiation given by a Siddha Guru connects us with a lineage of meditation Masters that stretches back to earliest times. Throughout history, such enlightened beings have lived in the world with one purpose: to awaken seekers to their own experience of the light of God. Gurumayi is the head of the Siddha Yoga lineage of meditation Masters. She received the full wisdom and power of this lineage from her own Guru, Swami Muktananda. It was Swami Muktananda, or Baba, who first drew together the teachings of the Siddhas in a path he called Siddha Yoga. Baba brought this path to the West in the early 1970s and bestowed *shaktipāt* initiation on thousands of seekers around the world. Everywhere he went, he taught the same message: "Meditate on your own Self. Worship your own Self. Your God dwells within you as you." Baba described this as his own experience, gained through the grace of his Guru, Bhagawan Nityananda, and a lifetime of spiritual practice. This is the work of Siddha Gurus: to uplift seekers and make real the true potential of human birth — the inner experience of God.

In *The Yoga of Discipline*, Gurumayi reveals a new dimension in the understanding of human perception: the dimension of inner freedom. Although the ultimate goal of this path is the transcendent experience of Reality, the keys to achieving that experience lie in the immanent capabilities of the human mind — in our ability to focus our attention inside, to discipline the activities of our senses, and to discriminate between what is merely pleasurable and what is beneficial. The teachings contained in *The Yoga of Discipline* build on a theme Gurumayi introduced at the Siddha Yoga New Year's Intensive for 1995. At the heart of the universe, Gurumayi said, lies supreme bliss, and to live in the experience of this bliss is the highest expression of human nature. Two of the talks that Gurumayi gave at that Intensive form Part One of this volume. By drawing our focus to the ultimate goal of spiritual practice, these talks naturally set the stage for Parts Two and Three, which describe discipline as the means to discover the same supreme bliss at the heart of our own lives.

The inestimable value of *The Yoga of Discipline* is that it destroys the illusion that life in the world is an obstacle to

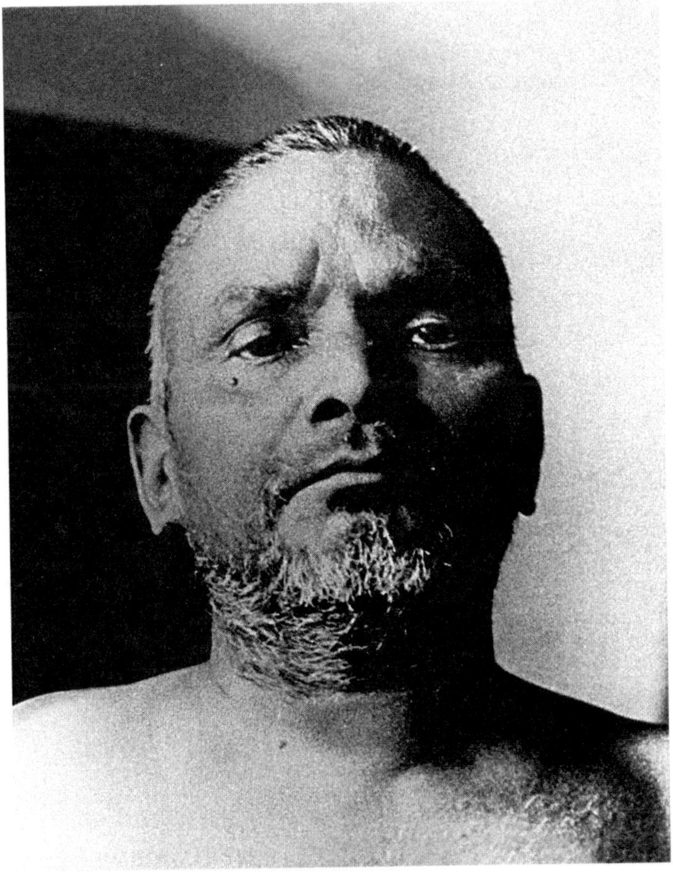

BHAGAWAN NITYANANDA

progress on the spiritual path and explicitly reveals how we can transform our thoughts and actions into sadhana, spiritual practice. Gurumayi defines a set of principles that each of us can apply in our daily lives, regardless of our background, or whether or not we have ever practiced any kind of yoga before. Through my own experience of reading and rereading these talks, I feel that I have begun to see with new eyes, to hear with new understanding, and to taste the sweetness of life more deeply than ever before. I urge you to treat this book as scripture, that is, as a work written on many levels and rich in both deep philosophic truths and practical guidance for daily life. These are words to digest carefully and with each successive reading new layers of meaning will be revealed.

May the wisdom of these profound teachings inspire and guide us, and may the grace of the Siddha Yoga lineage enable us all to live fully in the light of God.

David M. Katz

David M. Katz, Ph.D., is an associate professor of neurosciences at Case Western Reserve University School of Medicine in Cleveland, Ohio. He received his doctorate in neurobiology from the State University of New York at Stony Brook in 1981 and did postdoctoral training at Cornell University Medical College in New York City and the College de France *in Paris.*

1. The Sunrise of Supreme Bliss

The sunrise of supreme bliss shimmers
in every particle of the universe,
so why not drink a fresh cup of joy every day
and become inspired with new perception?
Remember, love and respect
must be renewed with each dawn.[1]

Note on Sanskrit Terms

For the convenience of the reader, Sanskrit and Hindi terms frequently used in Siddha Yoga courses and literature are presented in the same typeface as the rest of the text. Less familiar terms appear in italics with diacritical marks on the long vowels. In the glossary, as an aid to pronunciation, *all* Sanskrit terms are presented in the international standard system of transliteration. In addition, the Sanskrit scriptural passages quoted by Gurumayi appear in the Notes, also transliterated in the international standard system. Accompanying the Notes is a pronunciation guide.

Chapter One

The Foundation of Yoga

With great respect, with great love, I welcome you all with all my heart.

This morning at dawn the sky was breathtaking. Three brilliant, crimson stripes had painted themselves very neatly across the entire length of the deep blue eastern sky. They were shimmering with supreme bliss, reflecting the three stripes of sacred ash that yogis apply on their foreheads. This amazing sight has been occurring for the last few mornings. For yogis, these three stripes symbolize the three *gunas*, the three qualities of life, which they seek to transcend for the sake of attaining their own divine joy. It seems that the rising sun must have known the title of this Intensive, and therefore it was expressing itself across the sky in a very visible form.

The *Taittirīya Upanishad*, an ancient scripture of India, offers a beautiful viewpoint from which to see the sunrise of supreme bliss. It says:

> Brahman, the absolute Reality, is bliss.
> All these beings are indeed born from bliss;
> being born they live by bliss,
> and after death, they enter into bliss. [3.6.1] [1]

Baba Muktananda, who was the embodiment of bliss, elaborates on this verse. He says, "All beings are playing in this supreme bliss; they are born of it, and at the end, they merge into it. So bliss is at the beginning, in the middle, as well as at the end. But we don't get the sense of it. We don't have the knack of how to open ourselves so that we can experience that joy. You praise other people by saying, 'Oh, that person is so great, that person is such a high being.' But you do not praise your own Self that way. You do not have the confidence that inside you there is the great Self. We should have the greatest self-confidence."[2]

Confidence is a delicate term. It is one of those qualities that cannot be understood without humility. The right amount of the right kind of confidence strengthens you. You move forward in your endeavors; you are not afraid to develop your abilities. It brings you good fortune, as a magnet draws metal. But overconfidence weakens you; it makes you a laughingstock. You lose sight of your goal. You even lose touch with reality. That is not what Baba is talking about. He is referring to *ātma vishvāsa*, the confidence that arises from your true Self, from your trust in the supreme Power within, from your firm belief in God's creation. It is a refined sort of confidence, inspired by the higher intellect and rooted in Truth. This is *ātma vishvāsa*, true self-confidence. This confidence enables a person to see the glory of God in the universe.

The *Katha Upanishad* speaks from the fullness of this vision. Its purpose, like its tone, is very practical—to guide seekers to that glory. It says:

> First, accept that the Self exists, and accept
>   that it can be known.
> Then its real nature is open to experience. [2.3.12][3]

This is the foundation of yoga. First, you must have confidence in the fact that the supreme Self is within you. Not only is it always present—it is accessible. It can be known. Those who seek it can find it. Those who want to know it can know it. Those who truly long to see it can see it. Only then, when this absolute acceptance of the reality of the Self takes hold, is the real nature of the Self open to experience.

This is a great invitation. This is what true self-confidence means—having firm belief in the existence of the Self. When you have this self-confidence, it paves the way on the spiritual path. It is the first real step you take. You begin the search with complete faith in the possibility of finding the Self within, in knowing the Truth. That self-assurance must be there. You need a strong heart to walk the path, and your determination walks before you. Your self-confidence is not buried somewhere; it is not a memory from the past. It is right there with you, in front of you, supporting you all the way.

What would be the point of living without the experience of the Self?

Where would be the mystery and the joy if the great Self were not part and parcel of everything that happens?

What value would a human birth have if you were never to perceive the inner Self, resplendent as a jewel, within you?

What would your inner state be if you thought that life promised only suffering?

Why would you ever bother to serve another if you weren't convinced that it would generate joy, love, and peace for both giver and receiver alike? Many people say that they serve for the sake of service, that they are not actually looking for any reward. Still, they have the conviction that serving will somehow make them happy, will bring them merit; that by serving others, they will experience peace of mind and tranquility.

Finally, how could you tolerate the burden of physical existence, like the pull of gravity, constantly weighing you down with negative tendencies, if you weren't aware of the kingdom of God within you? How could you bear it if you didn't know what truly exists within?

The other day I ate half a banana and put the rest on the table. A few minutes later, I noticed that the skin of the part that had been removed was already dry and brown. When I realized what had happened, I was filled with gratitude and astonishment, and also a sense of how ephemeral existence is. Oxidation and decomposition set in so quickly! It is only the living core that gives meaning and radiance to the outer layer. As soon as that living core is gone, the husk dries out and breaks down into its basic elements.

Baba loved to point out that it is the light of the Self that makes you look beautiful, that gives you the power to move and speak. Once the light of the Self leaves this physical body, that's it. No one even wants to look at you anymore. Out of courtesy and tradition, they may come to view the dead body, but not with any great joy. And then, how long do they keep your body around?

The message of the banana skin reflects the teaching of Indian philosophy that the human body is enlivened only by the spirit within. It becomes lifeless when the spirit leaves. Therefore, use this body well.

The *Shiva Samhitā*, one of the scriptures of hatha yoga, also speaks of this, saying:

> When this body, obtained through destiny, is made the means of attaining divine bliss, only then does it cease to be a burden and become fruitful—not otherwise. [2.41] [4]

The supreme attainment of human life is divine bliss. Divine bliss is the nature of the Self. Have you ever wondered why you were born? The sages have an answer for this. They say it is your destiny. You have earned this human birth. It is the fruit of your hard work. In the past, you performed so many good actions, you accumulated so much merit that you have been given a human body, and with it, the chance to know the supreme Self. Not only a human birth but a sublime gift along with it: the power to know the Self. Now it is up to you; you must put your body to good use.

This human body is equipped with the incredible ability

to open doors to the subtler realms. Just as gold is found in a gold mine and lotuses in a pond, just as pine cones are found on a pine tree, wisdom on the tongue of a scholar, creativity in the hands of a painter, innocent laughter in a child, lightning in rain clouds, steam in hot water, and tenderness in a generous heart, in the same way, the great Self can be found in this human body. It does exist; and its nature, which is bliss, can be experienced.

And do you know what the best part is? This experience does not have to be a one-time thing. It can become an unfading source of inspiration, bringing forth ever-new and ever-fresh experiences. The bliss of the Self is inexhaustible. It is unlike anything else. A gold mine can run dry. The more gold you take out, the less remains—until all that's left is dirt and rock. But when you tap into the bliss of your own inner Self, the more you experience, the more emerges.

This amazing promise transforms a seeker's attitude toward his body. He no longer sees it as a burden, but as his greatest asset, the vehicle that sustains the inner journey. The body is a wonderful friend.

The *Katha Upanishad* goes on to say that the Self is not to be sought through the senses.

> The Self, the self-existent One, pierced the openings of the senses outward; therefore, a man looks out and not in. But a certain wise man, in search of immortality, turned his gaze inward and saw the Self. [2.1.1] [5]

Turning within is called yoga. Yoga is the divine discipline that gives a seeker the power to turn his attention within. It makes him understand the true purpose of the senses. It uncovers the glory hidden within him. It enables him to go deep into the cave of his own heart. It shows him the way to unite heaven and earth. Yoga gives a seeker the strength to uplift his energies and become mature.

In the *Bhagavad Gītā*, Lord Krishna gives a profound exposition on yoga. He imparts this knowledge to Arjuna, the greatest of warriors, at a moment when Arjuna has become weak in his dharma, his sacred duty. Lord Krishna renews Arjuna's spirit, elevates his understanding, and fills him with energy and strength by imparting to him the understanding of yoga. This wisdom, accompanied by the grace of Lord Krishna, his Guru, finally sets Arjuna free. This story of sadhana, this dialogue between Guru and disciple, is the *Bhagavad Gītā.*

All eighteen chapters of this sublime text are imbued with extraordinary luster. Just as you never get tired of hearing the song of a nightingale, and you never cease to be amazed by the sight of the Milky Way, just as the thought of the earth revolving in space always fills you with wonder, so has the incredible *Bhagavad Gītā* captivated its readers throughout the ages and made them ponder. Commentators, poets, and yogis all drink from its life-giving waters.

Chapter Six is especially relevant to a student of yoga. In this chapter, the Lord is determined to destroy Arjuna's ignorance and arm him with the right understanding of dharma. He gives Arjuna the highest teachings about his own nature. He speaks with tremendous eloquence about the necessity of realizing the immortal Self.

The great saint Jnaneshwar Maharaj's commentary on the *Bhagavad Gītā* is like adding fragrance to jewels. Imagine if diamonds, in addition to their brilliance, had their own distinctive aroma. That is what the commentary of Jnaneshwar Maharaj is like.

Jnaneshwar Maharaj describes how confounded Arjuna is by Lord Krishna's words. Arjuna says:

> O Lord, these signs of saintliness are not found in me.
>
> Moreover, if I were judged by such a standard, I would undoubtedly fall far short of it. But by hearing Your teaching, I may become great.

> I don't understand what You say, but hearing it, I revere it in my heart. What sublime qualities does a person need to attain this?
>
> May they also be in me! Will You, in Your great saintliness, make me Yours? Then Lord Krishna smiled and said, Why shouldn't I? I will do it. [6.139-40, 142-43]

Next, Jnaneshwar Maharaj gives a glimpse into what lies behind Lord Krishna's response. He says:

> Now listen to me. When Arjuna asked the Lord to make him one with the Absolute, the Lord listened to him attentively.
>
> He realized the great longing in Arjuna's heart, and He knew that the seed of dispassion had entered the womb of reason.
>
> Although the days of fulfillment had not yet arrived, still with the fullness of the spring of dispassion, the flower of union with God was ready to burst forth.
>
> Once this path is perceived, hunger and thirst are forgotten. Traveling on it, there is no awareness of night or day.
>
> Wherever the pilgrim sets his foot, a storehouse of eternal bliss opens before him. Even if he goes astray, he ultimately attains heavenly bliss. [6.147-49, 157-58]

This verse is so reassuring—"even if he goes astray, he ultimately attains heavenly bliss."

Chapter Six speaks about the yoga of meditation, the divine discipline. What kinds of images does your mind conjure up when you hear the word *discipline*? Something dry, severe, or austere? Something unnatural that goes against the grain? Something that always feels like swimming upstream? But this yoga isn't like that.

Let me tell you what is so astounding, exciting, gripping, intriguing, and inviting about yoga. Jnaneshwar Maharaj reveals it in his commentary on Chapter Six, where he describes what happens when the yogi arrives in the realm of the supreme Self. He says that a yogi "is heir to the land of the highest bliss" and that "the mind is seated on the throne of supreme bliss." He says that the bliss is "indescribable, immeasurable, and unceasing." He speaks of "the festival of supreme bliss" and "the harvest of all happiness." And he says "this bliss of yoga is within one's own Self."

This is the goal to keep in focus. This bliss is what you look forward to. When you hear the statement "The sunrise of supreme bliss shimmers in every particle of the universe," it is no exaggeration. It is completely true. It is the Truth. This reality must become your daily experience. Otherwise, you are in the same situation as the unlucky person who picks alcohol over spring water, and then wonders why he can never quench his thirst. No wonder the poet-saint Tukaram Maharaj said:

> When a yogi describes his experience of inner bliss,
> people are awestruck and wonder if this strange
> experience could be true.

Long ago there was a disciple, and when people talked about him, they said he had gone mad in his efforts to know God. When the disciple told his Master what people were saying, the Master answered with this story. Once a family gave a wedding festival in their house. The musicians sat in a corner and played their instruments, the guests danced to the music and were merry, and the house was filled with joy.

But a deaf man passed outside the house. He looked in through the window and saw people whirling about the rooms, leaping, and throwing up their arms.

"See how they fling themselves about!" he cried. "This house is full of lunatics!" For he could not hear the music to which they danced.

In Chapter Six of the *Bhagavad Gītā*, Lord Krishna discloses the mystical steps that lead to supreme bliss. By following the teachings of this chapter, the immortal fruit of the Self will become available to you.

First, it is a good idea to become clear about happiness. In the scriptures, several words are used interchangeably: *delight, bliss, happiness, joy, ecstasy*. But people tend to misconstrue their significance. Since almost all forms of enjoyment arise from the contact of the senses with their objects, people relate to happiness and bliss in these terms. And that creates a bit of a headache when it comes to understanding yoga. In yoga, one must go beyond the boundary of what is perceptible and pleasurable to the senses.

In Chapter Eighteen of the *Bhagavad Gītā*, Lord Krishna elucidates the three kinds of happiness. He scrutinizes happiness in the light of the *gunas*, the three strands that make up the rope of material existence. They are *sattva*, purity or light; *rajas*, activity or passion; and *tamas*, darkness or impurity. These qualities compose the entire world, and they color one's happiness too.

Describing the happiness associated with *tamoguna*, the dark quality, Lord Krishna says:

> That happiness which, both in the beginning and
> afterward, deludes the self,
> arising from sleep, indolence, and negligence,
> is declared to be tamasic. [18.39] [6]

Tamasic happiness is the darkest form of happiness. Its source is impure. As Kali Yuga, this iron age of darkness, continues, this sort of happiness becomes more and more prevalent. Under the influence of *tamoguna*, people are driven to eat unnatural food instead of finding happiness in fresh food. They prefer to eat things that invite incurable ailments and lead to bodily decay.

Rather than finding happiness in respecting and loving their elders, they take pleasure in insulting them. Tamasic happiness thrives on sarcasm, scandal, murder, bad-mouthing, smearing other people's reputations, provoking them, and destroying their good work. Tamasic happiness is born out of delusion, and therefore, its only source of joy is devastation, catastrophe. Then tamasic happiness rejoices. Fiasco—tamasic happiness is in love with it! Inflicting pain and suffering, garbling the truth, gloating over the troubles and failures of others—all this is tamasic happiness. It is a wretched happiness. It is the lowest brand of pleasure and sensationalism, and a perverse, twisted version of reality. Leading others astray, denying the existence of God, hiding from the light, and befriending the destructive and the deluded—these are all sources of tamasic happiness, the dark quality. Really dark, pitch-black.

Once, in a good-sized town, there were two merchants who were fierce competitors. Their stores were across the street from each other. The sole method by which each man determined the success of his business was not daily profit, but how much more business he had than his competitor.

If a customer made a purchase at the store of one merchant, he would taunt his competitor when the sale was complete. The rivalry grew with each succeeding year.

One day God sent an angel to one of the merchants with an offer: "The Lord God has chosen to give you a great gift. Whatever you desire, you shall receive. Ask for riches, long life, or healthy children, and the wish is yours. However, there is one stipulation," the angel cautioned. "Whatever you receive, your competitor will get twice as much. If you ask for a thousand gold coins, he will receive two thousand. If you become famous, he will become twice as famous." The angel smiled.

The merchant thought for a moment. "You will give me anything I request?"

The angel nodded.

The man's face darkened. "I ask that you strike me blind in one eye."

That is tamasic happiness, happiness derived from the darkest actions. Its source is impure and it is ruled by delusion.

Jnaneshwar Maharaj said this about tamasic happiness:

> O Arjuna, this kind of happiness is truly tamasic, of the nature of darkness. I won't say much about it, for it can hardly be experienced as happiness. [18.806]

That is his entire commentary, and it's well put.

The second kind of happiness of which Lord Krishna speaks is colored by *rajoguna*, the quality of passion and activity. He says:

> That which, through the contact of the senses with
> their objects,
> is like nectar in the beginning,
> and like poison at the end;
> that happiness is said to be rajasic. [18.38] [7]

dependent on outside pleasures

Most people in this world are used to rajasic happiness. In fact, it is the only kind of happiness most people are exposed to. When the subject of happiness comes up, this is what they think of. Rajasic happiness sounds wonderful in the beginning. The net results, however, are not so rewarding. This is the sort of happiness that fades quickly or spoils somehow. Because of it, a person becomes disillusioned. He expects every joy to end in sorrow, and laughter to end in weeping. When happiness is filtered by the quality of *rajas*—activity, attachment, passion—then sorrow is almost inevitable.

For example, a mother is so happy when she sees her newborn baby. But if for some reason the baby dies, she is thrown into the abyss of sadness. This is *rajoguna*, attachment.

Or, there is the college student who is delighted when he graduates with honors, and then crushed when he can't get a job. The economy is bad, no door is open. All his hopes are shattered.

There are many more examples. For instance, even after cultivating a field carefully, taking every proper measure, a farmer ends up with a bad crop, for no reason at all.

Happiness born out of *rajoguna*—in the beginning, nice, but later, not so pleasant.

A man discovers that his fiancée has eloped with someone else.

A newly built house goes up in flames.

Plans that were made with great care to re-establish an old tradition turn out to be futile, and the tradition dies.

The fine knowledge and skills that have been passed down though a family of craftsmen for generations are forgotten and gone forever.

Long hours of meditation don't seem to live up to expectations. You don't hear sounds; you don't see lights.

Many years of being a nice person don't seem to pay off.

So people begin to doubt the existence of happiness. "Is there any happiness in this world?" When they hear the scriptures talking about joy, love, delight, happiness, bliss, ecstasy, and peace, they react cynically. And, more often than not, they tell you about all the suffering in this world.

Years ago when Baba was in Boston, some Carmelite monks came to meet him. They were having a very nice conversation until the monks got around to the subject of suffering. Baba responded by talking about bliss and ecstasy. The monks thought Baba had not understood them, so they talked more and more about suffering. They got deeper into the subject as if they were trying to convince Baba of the rightness of their view of the world. And of course, the more they talked about suffering, the more Baba talked about bliss.

Finally, they said, "Baba, it seems to us that you are callous about people's pain. You simply don't pay enough attention to it."

Without any hesitation, Baba said, "It seems to me that you are callous about God's joy, and you don't pay enough attention to that."

The monks were speechless—which allowed Baba to go on and get his message across. He said, "Suffering is ordinary; it is *sāmānya*. What we have to do is tell people about bliss. Just because suffering exists, you don't have to elevate it by putting on a robe of suffering. Put on a robe of joy so you can uplift others."

As the monks were leaving, they shook hands with Baba and embraced him. They told him they thought the meeting was very fruitful and there was much for them to contemplate. Then they left—full of happiness. As an Italian saint put it:

> Leave sadness to those in the world.
> We who work for God should be lighthearted.

In the *Bhagavad Gītā*, Lord Krishna states very clearly that rajasic happiness comes from "the contact of the senses with their objects." Of course, in the beginning, it feels like real happiness. However, as long as it is conditional, and dependent on outside objects that give pleasure to the senses, then it does lead to disappointment or disillusionment. And inevitably, it will come to an end. Indulging your senses can never bring you to the ultimate happiness. In the words of Jnaneshwar Maharaj:

> If sense pleasures are given full rein, they burn up the field of religious duty and enjoy a feast of sensual indulgence.
>
> There is a poison which by name is sweet, but which proves deadly in its effects. [18.799, 801]

So rajasic happiness starts out tasting like nectar and ends up affecting you like poison. Sooner or later, it becomes utterly indigestible.

The third kind of happiness is sattvic happiness, and it is just the other way around. Lord Krishna says:

That which in the beginning feels like poison,
but in the end tastes like nectar;
that happiness, born out of the tranquillity
of your own mind,
is declared to be sattvic. [18.37] [8]

This is the purest happiness. In the beginning, a smoke screen of impossibilities and sacrifice denies you access. However, if you persevere, you experience the sweetest joy. Have you noticed when you chew on something very bitter—for example, bitter melon or certain bitter leaves that are good for health—they do indeed taste very bitter. When you first put wheatgrass juice in your mouth, it is unbearable. But then you chew and chew, and it becomes sweeter and sweeter and sweeter—so nectarean that you never want to eat another dessert made with white sugar. In fact, a dessert made with white sugar tastes very bitter once the sense of taste has been fully awakened. true!

Lord Krishna explains that sattvic happiness is born from the tranquillity of the mind. It is not dependent on the chaotic muck that you find in *tamoguna* or the frenetic activity that typifies *rajas.* Sattvic happiness arises from dispassion. It occurs once you separate yourself from the dictates of the senses. Then you are not tossed back and forth between the pairs of opposites: gain and loss, honor and dishonor, giving and receiving. Nor does this type of happiness depend on expectations being fulfilled. In rajasic happiness and tamasic happiness, there are expectations to be fulfilled, and you have to wait for a long time. Sattvic happiness is freer than that.

Lord Krishna says that sattvic happiness *may* seem like poison—it doesn't have to. What the Lord is emphasizing here is that this happiness lies beyond the senses. To attain it, you have to perform actions that discipline the senses. What do the senses do? They cry out, "This is poison! I don't like it!" However, if you continue to persevere, the aftermath of such effort is pristine and perfect joy.

What kind of person is appreciated in this world? One who perseveres. People always admire that quality in others, whether they are good or bad. What really appeals to your heart is that perseverance. In the same way, if you persevere in the yoga of discipline, sooner or later the senses do come around. They say, "Whoa. There's a boss here."

Jnaneshwar Maharaj comments on this verse, saying:

> When a person lights a lamp he must endure its smoke, and when he takes medicine he may find it unpleasant to the taste.
>
> O Arjuna, it is the same with this happiness, which results from the difficult practice of controlling the mind and the senses. [18.777-78]

Sattvic happiness arises from the discipline of the mind and the senses.

Once again, tamasic happiness is wretched and thrives on laziness and others' pain. Rajasic happiness seems like nectar in the beginning, but turns to poison in the end. Sattvic happiness is born of restraint, and though it may seem bitter at first, in the end it produces a fountain of nectar.

Beyond these three kinds of happiness is the pure bliss of the Self, which transcends the three *gunas.* Bliss is absolutely free from the stains of this world. Bliss is the very nature of Consciousness. When you say, "The sunrise of supreme bliss shimmers in every particle of the universe," you acknowledge its presence. You give it the honor that it is due. You make the experience your own. It is not someone else's; it belongs to you. Supreme bliss belongs to you; you actually take possession of it. Then whenever you or someone you know goes through something less than bliss, you begin to experience deep compassion. There is a point below which your spirits never fall. You are no longer devoured by maya, by illusion.

What kinds of happiness have you experienced in your life? There may have been some times when you experienced tamasic happiness. There may have been times when you experienced rajasic happiness. And then, once in a blue moon perhaps, you were happy for no reason at all. Just simply happy. You didn't see a deer in the woods. You were just happy.

What kind of happiness have you known best? Sweet happiness? Bitter happiness? Bittersweet happiness? Pure happiness? Impure happiness? Happiness that is mixed, both pure and impure? Something to contemplate.

With great respect, with great love, I welcome you all with all my heart.

Sadgurunāth mahārāj kī jay!

Morning talk
December 30, 1994

Chapter Two

In Pursuit of a Great Goal

With great respect, with great love, I welcome you all with all my heart.

In the sixth chapter of the *Bhagavad Gītā*, Lord Krishna instructs Arjuna about the means to attain the bliss of yoga. The name of this chapter is "The Yoga of *Ātma Samyama*," which literally means the yoga of self-control or the yoga of discipline. It can also be translated as the yoga of meditation. Meditation is discipline; it is self-control.

To experience real happiness, self-control is absolutely essential, and in this chapter that is exactly what Lord Krishna teaches Arjuna. He speaks as clearly and explicitly as possible, though his words are steeped in the subtlety of the most profound mysticism. He says:

> For the sage who desires to attain yoga,
> action is said to be the means;
> for him who has already attained yoga,
> tranquillity is said to be the means. [6.3] [1]

Do you remember how Lord Krishna described sattvic happiness? He said that pure happiness is born out of the tranquillity of your own mind. Here is the same point once again. He tells us that the sage who has attained the culmination of his practices turns to tranquillity again and again. He rests in that state. He is pervaded by the intoxication of the Self. The sage has risen above even sattvic happiness—he is not attaining happiness; he *is* the happiness. However, a seeker who is still climbing the mountain of yoga must allow himself to go step by step in his sadhana. So for him, action is the means.

What are the steps of sadhana? In the *Yoga Sūtras*, the great sage Patanjali specifies eight distinct limbs. They are *yama*, restraints or things to be avoided; *niyama*, daily practices that aid the development of inner purity; *āsana*, the postures of hatha yoga; *prāṇāyāma*, breathing techniques; *pratyāhāra*, withdrawal of the senses from their outer objects; *dhāraṇā*, concentration; *dhyāna*, meditation; and *samādhi*, deep absorption or the state of union with the Absolute.

Each of these is very helpful if we are to "drink a fresh cup of joy every day and become inspired with new perception." Purity, inside and out, is what allows inspiration to arise. You have to make space for it. You have to clear out the old before you can bring in the new.

The practice of discipline is the mainstay of purification. As long as the mind is not channeled in a positive direction, it compulsively paints one dreadful picture after another—of your past, your future, your character, and the world you live in. It drags you down into the dust. It takes any situation or relationship and turns it into the worst hell possible. Then you panic and look for refuge in undesirable actions. Wouldn't it be better to control the mind in the first place?

Truly, the path of discipline cannot be praised enough. On this path, the mind learns to keep its energies centered so it can perceive its own source, which is the light of Consciousness, *chitprakāsha*.

Jnaneshwar Maharaj speaks highly of students on the path of yoga, those who have practiced hatha yoga and breathing techniques and have also learned withdrawal of the senses, concentration, and meditation. He says:

> Then they will reach the end of the path. All desire for further progress will be satisfied, and those who seek the goal will attain it in the joy of the Self. [6.59]

Chapter Six of the *Bhagavad Gītā* defines the path of yoga for Arjuna, and also for us. After describing the necessity of discipline, Lord Krishna goes into more detail. He says:

> The yogi should constantly discipline himself,
> remaining in solitude, alone,
> with mind and body well restrained,
> having no desires, and without avarice. [6.10] [2]

Every verse of the *Bhagavad Gītā* is brimming with directions and divine advice about how to uncover the bliss of the Self. However, this verse is particularly rich in meaning. Just by accomplishing everything mentioned in this one verse, a true seeker can fulfill all the ideals of yoga and drink the nectar of *samādhi.*

By the same token, an unbaked person, one whose understanding has not cooked long enough, might find this verse a little intimidating. He might wonder if he has to stay all by himself forever to be a yogi. And how is he going to bring the activities of the unruly mind and the body under his control? How will he live without his desires? How can he be free from avarice? The more you think about it, the harder it seems, particularly when your body acts like it has a mind of its own. One mind you can deal with. Two minds—get some help! How do these yogis do it?

Arjuna had the same doubts about himself. When he expressed them to Lord Krishna, however, the Lord could see through Arjuna's words to his longing, and he knew the perfect way to encourage his disciple. Jnaneshwar Maharaj comments on the reassurances that the Lord offered Arjuna, saying:

> Multitudes of yogis have set out by various ways to find God, and the footprints of their experience have made an easy path.
>
> They have traveled steadily by the straight path of Self-realization, avoiding the side roads of ignorance.
>
> All the sages have traveled this path, seekers have attained perfection in this way, and those who know the Self have reached exalted positions. [6.154-56]

The teachings of yoga have already led many, many seekers to the goal. Therefore, you must not panic and revert to your old ways, thinking this path is too difficult to tread.

It is very important that you delve into the deeper meaning of each element that Lord Krishna includes in this verse. The first one is to constantly discipline yourself. How? By "remaining in solitude, alone, with mind and body well restrained." How can you restrain them? By having no desires and by being without avarice. As you contemplate these elements and put each one into practice, you will find yourself going deeper and deeper within. And there, a greater meaning will be revealed of its own accord and through the Guru's grace.

Restraining the body and mind can be done very effectively by practicing the eight limbs of *ashtānga yoga*. In fact, for deep absorption, the solitude that Lord Krishna recommends is essential. Constantly disciplining yourself means to purify your thoughts, your speech, and your actions. It does not mean putting your body through contortions or depriving your body of food and refusing to take care of it.

In yoga, the word *discipline* has a very specific meaning. It has nothing to do with the rigors of boarding school or military life—it's not that easy! Discipline in yoga truly means "purification." Lord Krishna is telling Arjuna to purify his thoughts, his speech, and his actions.

Generally speaking, a person lets his mind think whatever it fancies, he says whatever words the tongue wants to spit out, and he acts without much concern for the consequences of his actions, particularly the detrimental ones. That may be satisfying temporarily, but it is not yoga. Yoga begins with the watchful disciplining of one's impulses. The senses can be distracted so easily—one gust of wind, one gust of passion and the senses fly after their objects. And you say, "What's happening to me? I don't understand!"

Baba Muktananda placed great importance on spending time alone. He said, "In order to experience the true Self, one should remain in solitude for some time each day. If possible, one should go into complete seclusion for about seven days every two or three months. During these periods of solitude, one should abandon all thoughts and practice watching what is happening within. In this way, one gets into the state of Witness-consciousness."[3]

This is not just a matter of distancing yourself from people and buildings and professional obligations. It is a question of clear mental space. You must make space in the region of the mind. According to the Indian tradition, the mind consists of four psychic instruments: the intellect, the subconscious mind, the ego, and the conscious mind of the waking state. When you make space beyond all your mental activity, you discover the company of a deeper silence within, where you can hear the sound of your own breath—*So 'ham*, "I am That."

Have you ever heard the music of your own breath? That is when you swim in supreme bliss. Thoughts may play in your mind, memories of the past and thoughts of the future may come and dance, but you are absorbed in hearing the music of your own breath, the music of *So 'ham*. You are swimming in the ocean of bliss.

What else did Lord Krishna tell Arjuna to do? He began with discipline; then he told him to remain in solitude, and then he added the word *alone*. Being alone means separating yourself from the things that keep you from being with God. In this aloneness, there is no loneliness. Understand the difference between the two words. Aloneness, *kaivalya*: in this state there is no loneliness.

In this state, the true seeker or yogi is summoning the divine light. He is on the verge of experiencing his own wholeness. Deprivation, which is what loneliness is all about, is the furthest thing from his mind. So as a yogi, a seeker on the path, you cultivate this awareness: being alone, being alone with God.

"Having no desires" is the next teaching in this verse. That means becoming free from the clutches of sense objects, being free from the desires of the senses. For example, if the eyes see ice cream, you want ice cream. If the ears hear praises, you want more praises. If the tongue tastes strawberry shortcake, you want more strawberry shortcake. Such desires, big or small, have a tendency to balloon and go out of control. That is what you need to watch out for. It's okay to have ice cream, but you want more and more. Your eyes get bigger and your fingers get longer, and your whole being gets wider so you can embrace sensual objects. It's almost as if the universe is not big enough for your passion. That tendency is what you have to watch out for.

When desires are not under control, they drive a person into a horrible ditch. This is not surprising or difficult to understand. Everyone has experienced it to some degree—in diet or recreation. It's well known. However, a yogi, a seeker of the Truth, must develop the power to say no to unwanted desires.

Before we go on, let's take a moment to do a short exercise. Go back in your memory and find a time when a certain desire arose—one that you knew was not beneficial and yet you pursued it. What happened? What were the consequences? Follow the sequence of events just for a moment, with your mind's eye, and watch what happened to your heart, your mind, your awareness of God. Watch what happened to the way you perceived others and the world.

Now, go back in your memory and find a time when the same kind of desire arose, and also the awareness that it was not a beneficial desire. Only this time, you did not give in. You struggled against it. You put forth whatever effort was required. You turned within and asked for grace. And finally, you found yourself able to let go of this desire completely. It was as if you never even had it. It was gone. You didn't feel even a twinge as it left. Remember how that felt.

Lord Krishna goes on to say that a yogi is free from avarice. When you look at history, it is very clear that greed is the cause of the downfall of empires. Avarice can take over a country like a disease invading the body. A country wants to expand; it becomes greedy, ravenous for more and more land, more and more wealth. And what people are willing to do to add to their treasury becomes appalling. But for all their grasping, what do they really amass? Only vices. And then one day, they go under. Avarice is the warehouse of all the other vices. Obviously, this tendency is damaging to a yogi, to one who aspires to see the light of God.

You can see how valuable this one verse from the *Bhagavad Gītā* is. It not only reveals the high road to liberation, to supreme bliss, it also provides practical inspiration for day-to-day living. Through this verse, one learns to abide by the laws of dharma. Living by this discipline increases the love and respect you feel for other people. Very naturally, with each dawn you refresh your feelings of love and respect, you make them new once again. And then the very world you are living in becomes the house of God. By practicing even the smallest amount of discipline, you experience true happiness.

Jnaneshwar Maharaj comments further on this verse:

> A person for whom the day of nonduality dawns and never sets remains in the unceasing bliss of the Eternal.
>
> [6.105]

The key that unlocks the different aspects of yoga is

dispassion, *vairāgya.* This conviction is sprinkled throughout the *Bhagavad Gītā* and all the great scriptures. The poet-saint Tukaram Maharaj sings:

> Such a being who is weary of the charms of this world
> drinks the nectar of Brahman, the Absolute,
> and attains tranquillity within.

The *Yoga Vāsishtha* says:

> When the mind sheds its desires, it feels
> the sweetness of peace and bliss descend over it,
> as if it were the lustrous moon in the heavens. [2.13.6] [4]

For the fulfillment of yoga, to become free from desires, one-pointedness is vital. In this discipline, all the energies of the mind must be brought together so that purification can take place within and without. A scattered mind can never gather enough momentum to progress on the path of discipline.

We are talking about one-pointedness of mind, *ekāgra manas.* It is very important to learn how to bring the mind under your control. A stable mind is a tranquil mind. Attaining this depends on how you look at your mind, with what attitude you regard the mind, how much respect you give your mind, and how much you torture your mind. In yoga you must have the mind within your grasp.

Once someone asked Baba, "Baba, do you think?" "Whenever I wish," replied Baba. So in yoga the mind *is* within your grasp. You can ask your mind to do some things and not to do others. It is there to serve you.

In true meditation, consciousness is fully active, but the mind is quiet. Meditation should never be inert. When you meditate, your entire being is alert, vibrating with awareness. You watch your mind, you witness your mind, but you don't buy into its comings and goings. If you want to have a good meditation, it's very important to be able to keep your mind in one place for as long as you wish. The longer the mind can stay with one thing, the stronger and healthier it becomes.

If you examine the workings of the mind with a magnifying glass, on the one hand, it reveals how concentration requires a strenuous, sometimes almost torturous effort. But on the other hand, mastering the restlessness of the mind and giving it a proper object of contemplation cleanses the inner being and releases a stream of nectar. Finally, as you are led, little by little, to merge with your chosen deity, you experience your own glory, the glory of God, and the purpose of human life.

In the *Yoga Sūtras*, Patanjali gives a beautiful *sūtra* about the disciplines of yoga. He says:

> Practice becomes firmly established when it has been cultivated for a long time, uninterruptedly, and with earnest devotion. [1.14] [5]

habit

So the practice of one-pointedness, this *abhyās*, also contains devotion. Yoga is the practice of concentrating the mind until it becomes one-pointed—that is, until it can focus on a single object without wavering. Sometimes seekers meditate on a flame for a long time.

One day during a chant in the temple, I noticed that the candle flame before Bade Baba was very still and steady. It was clear that the people there were chanting with devotion and one-pointedness. After the chant was over, the flame was still incredibly steady. I was fascinated and happy that the people in the temple had such quiet minds. I wanted them to know it, so I drew their attention to this phenomenon. However, as soon as they watched the flame, it began to move and waver.

"Can you watch the flame with your minds completely quiet?" I asked them.

As they watched the flame with quiet minds, the flame immediately became steady—but not for long.

Again I asked them to become more alert and watch the flame with their minds completely quiet.

They did that, and the flame once again was steady and still. But they couldn't hold the quietness for long, and the flame began to move again.

So I said, "Forget about it. Don't watch the flame. Let's chant for a while." As we chanted, their minds became quiet, and once again the flame was steady. But this time I didn't say anything about it.

The mind has tremendous power. You can utilize its pure power for good things, for knowing God, for help in performing dharmic actions. The mind is the seat of the will. It rules the body. So by getting hold of the ruler, so to speak, and training it properly, then all things become possible. The energy within a human being can be harnessed in pursuit of a great goal.

Let us look a little further into this question of how the disciplines of yoga lead to supreme bliss. The *Chāndogya Upanishad* says:

> That which is done with proper knowledge, with devotion, in conformity with the scriptures, and with the proper method, becomes more forceful. [1.1.10][6]

In India, before a brahmin priest begins his worship, he installs the object of worship in his own being. In this way, he invokes the power and the grace of the deity within and without. He performs this practice with a one-pointed mind.

When you focus your mind on something, whatever it may be, you absorb its qualities. In a very real way, you take it into yourself. At the same time, you also infuse it with your own energy. You give it life. It is your *bhāv*, your devotion, your deep feeling, that gives meaning to everything.

Devotion to God is much more than a feeling. Through your devotion, God comes alive for you. Through your devotion, you also invite the one you worship into your body, into your mind, into your life. The formless takes on a form that you can relate to.

In Chapter Six of the *Bhagavad Gītā*, Lord Krishna says:

> Whenever the unsteady mind,
> moving to and fro, wanders away,
> the yogi should restrain it
> and control it in the Self
> with *niyama*, regularity. [6.26] [7]

It is the nature of the mind to be active. Have you noticed? It wants to flit from one object to another, like a butterfly from flower to flower. You cannot expect something to go against its own nature. You are only courting disappointment if you do. It is much more sensible to examine a thing—in this case, the mind—on its own terms. When you see what its qualities are, then you understand why it is the way it is. And you can begin to predict what it will do.

This is how the sages approached the mind. They saw that the mind has a tendency to latch on to something it likes or dislikes, and concentrate on that exclusively. If it likes something, it stays there. If it dislikes something, it stays there. From this tendency, the sages evolved guidelines for meditation that help the mind become immersed in pure Consciousness, in God. By following these guidelines, a meditator can learn to use his mind for a higher purpose.

As long as the mind has not realized its true nature, it will be unsteady. It will wobble. The mind is like the wind constantly blowing through a hollow bamboo. To control the fluctuations of the mind, you must be like a master flautist who blows into the flute and creates celestial music. What does he have to work with? Only the air circulating inside the flute. That's all—but he puts it to good use. The wind just keeps moving, but a master of the flute can control it. He gives the wind a sweet purpose, and then its existence delights the hearts of many. The sound of the flute resembles the divine inner sound, *nāda*. Its melodious vibrations are healing. This is very different from a gusting wind.

One-pointedness of mind is essential. Like the wind, the mind moves all the time. However, with the power of concentration you can give it a shape; you can make it harmonious and steady. The practice of one-pointedness is using the mind to control the mind. You don't have to depend on anything external. You take the help of the mind to support the mind.

Lord Krishna stressed the role of *niyama*, regularity, in restraining the useless wanderings of the mind. The *niyamas* are a set of observances that calm the mind and help make it one-pointed.

In his *Yoga Sūtras*, Patanjali lists the *niyamas* one by one:

> The *niyamas* are cleanliness, contentment, austerity, regular recitation of scriptural texts, and the surrender of one's limited will to the higher power of God. [2.32] [8]

Is this a lot to remember? Well, you want supreme bliss so you have to work a bit! We'll discuss these yogic practices for attaining supreme bliss, so you can apply them one by one. Then wherever you go, you will know how to derive supreme bliss from within, how to get to this state on your own. Grace, of course, is always there. Your effort is essential, too.

In his book *Light on the Path*, Baba Muktananda explains the effect of these disciplines very clearly. Baba says, "When a yogi, through the practice of *yama*, *niyama*, and *prāṇāyāma* and meditation, succeeds in attaining the state of mindlessness,[9] he experiences the same supreme bliss that the *jñānī* experiences through Self-knowledge. Thus, the yogi is intoxicated by *yogānanda*, the *jñānī* is absorbed in *jñānānanda*, and similarly the *bhaktā* becomes enraptured in *premānanda*. This is the ecstatic delight of love of all the devotees of God."

The first *niyama* is cleanliness. It's easy to understand the need for cleanliness of the body. But in yoga, what is more important is cleanliness of the mind. Of course, they often go together. There has to be cleanliness of the body, as well as the mind. When you look at people's rooms, for instance, you can tell at a glance how they keep their minds. In yoga, the mind is our top priority. The cleanliness of everything else follows naturally from a pure mind.

There are many, many tools to purify the mind, speech, and actions. One of the easiest and most powerful of them is the repetition of the mantra. This practice comes with a guarantee. If you repeat the mantra with a sincere heart, with deep devotion, it bears fruit immediately. Whenever a meditator realizes that his mind is becoming clogged with unnecessary thoughts, he must learn to empty it by repeating the mantra.

The mantra is a great purifier. It carries the vibrations of the Divine into a busy mind. It is not just a matter of blotting out useless activity, but of replacing it with joy and peace. Mantra repetition makes room for inspiration, for higher thought. Constantly emptying the mind is like purifying the mind. By repeating the mantra, you replace unnecessary thoughts with the power of the mantra.

When a thought is unnecessary, you know it. But sometimes you don't know how *not* to have such thoughts, so the best practice is to repeat the mantra. When you see that your mind is going far far away, and you need it for concentration, then take a moment and do *japa.* Mantra repetition helps, whether you are meditating or trying to work.

Many people complain that they cannot get into meditation. It's like a soap opera—"I can't meditate. I can't meditate." Actually, it's a foolish complaint because meditation is part of life. It does happen to you. If it didn't, you would never be able to go to sleep. In fact, you wouldn't be able to eat. Baba used to say that even for eating you need meditation. Whenever you concentrate on something, it is a form of meditation. So meditation is already a natural part of your life.

Whenever the mind is filled with thoughts, particularly

thoughts that drain you, repeat the mantra. Purify the mind with the repetition of the mantra. The mantra also purifies the body, the heart, the soul. You begin to experience a tingling vibration in your body when you do *japa* sincerely, when you take time to sit down and repeat the mantra for a while. Constant cleansing of the mind, the intellect, the subconscious mind, and the ego is vital.

What you say, what you eat, where you sleep, how you sleep, where you work, how you work, what you do, what you don't do—every activity must be filtered through the awareness of the great Self. When a meditator continually bathes everything he says and does in the power of the mantra, he aligns himself with the sunrise of supreme bliss in his own heart.

So this cleanliness of mind and body is the first *niyama*. It should be easy to remember when you wake up in the morning, the first thing you want to do is take a shower. Before you begin your meditation, worship, or any activity, think about cleanliness of mind and body. It is essential.

The second *niyama* is contentment. Contentment sounds like something within your reach, so clear and simple. However, attaining it calls for deep inner change. It is so convenient in life to blame others for your misfortunes. It is such a habit to be critical of people, to be critical of God's creations. It seems so natural to be cranky and to complain, so normal to express one's uncontemplated annoyance. One is passionately driven to fix the lives of others. These habits have become people's customary mental furniture, which they are used to living with. To make life more exciting, from time to time they move the furniture around. So when the sages say that for discipline, for yoga, for attaining supreme bliss, you must cultivate contentment and steadiness of mind, people are dumbfounded.

They answer, "But what will happen to my life? How will I live? If I'm not a nervous wreck, who will listen to me? How will I get things done? If I don't weave tapestries of desire, then how will I know what I want? How will I function? If I can't flare my ego like the hood of a cobra and strike everyone in earshot, then how will they know that I'm an interesting person?"

Well, the sages say, if you want to realize the purpose of human birth and enter the abode of supreme bliss, then you have to change your view of life. It's that simple—you have to change. Much of your life has been created from your unlimited supply of negative concepts. Purify them. Give your mind a break. Have you ever thought about it? Have you ever considered what your mind must think about *you?* Give your mind a break every now and then. It wants to be free from your clutches.

Consciousness is the very nature of the mind, and Consciousness is totally free and steady at the same time. So let the mind become still; it wants to become still and savor its own elixir. Let it be. Don't drag it off to go shopping with you. Let the mind become serene; then a fountain of joy will flow within you. When a meditator learns to strengthen the mind and the heart by invoking the presence of contentment within, he drinks from that fountain of joy.

You can learn about contentment by watching birds and animals and the miraculous workings of the universe. You can learn from simple things, such as watching the state of your mind when your best friend receives a Christmas present and you don't. What happens to your mind? If you can cultivate happiness at that moment and not get caught up in the six enemies, such as jealousy and anger, then you have come a long way. You are happy that your best friend got something. You are happy not to accumulate things you don't need. You are happy to have a best friend who is loved by so many. You are happy that your best friend is happy.

Contemplating in this way, you extract the elixir of contentment from the ocean of events, rather than the poison of envy. As the mind becomes accustomed to contentment, as this evenness settles in, it is like applying soothing balm to the wounds and bruises of the mind. Then the mind naturally becomes stronger, finer, and more pliable. It feels supported by your discipline. It is happy with your discipline. It is ready to plunge into the ocean of joy.

Once a blackbird found some food in the village and lit out into the sky with the food in its beak. A flock of his brothers and sisters chased after him and attacked the food, pulling it from his beak. The blackbird finally let go of the last piece, and the frenzied flock left him alone. The bird swooped and dived and thought, "I lost the food but I regained the peaceful sky."

One of the commentaries on Patanjali's *Yoga Sūtras* says, "It is said in the *shāstras* [the sacred texts] that just as to escape from thorns it is necessary only to wear shoes and not to cover the face of the earth with leather, so happiness can be derived from contentment and not from thinking, 'I shall be happy when I get all I wish for.'"[10]

Have you ever asked yourself what makes you feel content? Take a moment to think about it now. Ask yourself, what times of day, what kinds of activity put your mind at rest? Of all the people you know, which ones make your mind feel content, and when? What personal trait in yourself or others gives you the sensation of contentment? Take a moment and contemplate this.

Did you notice? You must have seen this over and again in your life: it's when you are free from selfishness that the harvest of contentment appears. It's when you are not thinking about yourself in a selfish way that you experience the tender shoots of contentment growing inside your heart.

Next on the list of *niyamas* is austerity, *tapas*, which literally means heat. This is the fire of yoga. First, it burns up the impurities in the body. Then it reveals itself as the great fire, the blazing light of the supreme Self. For a meditator, *tapasyā* also includes accepting whatever happens as the best thing for your sadhana, and not being disturbed by any discomforts, inner or outer, that you may experience.

Austerity develops endurance, which is the backbone of yoga. In yoga, you need that power of endurance. Constantly enduring whatever happens, never falling apart. You should never give yourself a chance to fall apart because when you do, it becomes a tendency, and it happens over and over. Endurance is an invaluable quality that strengthens a meditator and helps him overcome the obstacles on the path. The path is strewn with many obstacles, so you can't let one obstacle stop you. You have many obstacles to overcome, so you must gain strength as you walk the path.

Even though at times you might feel very tired and depleted, so tired that you feel you can't go on, even then, remember cleanliness, remember the purification that has already happened. Remember that austerity is good. It is the real fire that will burn up impurities and obstacles. Do not let yourself become completely exhausted. Without austerity, it is so easy to give in to temptations and fall back on the indulgences that are so much a part of the lower self and the world of sense objects. So a yogi, a seeker, must always remember to ascend higher and higher. There should be nothing in the closet to revert to. Many people think if they put their bad habits in the closet, somehow no one will see them. Then, if they really want to indulge themselves, they can. But it's better to keep the closet clean.

Austerity has the power to mold a person into a sturdy vessel capable of holding the immense energy of yoga. This energy, this *shakti*, is very strong. In order to hold it, you need a strong body, a strong vessel. To sum it up, every part of your being profits from austerity, which curbs the appetites and purifies the will.

The fourth *niyama* is *swādhyāya*, reciting scriptural texts and chanting mantras. To steady the mind on the highest goal, recitation of the scriptures and sacred texts is a great support. First, a meditator fills himself with the power of the great Truth. Then even if the mind wanders, it can't go any place where there is no awareness of the Truth. It seeks out pure thoughts. Sometimes it simply rests in a thought-free state.

When it has been washed clean by the chanting of mantras, the mind becomes more receptive to resting in the great Self. If you have recited the *Guru Gītā*, you must have noticed this: in the beginning, your mind may be perturbed, it may wander aimlessly, but when the chant is finished, your mind is serene. In the *gurukula*, we sit quietly for some minutes after the recitation of the *Guru Gītā* to give the body and mind time to relish the sweetness of the mantras and to savor the great silence, the serenity. Sometimes people don't give themselves time to enjoy serenity.

Many people shun reading holy books and chanting ancient hymns because they think it is old-fashioned. They think religious activity is obsolete and irrelevant in the modern world. They regard religion as a refuge for people with problems, people looking for easy answers, people with time on their hands. So they look askance at spiritual practice. It doesn't fit into their schedule, they say. It is not backed up by the latest scientific discoveries. It's something toothless old folks do. It doesn't look good in the neighborhood. It doesn't fit in with modern civilization.

Most people underestimate the tremendous power of *swādhyāya*. But they don't mind spending hour after hour on a therapist's couch. They don't mind traveling great distances for advice from astrologers or psychics who have never laid eyes on them before. It's so much safer to ask someone else, "Can you tell me about my life? Can you read my chart and tell me when I will get married?" instead of finding the answer within yourself. If you don't keep yourself open for a relationship, but you go to an astrologer and ask, "When will I get married?"—then anything too deep can be kept on the periphery. You don't have to go through personal transformation. You can just stay in the realm of the mind and avoid the process of deep transformation. Most people don't want deep transformation. They want others to tell them what is going to happen in their lives.

What about *you*? You and your mind and your strength and your good merits and your sadhana? What about your talents, your skills, your good intellect? Are you ignoring all your treasures and asking someone else, "Tell me, please tell me—what's going to happen to me?" I have nothing against psychics, but I am talking about you as a yogi, as a seeker of the Truth, a seeker of higher knowledge. Don't you want to utilize your own mind, your own intellect? See what your own intuition has to say. You do have it—open it up, let it blossom, let it flower.

In yoga the recitation of sacred texts is great medicine. It gives the mind incredible support. It removes your pain. Many people chant the *Guru Gītā* when their friends or relatives are on their deathbed so they can experience peace when they pass from this world to another. Unfailingly, they do experience that peace. Sometimes people chant the *Guru Gītā* for the benefit of others who are thousands of miles away, and the fruits of those recitations do reach those distant people. So you can imagine how much it must help you as well. It carries you deeper and deeper within to the source of bliss. It is the lullaby of the soul.

The fifth *niyama* is surrender to God, *samarpana*. A person spends most of his time and energy building up everything that will reinforce, protect, and extend his ego. Name and fame, professional reputation, material possessions, personal appearance, other people's opinion, and so on. How hard you work so that others will say something good about you!

However, there comes a time in each person's life when he suddenly finds that he is helpless before even a minute difficulty—a moment he simply can't handle, when he doesn't know what to do, when he doesn't have enough strength. Maybe it's the moment when he realizes he's dying. If a person has not practiced taking refuge in God, in discovering the great Truth within, in surrendering his limitations to the supreme Power, then panic sets in. All his activities become fraught with fear and depression and anger. No one seems to be loving or lovable. In his eyes, the universe becomes a cruel, indifferent place.

It is so clear why a seeker must learn how to surrender. If you don't know how to surrender to the supreme Power, then during your difficult times you don't know where to turn. *Samarpana*, surrender, is a magical practice. Without having to wait for a crisis, you recognize your own helplessness and ask for protection. When there is surrender, you don't have to wait for a crisis. All along the way, you are thankful, you are happy to be humble before God. The humility involved in this practice actually attracts God's grace. Without humility, it is very difficult to experience the tenderness of the great mind.

Do you ever worry that the path of discipline might alienate you from the world and from those you love? Well, this is not the intention. Nor is it a way for you to punish yourself for your so-called sins. It is not a torture chamber. It is not an extreme form of penitence that you follow out of the fear of hell. The path of discipline is not intended to make you feel that you are better than the rest of the world, either. It is meant to end delusion, not create a world of its own.

You must learn how to embrace others while you do your sadhana. You must not say things that will scare other people. You must not behave in a way that will reflect negatively on sadhana. If someone is not ready to listen to what you have to say about your sadhana, then don't say anything about it. You can remain quiet. Allow others to watch your transformation —this was Baba's advice. Then very slowly they begin to ask, "What kind of food do you eat? What do you drink? Where do you go on the weekends? What kind of makeup do you wear?"

Don't be afraid that you will have to renounce the world in order to make progress on this pure and beautiful path. You can put that fear aside. The yogis of ancient times performed many incredible and austere spiritual practices in order to attain the ultimate state. Still, that doesn't mean everyone has to put forth that much force, effort, and determination. Not everyone is cut out for that. Everyone is different. Do your sadhana at your own pace. You need not be an extremist.

In fact, Jnaneshwar Maharaj says, "Little by little, the yogi should come to rest with the intellect firmly held." In the *Bhagavad Gītā,* Lord Krishna assures us that even if you don't finish your sadhana in this lifetime, you will continue it in your next lifetime and begin where you left off. So go at your own pace without hurrying. It's a great assurance—that you can proceed slowly and gradually, at your own pace. The whole point is: Do it. Practice yoga. Observe the practices. They are highly beneficial. This is particularly true in Siddha Yoga, where grace is such a strong element in sadhana and the practices seem to deepen of their own accord. Here, you can walk the path of discipline with knowledge and devotion, and grace supports you every step of the way.

Constantly remember how much grace there is in your sadhana. It's like going for a walk and having the wind at your back. When that happens, it's as though you are not really walking anymore, as though the wind is completely supporting you. I love those walks. Before I go for a walk, I look for the wind and I say, "Coming with me?"

Once again, it is very clear from the *Bhagavad Gītā* that all the practices are aimed at making the mind happy. When the mind is happy, it can experience the sunrise of supreme bliss shimmering in every particle of the universe. It can actually drink a fresh cup of joy every day and become inspired with new perception. It is willing to renew love and respect with each dawn. It is ready to dive into the Great Void of liberation.

You have heard the teachings of Lord Krishna about the yoga of meditation, the path of discipline, and all its sublime fruits. You have also heard Jnaneshwar Maharaj's exposition, which is as sacred as the Ganges, and which flows through the *Bhagavad Gītā* like a river of light. Light added to light. This is why there is such beauty when you watch the sunrise. The light of your eye meets the light of the sunrise, and you see a golden disk shimmering on the horizon.

Contemplate once again the title of the Intensive: The sunrise of supreme bliss shimmers in every particle of the universe, so why not drink a fresh cup of joy every day and become inspired with new perception? Remember, love and respect must be renewed with each dawn.

Pay particular attention to renewing your love and respect with each dawn. If you make this a practice, then very naturally it springs forth. Each evening you can end your day and begin the night with the ecstatic understanding that even in your sleep state, God is present, and supreme bliss is coursing through your entire being. Even in your sleep state, it's there. God is present. You can be happy when you go to sleep and you can be happy during your sleep. Then the next morning, you are ready to start the day with another fresh cup of joy.

With great respect and great love, I welcome you all with all my heart.

Sadgurunāth mahārāj kī jay!

Afternoon talk
December 30, 1994

11. The Path of Discipline

Discipline gives total freedom;
it allows you to go beyond limitations,
to break through boundaries and reach the highest goal.
The path of discipline will not only save a person's life,
it will also give it meaning. How?
By introducing him to deeper joys and deeper longings,
by creating a silence in which
the whisper of the heart can be heard.
Truly, discipline is the road to liberation.

Chapter Three

The Road to Liberation

With great respect, with great love, I welcome you all with all my heart.

This morning one of the speakers welcomed all the Siddha students and all the seekers of the Truth. He also welcomed all the invisible beings, all the great Siddhas. We do experience their presence; we experience their grace and their blessings, we melt in their love. We are in their service; we are serving them. Their love encompasses this entire universe. If you love these great beings, these invisible hands, then you must serve that which they love, that for which they have compassion, and that is this universe. So we are in service, and this is why we will continue to live on this earth as long as God has a purpose in keeping us here.

The *Rig Veda* says:

> Sweet are the winds that blow,
> the seas scatter sweetness all around,
> our herbs are sweet,
> and the very dust of the earth
> is full of sweetness. [1.90.6] [1]

The *Rig Veda* also says:

> Sweet be the plants for us, sweet be the heavens,
> sweet be the waters and the air of the sky!

May the Lord of the Field
  show us honeylike sweetness. [4.57.3] [2]

At the end of the *Rudram*, there is a prayer that says:

O Mother Earth!
I will think that which is sweet,
I will do only that which is sweet.
I will select only sweet things
  for the worship of the gods.
I will speak only those things which are
  as sweet as honey to the gods
and to human beings who want
  to listen to good things.
Let the gods protect me from verbal faults
  and make my speech beautiful.
Let the ancestors also approve of it. [*Chamakam 11*] [3]

Sweetness. This entire universe is filled with sweetness. God wants us to experience this sweetness, to melt in this honeylike sweetness by having sweet thoughts, by speaking sweet words, by performing sweet actions, by letting the sweetness from our soul flow into other hearts. Every heart is made of sweetness. Sweetness is another name for the heart.

The theme for this summer is the yoga of discipline. Discipline is the churning process we go through in order to experience this great sweetness.

In the *Yajur Veda* the sages pray to God:

O supreme Lord, you are full of fiery spirit.
Give me fiery spirit.
You are vigor; give me vigor.
You are strength; give me strength.
You are discipline; give me discipline.
You are conquering might; give me conquering might.
[19.9] [4]

People from all faiths pray to God in their own way; they pray for a million things—various blessings, achievements, goals, and boons. Every time a prayer is fulfilled, a feeling of immense gratitude wells up. How long will this feeling last? That varies according to each person's ability to hold the power of gratitude, to sustain the transforming awareness of God's grace. In this prayer from the *Yajur Veda*, the sages pray for discipline. They regard it as an attribute of God. Discussing discipline in his book *I Have Become Alive*, Swami Muktananda said, "A life of discipline is a life of nectar; it is filled with joy."

Discipline is another attribute of God. While making Siddha Yoga available to seekers everywhere, Swami Muktananda placed enormous importance on discipline. In fact, in India his name and the word *discipline* are synonymous. Any time you hear the name *Swami Muktananda*, the image of a life of discipline springs to mind. And it also works the other way around. All you have to hear is the word *discipline*—and what appears in your mind's eye? The smiling face of Baba Muktananda. People used to tell me that every time they heard the word *discipline*, they would remember the photograph of Baba pointing his finger at them and looking straight into their eyes. As teenagers, we kept our distance from that photograph.

In the early 1970s, an English traveler wrote a seeker's guide to the ashrams and temples of India. In his introduction he said that the code of conduct at Swami Muktananda's ashram should be taken as a model for how to behave in holy places. His description of Gurudev Siddha Peeth included these comments on the food:

> Food is of good quality, mildly spiced Indian-style vegetables with rice, *dal*, *puris* and often fruit salad (a rarity in most ashrams) and tea and coffee. Servings are more than adequate. However, it is made clear that one

> should exercise restraint. As Baba says: "The two main causes of illness are too much food and too many thoughts." [5]

So here we have Baba's teaching: Too much food and too many thoughts become the cause of illnesses. They can also cause one to fall from the path of yoga. Now, I have been made very aware of the reaction that most people have to the word *discipline*. It brings up great resistance, and underneath that, in many cases, tremendous fear, the fear of a child. As soon as a child's intelligence is mature enough to understand the spoken language, he or she becomes the victim of the parents' reprimanding behavior. Every time the child does something out of the ordinary, something that does not fit the parents' particular expectations or rules, the parents think the child is misbehaving. So the child is disciplined in one way or another—sometimes gently and sometimes severely. This system of punishment continues for the rest of a person's life. Though the form may change, the feelings that are provoked stay more or less the same. The word *discipline* is associated in most people's minds with doing something wrong.

Discipline and punishment have become interchangeable for many people. This idea of discipline is something to dread, something to run away from. So much stigma has been attached to the word *discipline*. This has been created by people who have experienced discipline as something to dread. As children, fear was instilled in them, and this fear is still there when they grow up. And when they are preparing to die, they are afraid. "Is God going to punish me for all my sins? Is He going to send me to hell?" Even at the last minute of their life, before the breath finally leaves the body and merges into universal Consciousness, there is fear of punishment.

When people have this fear, instead of wanting to improve, they want to rebel. Instead of wanting to obey the principles of discipline, they want to break them. Instead of welcoming the prospect of discipline, they develop an aversion to the whole idea. Instead of seeing hope in the path of discipline, they visualize pain and torment.

If you look up *discipline* in the dictionary, you will find that it is derived from a Latin word meaning "disciple." Even though most of the definitions in the dictionary are not negative, still the punitive definitions are listed first as the more common usages: correction, restraint, repression, coercion, routine; being supervised, controlled, managed, regimented, indoctrinated. What comes to most people's minds? The school yard, the prison yard, the military.

Remember when your parents treated you severely? That's the discipline many people are accustomed to. This is why, when we celebrate Father's Day, some people say to me, "Gurumayi, we shouldn't celebrate Father's Day. I didn't have a good childhood. My father disciplined me so harshly that I can't bear to celebrate that day." Some people say the same thing about Mother's Day.

Finally, I have to tell them, "Listen, when I say, 'Father's Day,' I mean God. When I say, 'Mother's Day,' I mean God, I mean that great Principle. So celebrate Father's Day; celebrate Mother's Day—and expand your awareness."

As your mind expands and recognizes the universal Consciousness, then you will be able to forgive your father for what he did out of ignorance and to forgive your mother for what she did out of ignorance. Then you can give them your love so that they can make peace with God.

In short, almost everyone's first reaction to the word *discipline* is to contract. People assume a very defensive stance, as if they are trying to present a smaller target. And all because they associate harshness, cold-heartedness, or anger with the term *discipline.*

You will be happy to hear that is definitely *not* what we mean by discipline. It is vitally important to understand this. We are talking about divine discipline. From the standpoint of the spiritual path, the term *discipline* is alive with the joyful expectancy of divine fulfillment. It is like seeing dark clouds, pregnant with rain, gather over a parched land, a place where there has been a drought for many years. All the animals, wild and tame, and the little creatures who have shriveled up in the intense heat and dryness are filled with the expectancy of relief. Even the plants seem to tremble with anticipation. The dark clouds and all the uproar of thunder and lightning do not frighten these creatures. They know that it will be followed by the sweet release of rain that will put an end to their suffering.

It is no different on the spiritual path. When a seeker is ripe, when he or she has come to the realization that all his senses have been used up in the pursuit of pleasure, and his whole life, his whole being, has grown dry in the heat of worldly agitations, anxieties, and appetites, then he recognizes the value of a life of discipline. He knows that discipline will refresh him in body and mind, and that the fruit of discipline is total freedom.

You have heard great singers. Do you think they could sing the way they do without discipline? Because they have led disciplined lives, now they can go beyond what we think of as the limitations of the human body. They can reach people's hearts.

Discipline gives you total freedom; it allows you to go beyond limitations, to break through boundaries and reach the highest goal. The path of discipline will not only save a person's life, it will also give it meaning. How? By introducing him to deeper joys and deeper longings, by creating a silence in which the whisper of the heart can be heard.

Truly, discipline is the road to liberation. Only spiritual discipline can free a person from the chains of suffering that have been forged in the furnace of a sensual life. Sooner or later, without fail, every true seeker learns this. He comes to understand that by applying himself to spiritual discipline he is placing his life in God's hands. And at that moment, his sadhana takes off. As Baba Muktananda said, "A life of discipline is a life of nectar; it is filled with joy."

Sometimes, when you are doing seva, offering selfless service, you may start your day very early. You may go with very little sleep for a night or two. Nevertheless, you feel fine, you feel joyous. This is the sign of discipline. If you live a disciplined life, then when you have to work extra hard, you can do it because you have the support of discipline. Your body is disciplined, your mind is disciplined, your speech is disciplined. And so your soul enjoys total freedom.

The yoga of discipline is not about confining yourself to an unknown world filled with strange phenomena. Nor is it about doing penance for your sins. I want to clarify this: you are not following discipline to get rid of your sins. You are following discipline because you want to drink this nectar, this ambrosia.

Once there was an elderly lady who came to church every day to perform her penance. The priest had assigned her the recitation of a long passage from the prayer book. He was very pleased to see her taking this penance to heart. Every day she sat in the back of the church and read from the prayer book. One day he noticed that she was flipping the pages over at a great clip. He went closer and heard her say, "All the saints on this page, pray for us. All the saints on the next page, intercede for us. All the saints on the following page, hear our prayers. From all sins on this last page, deliver us, O Lord. Amen! . . . Ah, finished at last!"

This is not the method we are going to follow. The spiritual path is made up of disciplined practice, as regular as a heartbeat. That is what fills the inner journey, and it prepares the ground for the spontaneous unfolding of grace. It is discipline that leads you to the recognition of your own great Self. It is discipline that uncovers the wealth of virtues hidden within you.

Imagine being in a burning house, and then finally you escape into the open and fill your lungs with pure, fresh air. Then you know all about the wondrous relief of breathing freely. Finally, there is oxygen; there is fresh air. It is as good as drinking nectar. This is the kind of immense joy you experience when you follow a life of discipline, removed from the burning of the senses.

So the sages pray: "O Lord, You are discipline, give me discipline." What a heartfelt prayer! It is so necessary in Kali Yuga, in this Iron Age, which Baba called a "treasury of defects."

In this world, people have created a zillion distractions for themselves for the sake of happiness. But it often seems as if everything a human being invents to make life more exciting ends up depriving him of his own inner elixir, the fragrance, the taste, the sheer ecstasy of the nectar that flows quite naturally within him. A zillion man-made creations can take him in a zillion wrong directions. They can make him wild with fanciful imaginings. They can send his senses running outside, scrambling to devour everything in sight. Of course, the popular reaction to this point of view is, "Why stop now? Nothing is ever enough. More! More! We've come this far, why stop now? Let's keep going." And what is the end result? A confused life. A state of perpetual sensory overload that leads to exhaustion, dejection, depression; that leads to contempt, cynicism, shame, and on and on.

In the sphere of nutrition, it is said that when you go on a binge, it takes the body at least two or three weeks to return to its natural state, to function normally. Imagine what must happen when your senses constantly binge, when the arc of your appetites is always swinging between two extremes. The effect on your body must be enormous. What are the chances of ever returning to a state of well-being?

Discipline is like a shield that protects the senses. It creates an environment where goodness can thrive and a seeker can experience his own inner joy. Then, being on this planet is no longer drudgery, nor is it without purpose. Discipline allows a seeker to lead his life with great maturity and awareness—with love, respect, and freedom.

The yoga of discipline. Yoga is that which unites the mind to the supreme Soul. Yoga annihilates the separation between a seeker and what he is looking for. Yoga can also be loosely translated as the divine path. So the yoga of discipline can be understood as the divine path of discipline. A life of discipline is a life of nectar; it is filled with joy.

The knowers of the Truth have said that there are two ways to lead your life. The first one, lack of restraint, leads to misfortune. The second one, self-control, leads to abundance of every kind and spiritual wealth. Now, you make your choice.

This message is so simple. However, living with self-control is much more difficult than just letting life be. The simple truth is that a lack of discipline brings misfortune; it fools you into leading a life that you don't want. Everything you detest, all the suffering you want to run away from, is produced by a life without discipline. Even though everyone is aware of the calamities that a life without discipline invites, still, making that little shift toward another way of life seems so hard. But it's just a little shift. It's not a sudden change from first gear to fourth. It can be done gently.

The yoga of discipline is pivotal for you. Explore it. Protect it. Be very vigilant. Maintain the yoga of discipline. No matter how tired you are, you can still have the presence of mind to be nice. You can still have the presence of mind to smile and to share the hidden happiness. I call it "the hidden happiness" because you may not be in a good mood at a particular moment. But that happiness really is there deep within you. So share it with others.

You don't have to be in the *gurukula* to practice discipline. You can follow discipline even if you are on vacation with your family; if you are with your friends, with your colleagues.

Even if you are working at your office or at home taking care of your children, you can still practice the yoga of discipline. You can practice in your own way at your own pace, and that will make you feel that you truly can be disciplined.

When you leave the *gurukula*, you should have this awareness: "Yes, I can follow the yoga of discipline. I am worthy. I am deserving. I don't have to live in the Himalayas. I don't have to live in a cave. I don't have to live in a remote place where I don't hear one human sound." No. You can have this feeling: "Yes, I can do it, I can do the yoga of discipline. I can take the ashram home. I can take the Guru home. I can take the practices home. I can do it. I can follow the yoga of discipline just the way I am, just the way I think. God loves me just the way I am. God wants my love. I long for His love, and I know God wants my love, too."

So have this experience within yourself, and believe in this, truly believe in this. God loves your love. God has a purpose for you, and that is why you are here.

Now that we have explored the idea that discipline is nothing to be afraid of, we can embark on this endeavor with courage. Now that we have contemplated how discipline leads us to freedom, we can launch this effort with enthusiasm. Now that we have seen how discipline is a great means to liberation, we can pursue the yoga of discipline with willingness, fortitude, and fervor. Now that we have looked at all this, let us begin.

With great respect, with great love, I welcome you all with all my heart.

Sadgurunāth mahārāj kī jay!

June 24, 1995

Chapter Four

Teach Your Eyes How to See

Discipline in Seeing I

With great respect, with great love, I welcome you all with all my heart.

The lure of the senses is tremendous. Baba Muktananda used to quote a poem about how different animals are addicted to different sense pleasures. He said: " 'Take the case of an elephant: an elephant is a slave to the sense of touch, and he even loses his life because of clinging to the pleasures of touch. The deer is a slave to the sense of smell, and for smell he lays down his life. A serpent is a slave to music, to the sense of sound, and he loses his life for the pleasure of sound. A fish is a slave to the sense of taste, and a moth to the sense of sight, and they lay down their lives for the pleasures of taste and sight.'[1] The poet says that each of these creatures lost his life because he was a slave to only one sense pleasure. 'How pitiful your plight is, O man, because you are addicted to all five different forms of pleasure. How can you ever save yourself?' "[2]

This is why we follow the yoga of discipline. Today we want to look at discipline in seeing. In the Upanishads it is said, "May everyone see only auspicious sights."[3] The eyes are very important; perception is very significant. The world is as you see it. Therefore, how you maintain your outlook, what you see, is essential. Just because you have eyes doesn't mean that you should take in whatever comes your way. It doesn't mean you should see anything, everything, anywhere, everywhere. That is not discipline in seeing. It is very important that you teach your eyes what to see and when to see.

In the *Viveka Chūdāmani,* the sage Shankaracharya takes up the subject and says:

> The objects experienced by the senses
> are even stronger in their evil effects
>   than the poison of the cobra.
> Poison kills only when it is absorbed into the body,
> but these objects destroy us
>   merely by being seen with the eyes. [77] [4]

The eyes are very powerful. You may not be hungry, but you look at some food and immediately your eyes say, "That looks so good. It's time to eat!" Or you are not feeling lustful at all. You're feeling fine—not even lonely. But then, a very beautiful woman walks by, or a very handsome man. Your eyes fall on that person and you think, "Oh my!" Now, you weren't doing anything at all! Your eyes just fell innocently on that moving object.

So Shankaracharya said, "Poison kills only when it is absorbed into the body, but these objects destroy us merely by being seen with the eyes." Your eyes see, and you want everything you see. The eyes are very powerful.

People often follow a religion or perform spiritual practices because they think they will attain heaven. Of course, everyone does need to prepare for life after death. However, if you follow a religion, if you follow a spiritual tradition only because you want heaven, then, as Baba Muktananda wrote in his book *Mukteshwari*:

> Even in heaven there is no happiness
> when Creation is limited by the eye of man. [288]

If your sight is limited, if your perception is limited, if it is filled with impurities, then even in heaven you cannot find happiness. It is said that a crow in heaven, for example, eats only garbage; whereas a swan living on Lake Manasarova consumes only pearls, even on this earth. [5]

So it all depends on what *drishti* you have, what outlook you have. The world is as you see it. If you cannot find happiness in your attitude, in the way you look at things, then you cannot find happiness anywhere else either.

There was a great saint called Sheikh Sa'di, who was also a great scholar. When he was a very young child, he went to Mecca with his father. They got up early in the morning at two-thirty to do their *namaz*, to perform their prayers. However, when Sheikh Sa'di saw that so many other pilgrims were still asleep, he looked at his father and said, "O Father, look at these wretched people. They came all the way to the house of God, all the way to Mecca, but they are fast asleep. They have come here just to sleep! Look at them!"

The father looked at Sheikh Sa'di with great compassion and he said, "Sa'di, my son, you should have stayed home. It would have been much better for you to stay home than come here and criticize the devotees of God in His own house."

When Sheikh Sa'di heard those words, even as a young child, his heart caught on fire. He knew he had to understand the laws of God. At that moment he dedicated his entire life to this pursuit.

Tukaram Maharaj in one of his *abhangas* said:

O Lord, do not let my eyes desire
  to look at others' sins.
It would be much better to be blind.

This is the understanding of the saints. If you cannot use your eyes to see God's glory in this universe, to see the beauty of the Self in this universe, if you cannot use these eyes to have the darshan of the Lord, then what is the use of these eyes? So Tukaram Maharaj said, "Do not let my eyes desire to look at another's sins." It is so beautifully worded. "Do not let my eyes desire." It is not just your mind that desires something or your heart that desires something. The eyes too desire; they want to get hold of what they see.

Or when the eyes see something, instead of speaking well of it, they speak badly. The eyes can speak much louder than your voice. The power of a look is horrendously great. The great American philosopher Ralph Waldo Emerson said, "An eye can threaten like a loaded and leveled gun, or it can insult like hissing or kicking; or, in its altered mood, by beams of kindness, it can make the heart dance for joy."

With these eyes, you can create new worlds, like those created by the vision of great souls. With these eyes, you can threaten another person. These eyes can make someone feel horrible, even if he was feeling good before you saw him. The eyes communicate so much.

Look at dogs, for example. When they want their way, they look at you and they make their eyes so soft. Even if you are angry with them, you see those soft eyes, and you say, "Okay, you can have a piece of toast." They can't speak, they can't come and hug you. The only thing they can do is use their eyes — and their eyes do everything. When you try to give them a hard time because they haven't been behaving properly, they look at you as though there has never been such an idiot in the entire world as you. Just with their eyes, they make you feel like a little worm. But then the next moment, they look at you as though you are the living end. Without you, the world wouldn't exist. They come and sit at your feet and make you feel that you have everything. Just having that dog, you have everything.

The eyes communicate so much. If you are not careful with your eyes, you will not know what they are communicating, what message they are sending out, what energy they are giving to the world.

There was a Sufi saint called Dhu al-Nun, who used to tell a story about his inner awakening. When he was a young man, he was walking along the bank of a river one day, and he noticed a huge pavilion by the water. He didn't pay much attention to it. But when he finished his ritual bath, he noticed the pavilion again. There he saw a beautiful woman and he wondered who she was. He kept looking at her as he walked along. Then, he noticed that she was looking at him too.

Finally, when he reached the pavilion, he spoke to her. "Oh, my dear one, who are you?"

She looked at him and called out his name. "Dhu al-Nun!"

He was very surprised. "How do you know me? What do you want of me?" he asked.

"Dhu al-Nun!" she said again. "When I first saw you, I thought you were a madman. Then I thought you were a scholar. Then I thought perhaps you were a mystic. But now I see that you are none of them."

Dhu al-Nun was shocked. "What do you mean?"

"When I first saw you, I thought you were a madman, but I changed my mind because you took your ritual bath. No madman could ever perform any kind of ritual properly. Then I thought you must be a scholar. But I realized that that couldn't be true either. No scholar would gaze openly at something forbidden to him. Then I thought perhaps you were a mystic, that you were God-intoxicated, and that everywhere your eyes went, you saw only God. But I realized you were not a mystic when you asked me who I was. A mystic would never see anything but God."

"At that point," Dhu al-Nun said, "fire blazed in my heart. I flung myself into austerities in order to know the Truth."

The eyes have such a tendency to grab what they see: they see something, and they want it. Therefore, a seeker must live his life in the discipline of seeing. You must teach your eyes what to see, how to see, when to see. For this reason, seekers spend time in solitude. For example, in the *gurukula* we have the meditation cave, a room that is kept dark and silent for meditation. There you close your eyes against the weariness of the world, the troubles of the world. You give yourself time to contemplate by taking the eyes away from all forms and objects. You give the eyes a chance to contemplate their own existence. By resting your eyes, you give the mind some peace also. Wherever the eyes go, the mind has to go with them to make sure their command is followed. By taking the eyes away from all that is physically seen, you give them a profound serenity. And as the eyes contemplate why they exist, they understand a greater Truth.

Baba Muktananda said: "When, through the grace of my Guru, Nityananda, I saw the light of pure Consciousness, it settled in my eyes and transformed them. This light is known as the lotion which enables blind eyes to see for the first time." [6]

Kabir sings of this lotion:

Since I applied the lotion of my Guru's grace
all that I can see is Rama, Rama,
  the Lord Rama everywhere.

It is very important to rest the eyes from physical objects and forms. Since the eyes travel at great speed, it is necessary to slow them down so they can relearn the purpose of their existence. They can retrain themselves to see what must be seen, to perceive what must be perceived.

Discipline in seeing. When you are being offered food, at that moment just pause for a split second. Do you really want to eat that? Also let the person know exactly how much food you want. Don't just blindly take what he gives you. He doesn't know the size of your stomach or what you can digest; he doesn't know your taste or your constitution. You need to help him; you need to support this process for yourself—this is part of discipline in seeing. When you are offered food, take only as much as you can digest. You don't want to throw food away; food is prasad, it is God's gift. There are millions of people in the world who starve to death. We are very fortunate to have food every day. We must respect and love food. We do this by disciplining our eyes; we take only the amount we can handle. In this way, we let the body have its freedom. The body can have its freedom only if we do not give it too much to digest. So follow this discipline of seeing in the way your soul would want you to, seeing in the way God would want you to, seeing in the way that will bring you greater happiness in the long run.

Discipline in seeing. When you are moving through a crowd of people, maintain discipline in seeing. Be sure that you are not bumping into someone, you are not hurting someone inadvertently, you are not rushing in a way that pushes someone aside. You can maintain discipline in seeing by respecting the other person with your eyes.

There are many people in the *gurukula*: many nationalities, many children and youngsters, many monks, some brahmins, great dignitaries and scholars, many wonderful men and women, including some seniors. What kind of feelings do you have when you look at them? Do your eyes respect them? Or do your eyes neglect them? When you have discipline in seeing, you see everyone, and you act like a proper human being in whom God dwells. You wait, you pause, you act with awareness. Discipline in seeing becomes part of everything you do.

What else can be done? Choosing what you read. You don't have to read every novel that comes along. You can choose what you're going to read. And what about movies and television? The senses are attracted to those things. You may say, "Well, why should I limit my God-given freedom? My senses want to watch violent movies; my senses want to watch somebody being killed—just in the movie, of course, not in real life." This is where you need discipline. You need to be careful about what you take in because toxins and impurities accumulate in your body. Then even digesting your food becomes very difficult because so many harmful energies have been allowed inside your system.

Where else can you follow discipline in seeing? By seeing good qualities in people, by not criticizing them. But if a criticism does arise in your mind, don't put yourself down. You may think, "What can I do? I know I should see only good qualities in others, but look at that guy! It's so obvious what's wrong with him!" Then an instant later you think, "Oh no, I saw something negative in him! What a wretch I am to even have this thought."

You don't have to go through that drama. Just say, *Om Namah Shivāya, Om Namah Shivāya* until the thought dissolves. Don't act on the thought. Repeat the mantra and you can also drink a little water. Don't put yourself down. Just remember your mantra and make it a practice to say something good to that person.

Discipline in seeing. You can remember to discipline your eyes by pausing. For example, in India when we go to a temple, we first pause at the door. We touch the ground and then we touch our hearts. We acknowledge that the presence on the ground is also in our hearts. Then we walk with reverence and devotion until we come to another door, and once again, we touch the floor and the heart. Then finally after going through many doors—that's how temples in India are often built—you come to the inner part of the temple. And there, you bow. You take your time; you bow as long as you want. Then, finally, you rest your eyes upon the image of the deity. Having purified yourself in this way, through reverence and devotion, continuously acknowledging the presence within and without, then—when you know your eyes have become focused and are ready to receive the Truth—you rest your eyes upon the deity.

By pausing and repeating your mantra, by pausing and repeating the chants you know, by uttering your prayers, you create an ablution for your being, for your mind, for your heart. Finally, you are ready to offer your being at the feet of the Lord. This is another form of discipline in seeing.

When you first wake up in the morning, instead of rushing out of bed, pause and repeat your mantra. Then rest your eyes upon the *mūrti*, the statue of a deity, or a photo or any object of worship. It could be a photo of your chosen deity or of your Guru—whatever is closest to your heart on the spiritual path. You let your eyes rest upon that, and then you begin your daily routine, whatever it is—brushing your teeth, taking a shower, going to meditate. After that, you pause.

In the ashram when people come for the first time, they ask why we have so many photos of the Guru and so many statues in the garden. There is a purpose: it is so we will always remember, so we will see with discipline. Once the eyes see the form of the Guru, then everything the Guru upholds, everything the Guru stands for is invoked. When you see the statue of a deity, everything that the deity stands for, that the deity contains is invoked. And then, that is what you see, that great energy. Disciplining the eyes in this way increases your strength and courage.

The poet Rahim said:

> The beautiful form of the Beloved
>   has settled in these eyes.
> There is no room left for any other beauty.

When you behold the Truth with your eyes, when you behold God with your eyes, then all that is negative, all that is destructive and evil, will walk away from your life. Only glory and auspiciousness will dwell in your house.

In response to a question about why God is so difficult to perceive, Baba Muktananda once said: "What form would you like to see God in? He has taken the form of bread in this piece of bread. Don't try to see Him as stone in bread. In fruit you should see God as fruit, and in yourself you should see Him as yourself. Who says that God cannot be seen? Don't try to see Him as different from the way He has manifested Himself. Try to see Him as He is." [7]

And elsewhere, Baba said: "Whatever you do, you should see your own divinity in everything. Don't look at anything as different from your divinity. All that you need to do is pray inwardly, to honor every form." [8]

As householders, as people living in this world, there are so many things you have to do. You are not living in a monastery like a cloistered monk who has the privilege of seeing only nature with all its beauty. You have to do quite a few things that are unpleasant. How are you going to cope with these forms and objects? Baba said, "See God in them." All you need to do is pray inwardly to honor every form. Whatever happens, see the Lord there.

In Siddha Yoga, we meditate. Meditation is the highest goal. Baba said: "It is a magnificent path. Man should experience for himself the knowledge of the *sahasrāra*. He should see the light that spreads there, brighter than a thousand suns, he should see the multitude of divine lights there." [9]

In the *sahasrāra*, the spiritual center at the crown of the head, you see your own inner light. This is the way you perceive your own inner divinity. When you are with God, that's all you see. When you are with the Guru, that's all you see. Divinity comes and resides in your eyes.

Once there was a student who came every day and sat before his Master. One day the Master said to him, "Bring me that book from that window."

"What window, sir?" asked the student.

"That window over there! You've been coming here for so many years, and you don't know where the windows are in my house?"

The student folded his hands and said, "Sir, when I come

here and sit at your feet, I see only you and the wisdom you are imparting to me. I don't know anything about your house. I have seen nothing except you, nothing except the teachings."

When you have such focus in your spiritual practice, you will receive That. Baba used to say, "Don't let your eyes wander all over the room. Bring the eyes back into the true focus." The eyes are beautiful pools, and in these pools you don't want scorpions, alligators, and vicious creatures. You want these pools of your eyes to hold the energy of God, the magnificence of this universe. And then you want to share that energy with everything in your world.

The poet-saint Eknath Maharaj sang:

> One should hold on to only one feeling —
> God is ours, God is ours.
> One does not have to make any effort;
> wherever one goes one will experience
> God's presence.
> One can see God everywhere — in meditation,
> in the mind, in sleep, in people, and in plants.
> Janardan's Eknath says, Wherever I look, I see God.

"Wherever I look, I see God." Disciplining how we see; the practice of seeing divinity in everything. Seeing divinity does not mean seeing only one form of God, one form of the Guru. Divinity may appear as a good feeling, or a generous attitude, or a helpful nature. It may appear as many wonderful forms.

What is important is the energy you perceive, the energy you communicate. Through your eyes, you can love someone; through your eyes, you can kill someone. Through your eyes, you can create a great, wondrous world for someone. Through your eyes, you can steal someone's soul and leave him empty. So disciplining the eyes, disciplining how we see is essential for the good of life.

May everyone see only auspicious sights. May everyone

see only auspicious sights. May everyone see only auspicious sights.

With great respect, with great love, I welcome you all with all my heart.

Sadgurunāth mahārāj kī jay!

July 4, 1995

Chapter Five

WHO IS LOOKING THROUGH YOUR EYES?

Discipline in Seeing II

With great respect, with great love, I welcome you all with all my heart.

We have been contemplating the direction in which our eyes want to go and observing their insatiable appetite for the enchanting. Of course, what an ordinary person might find enchanting is different from what would enchant a yogi. Haven't you found it illuminating to become aware of what your eyes look at? Those of you who really focused on discipline in seeing, have you noticed how consistently the eyes look outward?

Baba Muktananda used to quote a poem about how certain animals are completely addicted to one sense pleasure or another, and how the plight of man is even more pitiful because he is addicted to all five of the sense pleasures. If a person does not know how to keep the senses of perception in check, they can carry him away at the drop of a hat into the wilderness of *samsāra*, the world of illusion. Controlling the senses is no simple matter. It is quite difficult to see something without absorbing it into your system. The eyes are the windows of the soul, and most of the time the windows are wide open, so anything at all can blow in. Very few people are able to control this. Therefore, for most seekers, the challenge is to keep the eyes from resting on something that they don't want to imbibe. It is very difficult to protect yourself from the things that appear before you when they are not what you want to see. The intense desire of your eyes is forever pulling you toward sights that will get you into trouble.

Of course, the eyes can be the means of carrying the beauty of the universe from outside to inside, and that is wonderful. If you are able to use your eyes to perceive the miraculous power of this universe, you are in a great state; you don't really need to learn discipline in seeing. If you are someone who truly understands that everything that meets the eye is a play of Consciousness, you have transcended the traps and snares of your own mental creations. And that is a great blessing. You don't need to exercise discipline in seeing. You are in a fantastic state, so let it be.

Unfortunately, this is not the case with most seekers. On the spiritual path, each seeker has to overcome the inevitable difficulties of appearances, and what he thinks he sees. It's not what you *see* that gets you into trouble, it's what you *think* you see that gets you into trouble. Your eyes come in contact with the world—but what do those eyes really see? And how do you interpret it? You don't always know what to do with the information provided by your eyes.

In the *Viveka Chūdāmani*, "The Crest Jewel of Discrimination," Shri Shankaracharya explains how you can see clearly through your eyes:

> In order to know a jar is a jar,
> are any special conditions required?
> Only that our means of perception,
> the eyes, shall be free from defect.
> This alone reveals the object. [530] [1]

The eyes free from defects. When you find faults in others, Baba Muktananda used to say, where do those faults really reside? Do they reside in that person, or do they reside in your own eyes? When you see something bad, where does it really exist? Does it exist in that person, in that place, or in that time? Or in your eyes? A jar is a jar. If you see a jar as a machine, whose fault is it? Is it the fault of the jar or the fault of your eyes? Where do the defects reside? Think about this.

Those people who have been pursuing the practice of discipline in seeing have shared with me what a tremendous experience it has been for them. It has changed their dreams. They have been dreaming about the Siddhas. They have been having great visions in meditation, because they are making sure the eyes go toward those objects that are pure, those objects that are great. They also said that even when their eyes fell on something dirty, for example, they didn't say, "Yuck!" They were able to just clean up the dirt. It wasn't something horrible; it didn't make them cringe. There was a shift in their awareness. It is very purifying, this discipline in seeing. Some people spoke about their mental images changing. If they were in a crowded place, they would think of a lake with swans, or the wind blowing through the trees, or the sound of the mantra reverberating in the air. Or they would see a mountain with its stillness and its medicinal herbs; they would feel the healing power of the mountain.

As they shared their various experiences of discipline in seeing, Baba's words kept coming to my mind: "A life of discipline is nectar; it is filled with joy." When you pursue true discipline, it creates a fountain of life for you. You can dive into the pool of nectar and drink and become intoxicated. Your entire being becomes lighter. You dance with joy.

As long as the true Principle behind the eyes is not recognized, then one's vision is filled with distortions. Unless the eyes have been purified by spiritual practices, what they see does not convey the correct understanding. Without the discipline that comes from spiritual practice, you can't tell a false impression from the real thing. It's like seeing a snake in a rope. Do you remember this famous story from Vedanta?

One night a man named Janghu went for a walk along a

country lane. He was thinking about this and that, imagining what he might do in the future. All of a sudden, he jumped with fright. A short distance from the path, a huge snake had slithered into view. It had frozen when it saw Janghu. In fact, it was clearly poised, motionless, ready to lunge forward and bite the poor fellow.

Janghu let out a scream and ran off toward the village, yelling for help and warning everyone not to walk in that direction. A couple of villagers said they would take their lanterns to see if it was really poisonous.

But Janghu wouldn't hear of it. He told them he knew all about snakes, and that if they went there, they would die. He was sure this was the dreaded snake his grandmother used to tell him about. It was surely the one that had killed so many children, poisoned farmers in their fields, and attacked innocent travelers. His descriptions of it grew more monstrous by the minute.

Then Janghu got another idea. He would be the hero! He would save the village from this dreaded serpent by killing it himself. He could just see himself dealing it one mighty blow after the next. Totally energized by this heroic vision of himself, he marched off into the night. As he walked, he looked for a heavy stick to beat the snake with. He saw the perfect branch on a tree and grabbed it firmly to pull it down. Then he let out a cry and fell to the ground. The branch he had grabbed was no branch at all but a huge snake, which quickly dealt its fatal bite to the would-be hero.

Meanwhile, the other villagers with their lanterns inched closer and closer to the original snake, trying to scare it back into the bushes with their cries. But it didn't move; the snake just wouldn't move. Finally, they went right up to it and beat it hard. But there was no reaction — because there was no snake. It was a thick rope someone had dropped on the road and forgotten.

Janghu only *thought* he had seen a snake.

Projections, illusions. You think you see, but do you really see? You think you are watching. But are you really watching? You think you have the power to look. But are you really looking?

So discipline in seeing is essential. Everything you see is not what you think it is. You can be so enamored with your own perception that it becomes the cause of your downfall. Doesn't this happen to people who fall in love? A man thinks he has found the most beautiful woman. He describes her to his friends with all the adjectives that he learned in the sixth grade. One day he finally sees the woman smile. And that's it —she has horrendous teeth. Or a woman sees a man from a distance. "Ah, the prince of my heart! I knew one day I would find him. What a jewel! I can't wait to tell my mother. She always told me I would find my prince at the right time." Finally, she gets a chance to follow these fantastic vibrations that are coming out of nowhere. And she looks up at the man—only to find that his nose is crooked.

In his book *Mukteshwari*, Baba Muktananda wrote:

> The sins of the organs of perception
> are greater than the sins
> of the organs of action.
> Muktananda, keep your eye pure. [283]

In other words, the five senses of perception impel the five organs of action into pursuing whatever impresses them. In Sanskrit, these senses of perception are called the *jñānendriyas*: the powers of hearing, feeling, seeing, tasting, and smelling. The five organs of action are the *karmendriyas*: the powers of speaking, grasping, moving, excreting, and procreation. Once again, perception triggers action.

However, there is a catch, a slip that occurs more often than not. What you perceive—and then act on—is often a projection, and projections are symptoms, not of external reality, but of your own inner state. When your eyes are truly filled with love, everything appears to be the embodiment of love. It doesn't matter whether something is beautiful or ugly: you are able to see the God-given beauty in everything. When your eyes are filled with ugliness, you simply cannot see the beauty of the universe. No matter how spectacular the beauty is, you find it very difficult to appreciate.

What's more, these projections are almost always colored by the way you have led your life. During a *yajña*, a fire ritual, particularly when the sun is shining brightly and the fire is blazing high, you see this thick, shining, crystal wall between you and the fire. This wall is formed by the haze of heat. Similarly, if you are someone who likes to dwell on anger, then you see everything through a haze of heat rising from your anger.

If you are someone who likes to entertain a critical attitude, you see everything through a thin curtain of judgments. If your eyes are tired from sleep deprivation, everything you see irritates you. If you have been brought up in a home without harmony, you can't bear to see others' happiness.

How many people can look at life with a clear, uncluttered view in every direction? How many people can see with 360 degrees of unobstructed vision? Very few. Everyone has his own angle of vision, his own point of view. Everyone's house has a different kind of window through which he perceives the world. Your vision also depends on where you live: in a valley, on a mountaintop, in a crowded city, in the open countryside, in a desert, or in a haunted house. Your perception is affected by your outer environment and by the ecology of your inner world.

Through yogic discipline, you begin to climb upward, as well as going deeper within, toward a more expanded and more profound view of life. You have a different kind of perception, a divine perception. How do you acquire this divine perception? You do self-inquiry, *ātma vichāra*. You ask yourself: What are these eyes for? What is the purpose of seeing?

What will I achieve from the different perspectives available to me? Where will this process of seeing take me? How can I best utilize the means of perception, this part of myself, which I am becoming more and more aware of? Is the purpose of my perception just to help me get through a day? Or is there something more that I must see with these eyes? Does my happiness depend on what my eyes perceive? Am I happy only when I see something I want to see? Or am I independent of this, separate from my sense of perception? Who am I? Am I the eyes that see? What am I supposed to do with these eyes? Do I have the power to think about such questions?

You can do more *ātma vichāra*, further self-inquiry: Where do I invest my time? Should I try to see everything in the world? Everything that exists in this materialistic world—am I supposed to see it all in one lifetime? Should I feast my eyes on everything presented before me? Or is it better to discipline my eyes and to be selective about what they see? But then, does this mean turning my back on every unpleasant sight, like walking away from a crying child? What does it mean? How do I decide what I should be looking at? How can I know in advance whether something I see will wreck my life? How can I tell when my eyes are acting as if they were bigger than my stomach? What is the point of protecting my eyes from the affairs of the world? If all is Consciousness, if all is God, is there anything I should never see? Do I really know what I want to see? And, if I do, do I have the freedom to make it happen?

Ask yourself: What is the purpose of seeing? What is the goal of these beautiful instruments, these eyes, the means of perception? What are they for?

Contemplating in this way, a seeker receives a greater understanding. He learns to live a greater life; he learns to understand the purpose of his eyes, the real purpose of vision. Why the eyes? Why the seeing process?

In his *Mukteshwari*, Baba Muktananda described one of

the great mysteries of true vision:

> He who lives in the eyes
> and through them sees form,
> whose seat is the eyes,
> who is the eye of all,
> who is the great light —
> Muktananda, that is the conscious Self. [587]

This awareness is the astonishing culmination of lifetimes of sadhana and self-inquiry. Having ventured deep into the mysteries of life, great beings like Baba finally attained the highest understanding. They understood the true purpose of perception, of seeing, of looking. They not only recognized the Power behind the senses and the world, they became one with it.

As the *Shvetāshvatara Upanishad* says:

> It is Witness-consciousness alone that is formless. [6.11][2]

Witness-consciousness, *sākshī bhāva.* The One who is seated in the eyes, that One truly sees. That One abides in the eyes, and therefore the eyes have the power to see. This Witness-consciousness is the propelling force of the universe.

In Baba's verse from *Mukteshwari,* he describes his own experience of the Witness in words that are reminiscent of the ancient sages. No matter when this experience takes place, it is always the same. It is beyond time. You could be attending a meditation program, or preparing food in your kitchen, or answering the telephone. Or you could be just taking a quiet walk. All of a sudden you realize Witness-consciousness, this *sākshī bhāva,* the pure space within. You realize the Power behind the senses.

As long as a seeker does not recognize the true Seer, the Witness, that which abides in the eyes, then his gaze goes everywhere, without any real purpose, like wheels coming off a cart all at once and rolling in four directions at four different speeds. How long before they stop? It is the same with eyesight. If the One who dwells in the eyes has not been perceived, then perception becomes senseless; it does not have any greater meaning at all. If that One is not communicated through the eyes, if the relationship between that One and the eyes is weak, then what the eyes see is not beneficial to the soul in the long run. That One, that Principle, needs to be communicated through your eyes because it is that Power that enables you to see. So meditate on this great One who is changeless, who is untainted, who is immutable. As you meditate on this Principle, you realize the true purpose of the eyes, the true purpose of perception.

Witness-consciousness is called the inner eye, or the third eye, or the light of the eyes. It is also known as the eye of wisdom, the divine eye, or the celestial eye. Baba Muktananda further explains Witness-consciousness. He says: "Witness-consciousness implies watching without being affected, without making any judgment. Say, for example, there are two people quarreling and one person is watching. The one watching, who does not get involved, is the witness. Similarly, the indwelling Witness is the One who observes all the activities of the waking state without getting involved in them." [3]

Haven't you had this experience? You are watching two people quarreling. It's a really big fight, and there's no way you could get involved—you wouldn't come out alive. So you watch, you pray, you give your blessings, you extend your love, your respect—but you just watch. You can tell who is in the wrong and who is in the right, but you are not involved. You are completely detached, and this gives rise to joy within because your energy is not affected by this fight happening right before your eyes. You are merely observing. You are in the state of Witness-consciousness. You are the Witness. Although you know who is wrong and who is right, you say nothing; you know there is more to the story. There is a greater law of karma operating. And if you have kept a truthful journal of your own life, you must have noticed how you are causing every incident, every event in your life. You are the cause of every action in your life. You are the one who sets it in motion. If you didn't, it wouldn't be there. There is great power in understanding the law of karma.

As a witness, you have the power to think clearly. Not like Janghu who was just thinking random thoughts, a bit of this and a bit of that; who saw a snake in a rope and a branch in a snake; and who finally had a deluded death. When you are a true Witness, you have great thinking power because this Witness is also the Power in the mind. It is the Power in hearing as well. This is the very Power, the Principle, the One the scriptures talk about.

Baba's description of someone observing two people quarreling is a perfect example of the Witness. The Witness remains unaffected by whatever goes on. Whether events are distressing or enjoyable, the Witness is unmoved, unchanged, sublimely impervious. The Witness doesn't grow big or small according to outside circumstances. The Witness doesn't become happy or unhappy with what it perceives. Praise or blame, gain or loss cannot involve it. The Witness observes the dream state, as well as the deep-sleep state. When you wake up in the morning, it is the Witness who allows you to say, "I had a dream." Otherwise, how would you remember it? You were asleep. When you wake up from the state of deep sleep, you hear yourself saying, "I slept soundly. It was so great." Who is it that is saying so? If you were fast asleep, how would you know you had such a deep sleep? It is the Witness who is continually watching over you, continually watching everything, who makes you understand, "I had a dream. My sleep was sound. I really feel good now." Otherwise you would not know. It is the Witness who gives you this knowledge.

It is the same Witness who observes all your activities, good or bad. But it is not affected by the good or evil nature of what you do. It remains completely pure and free from attachment. Yet because it is present, the eyes are able to see. So who sees through the eyes? The Witness.

When the Seer and what is seen become one, when you recognize the unity between them, great ecstasy explodes within. Your perception is cleansed; it becomes divine. Through the knowledge of the Seer within the eyes, you attain divine perception. Then you know who is looking through your eyes. Jnaneshwar Maharaj describes this pure vision in his *abhanga.* He says:

> I am the Witness; I am the blue light in the Void.
> Still I remain different from everything.
> When the sight turns inward, hear what it beholds:
> The inner eyes see what lies beyond the mind;
> then I experience my attributeless being.
> Jnanadev says, Nivritti gave the wisdom in which
> I saw the whole universe within myself.

"I am the Witness; I am the blue light in the Void." The saints describe the Witness in so many different ways. Some saints say the Witness is as dark as thunderclouds, or iridescent, or as soft as velvet. As I was coming to the program this morning, the black swan, with its beautiful, reddish-pink beak, was standing majestically right by the path. As I saw the iridescent black color, I kept remembering what the saints say about the Witness. The swan was standing there so still—black; wonderful, gorgeous black; heart-warming black. Like the Witness, Witness-consciousness. The animals and the birds, all of nature, are constantly bearing witness to your life. The elements—fire, water, wind, and so on—bear witness to your existence. They are in this world, but completely uninvolved; they extend great help, wonderful support, life energy. Nature is one of the greatest examples of a witness. There is continuous flow, yet it is steady. Ceaselessly, it moves, but it goes nowhere. There is no place where it is not. There is no thing in which it doesn't exist. It just is. The Witness. And it is the same Witness in all. When you want to see the form of the Witness, you may see it in different colors. But it has its own color, which is beyond the perceptions of the senses. It just is. It is the experience—the experience within itself.

The great saints who were ardent devotees of the Lord perceived Witness-consciousness as their Beloved. They implored their Beloved to appear in a form that they could worship, one they could watch, one they could adore. With all their heart and purified will, they prayed that the Witness might take a form and become a tangible reality that they could behold with their physical eyes. These poet-saints understood that the true purpose of their eyes was to see the form of God. They vehemently refused to look at anything that was not sanctified. They lived with one strong yearning: wanting darshan, the vision of God; never having enough of it; wanting to behold the Truth in all its splendor. Through these intense acts of remembrance and surrender, they did, in fact, see this entire universe as the light of God. A Sufi poet-saint said:

> O Lord, please let me see You,
> for You are dearer to me than my own breath.
> You are truly the light of my eyes.
> Night and day I remember You incessantly
> with the hope that You will fulfill my wish
> to behold You.

Narsi Mehta, a great poet-saint from the Indian state of Gujarat, sang:

> O Lord, please appear to me!
> Don't you see how thirsty my eyes are!
> O You who are everywhere,
> please come into the gloomy temple of my heart and
> kindle your flame of love.

The Sufi poet-saint Amir Khusrau sang:

O my *sadguru*, this is the desire of your disciple:
that my eyes may have the constant vision of
your own form
until my last breath.

Ram Tirth, a modern saint, sang:

Since the eyes of my heart were opened,
I am able to see deep within.
Even when I look at the world around me,
I find my Beloved wherever I turn.

In the language of the saints, it is when the inner eye opens, when the eye of the heart, the subtle eye, becomes active, that a person truly begins to see, truly begins to understand, truly begins to live in the light. The eyes begin to fathom the mystery of the Truth. The beauty in the songs of these saints comes from their experiences of the Beloved, of the Witness, of absolute Consciousness embodied in a human form. This experience is so intoxicating that in their songs they revel in the ecstasy of that darshan. Through their songs, they want to awaken seekers, to help open their eyes to the Truth so they can behold the splendor of the Divine.

Once, during the time of Shri Ramanuja, there was a famous wrestler. Now Ramanuja was a great scholar as well as a great devotee of the Lord. He had written many philosophical texts. One day as he was sitting on his porch, he saw this famous wrestler holding an umbrella over a prostitute as she walked down the road. The sun was scorching and he was protecting her from its rays. When the sage saw this sight, his heart melted, and he understood that the wrestler was a devotee of beauty. He called him over and asked, "Why? You are such a good soul; you make such contributions to society; you have done so much for so many people. Why do you shamelessly walk like this on the street? Everyone ridicules you. They laugh at you and make fun of you."

"She warms my heart," said the wrestler. "She gives my heart something that nothing else in this world does. I receive something from her that I can't do without."

"You are worshiping beauty," said the great teacher, the *āchārya*. "You are worshiping the goddess of beauty, aren't you?"

"Yes, that's it," said the wrestler. "There's something about beauty. When I see something very beautiful, I go wild. I want to hold it. I want to carry it in my heart. I want it all the time."

The *āchārya* asked, "If I were to give you something even more beautiful, more splendid, would you accept it? Would you let the prostitute go her way, and would you begin to live your life as a true human being should?"

Touching the feet of the sage, the wrestler said, "If you make such a promise, I also promise that, yes, I will follow the beauty you show me."

"Come inside," said the sage. He had the wrestler sit in meditation. He touched his head and recited some mantras. "Just sit here for a while."

The wrestler did. Lo and behold, he had the darshan of the Lord. Right before his eyes, he saw the most astounding beauty with his own eyes. Not only that, his entire body became light. He sat in this state of awareness for hours and hours. Then, finally, when he came out of meditation, he began to perceive the same divine, astounding, splendid light everywhere. There was an incredible shift in his heart. He saw the entire universe as God. He began to see all men as gods, and all women as goddesses. He began to feel love for the first time in his life. His eyes were moist with the love of God. He couldn't believe he was having this immense experience of love. His entire body was trembling. He fell at the feet of the sage and said, "If such beauty, such love, exists in everyone's life, why is it hidden? Why doesn't everyone know about this?"

The sage just smiled and said, "This is your time. It's your time to have this experience."

The beauty of the Lord is so captivating that His devotees want to see Him, want to have His darshan all the time. It does something to the awareness; it does something to the heart.

A devotee of the Lord sang:

The mind is immersed in the splendor of the Lord.
The mind is immersed in the splendor of the Self.
The mind has merged in Rama, the Lord.
The mind is immersed in the radiance of the Absolute.

The eyes are riveted on the Lord's feet,
as the bumblebee is captivated by a lotus.
The transient ripples of worldly existence are stilled.
The mind has turned within and become intoxicated.
The eyes are riveted on the Lord's feet.

"The eyes are riveted on the Lord's feet." Discipline in seeing—let your eyes see God alone. Look for God alone. See only God in yourself. See God in each other; see the splendid beauty, the astounding beauty.

Remember Baba Muktananda's words: "A life of discipline is nectar; it is filled with joy." As you go about your day, watch your eyes. Be the Witness. Give your eyes rest, over and again, by meditating, by doing *japa*, by allowing the purest, the most beautiful feelings to arise in your heart. As you watch another person, give your blessings. As you see something, extend your support, your help. The energy flows out very fast through your eyes, so be the Witness. Let the eyes give the most beneficial blessings. In order to do that, keep your heart in the Witness state as well.

In everything you do, let there be the awareness that the great energy is watching over you. Discipline in seeing—it's a great practice. I promise you, if you pursue this yoga of discipline in seeing, it will purify the way you see the world. Your vision, your dreams will be filled with ecstatic events. Your thoughts will be filled with uplifting words. Your entire body will be able to perform hatha yoga postures it never could have done before. How the eyes perceive makes a very big difference. So have some control over your eyes. The eyes dictate the posture of the body, so if your eyes become still and steady, if the eyes have a purpose, a focused goal, then they give power to the body as well. The discipline of seeing is very important; it's a great practice.

With great respect, with great love, I welcome you all with all my heart.

Sadgurunāth mahārāj kī jay!

July 8, 1995

Chapter Six

What Enters Your Ears Goes Straight to Your Heart

Discipline in Listening I

With great respect, with great love, I welcome you all with all my heart.

We have been discussing discipline in seeing and the importance of where we place our visual focus. When Swami Muktananda spoke about his Guru, he would often point out that although Bade Baba's eyes were looking outward, the focus was inward. He was in *shāmbhavī mudrā*. Whenever you want to remember discipline in seeing, just visualize the divine face of Bade Baba. It will give you the awareness of what that discipline is, of what it is that you must watch all the time. Even though his eyes appear to be looking outside, the gaze is turned within. Just by watching those eyes, you merge into Consciousness.

The eyes of such great beings truly reveal that they have merged into the Absolute, Brahman. Their eyes do not wander aimlessly; they have found their focus, they have found their Truth. So when you meditate on the divine eyes of those great beings, you too experience Brahman, the Absolute, your own great Self.

The *Bhagavad Gītā* says:

Here in the practice of yoga,
  no effort is lost,

> and no progress is ever lost either.
> Even a little of this discipline
> protects one from great danger,
> from great fear. [2.40] [1]

This is a beautiful *shloka*, a great verse. It gives you such assurance, such support. The dharma of discipline redeems you.

Why is the yoga of discipline so essential for every seeker of the Truth? The very fact that you are a seeker means you want to know the Power behind the universe. You want to unearth the mysterious laws behind events. You want to understand the independent joy that you come across every now and then. Think of a time when, all of a sudden, you were happy. You didn't do anything to make yourself happy, but you were happy. This happiness is called *svayambhū*, spontaneous. It is self-born joy. As a seeker you want to know what causes this. There have been times in your life when you have had a glimpse of unconditional love. Without any cause, you experienced love for someone. Without any reason, suddenly you loved the entire universe. For a few seconds this state lasted, and then it disappeared. You want to know what this is; you want to become anchored in this pure state of love.

Your heart has a very deep yearning to find its true owner, its true Master. To discover the Master of your heart, to make it a reality is no small endeavor. Both the goal and the means of attaining it are very lofty. The path and the goal are not different. When you finally realize the Truth, the path and the goal are one and the same. Therefore, when you do sadhana, it should not be halfhearted; your full focus must be there. The path is as important as the goal. The process of sadhana is as significant as the goal.

The major difficulty resides in the inclination of the senses to look outside for their entertainment. There is also the natural law of gravity holding you down. Constantly, you are pulled down. You try to sit for meditation with an upright, elongated spine, and before you know it, deflation occurs. And then you remember, "Oh, yes, elongate my spine." So once again you sit up straight, and then before you know it, gravity has pulled you down again.

There is another difficulty. Because of the outgoing tendencies of the senses and the downward pull of gravity, a seeker often finds himself in a quandary. What he is looking for is beyond the reach of the senses, yet he must master his senses to attain the Truth. Isn't this a paradox? What you want to know—the Truth, the light—is beyond the senses. In fact, all the scriptures say it is beyond the mind, beyond the intellect, beyond the five senses of perception, beyond everything. Nevertheless, you must use all your senses to know the Truth. It is a paradox.

A seeker is constantly struggling with this paradox. It is like this, but then it is like that. It is beyond the senses, but then, without the senses, how will you know it? Even if you find the Truth, you are not there to delight in that experience. You must lose yourself in the Truth to know the Truth, but then you have to be there to say, "I'm ecstatic. I've seen the face of God." How can you do that if you lose yourself completely? This is what a seeker constantly struggles with: "Am I there? Am I not there? Should I be there? Should I not be there? Is my ego in the way, or is my ego useful?"

A seeker must turn the senses around and redirect them toward his own heart. And that is about as easy as putting out a volcano with a bucket full of water. Impossible. Unthinkable. This is why it is such a heroic undertaking to turn the outgoing senses around so that they can make the inward journey. You need courage. This is why the Upanishads say that you have to be courageous to do sadhana. Only a courageous soul is able to pursue sadhana.

The very thing that is the source of distractions is the same thing that can take you to the goal. Take the example of a friend who seems to be undermining everything you do. Yet this same friend, who seems to be such an obstacle in your life, could end up being the person who inspires you to see God. In that case, he would be a true friend.

How does one control a wild bull? Think of a really ferocious animal, crazy with rage, foaming at the mouth, and charging right at you with tremendous speed. The senses have the same wild fury, the same savage momentum. How can you bring them under your control and make them see the radiant Truth?

During Baba's time in Gurudev Siddha Peeth, some devotees gave him a young elephant. The elephant was called Swami Vijayananda, and as a teenager, he was wonderful. As the years went by, he grew bigger and bigger, and they had to keep building bigger sheds for him. During his mating season, he went completely mad. No matter how much his trainer tried to subdue him, it didn't work. The elephant wouldn't listen to anything. All the discipline of the entire year went down the drain. So that he wouldn't run amok in the village, the elephant had to be chained when he was in heat. But there was so much force in his passion that he would rub his legs against the chains and create huge wounds. The only person who could control him was Baba. However, Baba was traveling on his world tours, so he often wasn't there to control him. Vijayananda knew only one thing, and no one could change his mind.

Baba used to describe how animals were slaves to one particular sense pleasure or another, but human beings are addicted to all five sense pleasures. So as human beings, you have a very difficult task ahead of you. But you do have the chance to transcend the powerful senses and taste the nectar of the Self.

Discipline in listening. The *Rig Veda* says:

> O Lord, may we ever hear auspicious words
> with our ears. [1.89.8] [2]

This earnest plea invokes God's grace so that we may hear only that which is auspicious, consoling, and nourishing for the soul. The sense of hearing is another one of the five senses that is outgoing by nature and indiscriminate in its choice of objects. It is not easy to keep your ears from becoming involved in everything they hear. Words are very powerful; they engage the mind. If you do not know how to choose what words to take in, you are at the mercy of your environment. Sooner or later, this filling of your mind with indiscriminate words takes a terrible toll.

In one of his insightful songs, the great saint Sundardas describes the various effects that words have on us. He says:

> When some people speak, we are happy,
> for their words are as soft as flower petals
> and are pleasing to the mind.
> But there are other people who utter words
> that are as sharp as the edge of a sword
> and create a feeling of enmity
> in those who hear them.
>
> Some people speak with such bitterness
> that their words pierce the mind and cause pain.
> Sundardas says, There are
> different types of people:
> some are superior, some are mediocre,
> and some inferior.
> And they all speak accordingly.

When this is the case, you need to be very vigilant about this great faculty of hearing. To whom should you give your attention? How will you utilize this incredible mechanism, the sense of hearing? Whatever goes into your ears creates a fountain of life or a furnace of hell. You are responsible for your own mind and the way you choose to live. You have free will; you can live the way you choose to live.

Think of the owner of a house. He or she makes sure that the house is safe. The beauty and security of the house and its residents have to be protected. Therefore, not everyone or everything is allowed inside. The owner of the house expects people to arrive with a proper invitation at the right time. He keeps the house safe from all sorts of intruders—burglars, insects, bats, and other wild creatures. To a certain extent, he is on guard. He makes sure nothing creeps in through the doors and the windows. He is always watching over his house, inside and outside, for the beauty and safety of the house. Why? So that he can live happily and at ease in his own home, so that he can relax. For his own peace of mind, he maintains his home diligently. He cares for the roof. He replaces broken windows. He tends the lawn. He creates and protects the atmosphere out of love for his family.

If the owner of a house does not do all these things, sooner or later his place becomes dilapidated, a roost for scavengers, a hideout for thieves, fertile ground for infestations of all kinds: cockroaches, termites, vagrants. It becomes an ugly sight. No one even wants to hear about it.

The same thing applies to your body in which you dwell your whole life long. You have a house—your body. You have chosen this body. Each one wills what kind of body he wants to be born into. Some of you may wonder, "Is there such a thing as reincarnation? Is it really true? Do I have the power to choose the family I will be born in?"

Yes, you do. I hear so many people say—people who don't believe in religion or in any spiritual tradition—"In my next birth, I want to be like so-and-so. In my next birth, I want to be born in a family like this." You do have these desires. This is how you choose. You may think you are just making a casual statement or an off-the-cuff remark. But it is recorded in the universe. Every thought of yours, every feeling of yours is actually recorded—and each one influences what you get in return. It's like putting money in the bank and then later getting it back, multiplied many times. Everything you say and think and do is recorded in the universe.

There is a sweet family in Australia, people who have been Baba's devotees for a long time. One of the daughters recently wanted to go back and see her family house, which had been sold many years before. Her mother had run a Siddha Yoga Meditation Center in this house, and many devotees had come and chanted there. At the time, the daughter was a very little girl and she was embarrassed about her mother meditating, doing yoga, and following an Indian Guru. She was so embarrassed that she didn't want to bring her friends home. And if she ever did bring them home, she had to steer them so their eyes would not wander into the meditation room, where they would see all those weird pictures.

So the girl had lived in this house as a stranger. Now that she practices Siddha Yoga herself, she felt she needed to make peace with the house. She needed to let the house know that even though she had been arrogant, had refused to believe in what her mother was doing, and had been resistant to any spiritual practice, still the house had been compassionate. It had given her prasad, the blessing of a spiritual home. Now that she has so many meditation experiences of her own, she wanted to offer her gratitude to the house where she had lived as a child.

She went to the house, met the woman who owns it now, and explained that she had come to see her childhood home. Now, the new owner had never met this family. She had bought the house from someone else, but she said, "Oh, good. I've been thinking about your family. Please come in." Then she asked, "What did you people do in this house?"

The young woman was horrified. She thought, "How can I explain what my mother did?" So she paused, repeated the mantra to herself, watched her breath, remembered the teaching about equipoise, smiled, and finally said, "Do you know anything about meditation?"

"Yes!" said the owner. "In fact, I'm a meditator."

"Oh, good. But why do you ask?"

"Well," said the owner, "first I have to tell you I'm not crazy. I have a profession, I have a family. I'm a very responsible person. But ever since we bought this house, I wake up in the middle of the night, and I hear this music." Then she hummed the first line of the chant *Muktānanda Mahān.* "Can you explain? I wake up my husband and ask him, 'Can you hear it, can you hear that music?' And he groans and says, 'No, I don't hear anything.' But I keep hearing this strange music."

By now the devotee was very happy. She felt she could forget about equipoise and dance for joy. Then she explained that over the years many devotees had sung that chant in the house. To this day, even after so many years, that house is still holding the vibrations of that chant because that was what people had done in that house. So remember, everything you do and think and feel is recorded.

Listening initiates a very powerful process. There is the simple dharma of being human, and that entails listening to the advice of elders, listening to the loving corrections of parents, listening to the knowledge imparted by teachers, listening to the joys and sorrows of friends and neighbors. All this is a form of giving to the world, giving by being receptive to what it wants to give you, by being patient and open. When you are unable to provide this power of listening, then you are considered cruel or apathetic, unresponsive, hard-hearted, or self-centered. Basically, when you turn a deaf ear to others, it paints a very bleak picture of *you.*

Listening is a great art. On one hand, you have to keep yourself present in order to listen; on the other hand, you have to be very discriminating to protect yourself from being depleted. How much can you listen, after all? The world is full of opinions. Some are useful and others are hopeless. Some are valuable and others are condescending. Some are uplifting and some, destructive. Some take you to heaven and others, to hell. So the task that lies before you is not simple.

However, unless you exercise discipline in listening, you will be carried away by waves and waves of words, until one day, you will end up feeling that some essential part of you is stranded on the beach, while the rest of you is lost at sea. You are listening and so much is coming at you with such force that you bury your face in your hands and wonder how to solve these mammoth problems. How are you going to solve it all? How are you going to be there for every person?

With disciplined listening, you know what to let in and what to keep out. You create a boundary that is wonderfully flexible; it moves the way you want it to move.

A disciplined listener is a good listener. A long time ago in China, there were two friends, one who played the harp skillfully and one who listened skillfully. When the musician played or sang about a mountain, the other would say, "I can see the mountain!" When he played about rivers and streams, the listener would say, "I can hear the running stream!" But one day, the listener fell sick and died. The harpist cut the strings of his harp and never played again. As people say, it takes a great man to make a good listener.

The great saints know that God is the greatest listener in the universe. In their prayers we hear them singing to God. As Mirabai says:

> O merciful Lord, says Mira, hear my plea,
>   and give me Your darshan
> at the dead of night by the river of love.

And Narsi Mehta, another saint, sings:

> O Lord, please hear Narsi's prayer
> and put an end to my sorrows and pain.
> O Lord, my speech is crude,
> without the least bit of sweetness,
> yet I have come to You

so that You may hear my pleas.

God is always listening. In fact, the poet-saint Kabir said:

I don't know what you think God is like.
At dusk, the priest calls out in a loud voice
  to the Lord.
Why? Do you think your Lord is deaf?
He can hear the anklets that ring
on the delicate feet of an ant as it walks.

"The Lord can hear the anklets that ring on the delicate feet of an ant as it walks." So God is always listening. He is the best listener in the universe. When you see the paintings of the saints, you see the image of the Lord listening with rapt attention to every word they sing. Have you seen the paintings of Surdas in which he is singing, lost in ecstasy, and the young Krishna has put his flute down to listen? That is how it is—the Lord is always listening to the prayers of His devotees. Not a single heart goes unheard. That is the truth.

In his book *I Have Become Alive*, Baba Muktananda said: "Through discipline and regularity, you can conserve the strength in your body and make it grow, so that you can use it for the pursuit of God. God has placed the same power in all bodies. There is no partiality in God's distribution. He has given as much power as He has kept for Himself. However, we waste the energy God has given us through the senses and the mind. As we do this, we become weaker and weaker."

Baba went on to say: "Most people drive their body and their senses day and night. They keep looking at things that are not necessary for them to see. They keep listening to things that are not necessary for them to hear. Above all, they think so many unnecessary and useless thoughts. In this way, their energy is scattered."

When you do this, you feel depleted and exhausted. You become weaker and weaker. Very often, the reason you feel weak is because this energy has been squandered through the senses. How? By failing to exercise the fundamentals of proper discipline.

But this is something many people don't notice and don't want to understand. They go on seeing anything, hearing anything, smelling anything, saying anything, touching anything. They neglect to notice how susceptible to disease they have become, how exhausted their whole system is from all these small infringements on discipline. When discipline is neglected, the body falls prey to all kinds of germs.

Even then, most people will not listen to the scriptures, to the words of the great beings. When there is no discipline in listening, the Truth just cannot penetrate. It gets lost because the power of the mind has been debilitated by the indiscriminate way in which people have used their hearing. They have literally worn out their capacity to listen.

Listening does not happen with the external ears alone. It is a process that takes place within. If the senses have been squandering energy, you do not have the power to listen, you do not have the power to concentrate. Discipline is like building a reservoir so that water can be contained. Discipline helps the body conserve its energy.

A seeker ought to contemplate why he has two ears and a keen sense of hearing. What is he supposed to use them for? What kinds of things should he pay attention to? To whom should he lend his ear? How far must he travel to hear the Truth? How will he know when to close the gates of hearing and when to keep his ears open? When will he learn that the words and sounds that enter his ears affect his heart? Whatever enters through your ears goes straight to your heart. How can you shut out negative words without putting your fingers in your ears? What do you do to turn down the volume of the noise inside? How much can you listen to your own thoughts?

It is very important to establish boundaries for your senses, to be able to say freely and with firm conviction, "I don't want to hear this. I don't want to listen to that." And it is just as important to be able to say, "Wait, this may not be flattering, but this is something I must hear. This is good for me. I should pay attention to this. I must listen." These are two sides of the same issue. Discipline in listening is a two-way street.

How can you purify the sense of hearing, the sense of perception? How do you create these beautiful subtle boundaries so that you know what you must take in and what you must not take in, what really belongs to you and what does not belong to you? Not everything the world says is meant for you. The world is full of opinions but they are not all for you. They are not *you.* There is something else blazing inside your heart—and *that* is you. That is what you must listen to. And in Siddha Yoga, that is the mantra.

Sundardas, the great saint, once again beautifully gives us a profound message. In his song, he says:

> Becoming pleased with me, my Guru bestowed
>   his grace upon me
> by giving me the mantra.

"Becoming pleased with me," my Guru gave me the mantra. So there is that step. You perform that action by which you learn how to please the Guru. It is not external flattery—it is through discipline. "My Guru bestowed his grace upon me through the mantra."

Sundardas continues:

> Just as darkness is dispelled when the sun rises,
> in the same way, the Guru removed my ignorance.

The sound of the mantra washes away the impurities of the past. Everything that has been collected inside you, everything that has entered you is purified and swept away. This is why we have saptahs in which we chant for days on end. We completely immerse ourselves in the ocean of the mantra.

The mantra is very purifying. If you want to hear something, hear the vibrations of the mantra. If you truly want to listen, then listen to the sound of the breath that carries the vibrations of the mantra.

The power of the mantra dissolves whatever grudges you have been holding. It erases all the harsh words you have heard through your ears. It is a way to forgive yourself for having allowed your ears to hear harsh words. The mantra is the best purifying force. The mantra creates a subtle protection that you need. If someone is saying something unpleasant to you, good manners don't allow you to put your fingers in your ears. On the other hand, you shouldn't be taking all that in. It is not meant for you; it is not you. So you need this equipoise, which comes about only through discipline in listening, through constant repetition of the mantra.

The poet-saint Lalleshwari described how this practice can permeate your entire universe. She said:

> O Lalli!
> With right knowledge,
> open your ears and hear
> how the trees sway to *Om Namah Shivāya*,
> how the wind says *Om Namah Shivāya*,
> how water flows with the sound *Namah Shivāya*.
> The entire universe is singing the name of Shiva.
> O Lalli! Pay a little attention.[3]

"Pay a little attention." Isn't that filled with compassion? Just a little attention—not much, just a little.

The other day when I was taking my morning walk, some beautiful rain showers began. We were becoming more and more drenched. All of a sudden, stillness pervaded the atmosphere. And out of nowhere—if one can ever say that in Siddha Yoga!—out of nowhere, I began to hear these words, "Have you heard the sound of the raindrops? Have you heard the sound of the wind blowing through the leaves?" At first, I wondered if the person walking with me were singing a song or saying something, but no, she was just walking quietly, silently, reverently. Then I looked into the woods, and there I saw the leaves and the trees smiling, the deer frolicking. It was beautiful—the stillness, the fragrance of the plants. And I remembered Lalli's words. *Om Namah Shivāya,* they are singing *Om Namah Shivāya.*

Have you heard the sound of raindrops? What is the sound of raindrops? It is the sound of the mantra *Om Namah Shivāya.* What is the sound of the wind blowing through the leaves? It is the sound of *Om Namah Shivāya*—the mantra, the vibrations of the mantra. What is the sound of the heart? As I listened to the sound of the raindrops and the sound of the wind blowing, as I became more and more immersed in this sound, it was very clear: the sound in my heart and the sound of the woods were one and the same. We were chanting the same mantra. Just that sound, *Om.* It was resounding so sweetly, so quietly, yet so perceptibly. I just had to walk a little more slowly and breathe a little more quietly so I could hear the whisper. And then, once I became even quieter, the sound of the mantra became louder, reaching a crescendo. I wanted to fly through the sky. It was an incredible, ecstatic experience of the mantra.

Discipline in listening. How to do it? Another way to be disciplined in listening is not to keep bad company. Mirabai said:

> Give up bad company
> and keep the company
>   of those who love God, instead.
> Listen to their conversations
>   and discussions about God.

When you take an Intensive or one of the courses offered in the *gurukula,* you are having satsang. You are keeping good company. They say that even to hold a scripture in your hand, you are keeping good company. You are holding something sacred, something very holy. So you can imagine coming to a place where spiritual subjects are openly discussed, without any fear. You freely immerse yourself in the discussions and in the conversations about God, the Self, your own personal experiences. You have the divine spark within, and that must blaze very high. To keep it burning very strong and pure, you come to satsang and take part in it. You drink the nectar of satsang. This too is discipline in listening.

When you take a course with one of the swamis or scholars, you listen to the Truth. Something penetrates, something goes deep within, and then when you meditate, it's there. You have the realization of what you heard about in the course.

In the Intensive, your Kundalini energy is awakened. If you have taken many Intensives, your experience becomes more and more tangible. You experience greater and greater purification. There is another revelation, another insight. You experience yourself becoming more and more anchored in the knowledge of the Truth, and this gives you a divine confidence, a divine conviction about your own great Self. These are the fruits of discipline in listening.

All of the poet-saints tell us in songs and scriptures that the real purpose of the senses is to know God, to revel in His glory. The great saint Kabir revealed the key to making the senses a boon rather than an obstacle in a seeker's quest to know God. He said, "Don't consider these senses of perception to be an obstacle. They are actually the means to know God, to know the Truth." Kabir went on to say:

> Don't be deluded.
> Chant the name of God!
> You have been given eyes to see the Lord.
> You have been given ears to hear the true teachings.
> You have been given a mouth to praise God,
> to sing God's praises.

You have been given hands to offer selfless service.
Kabir says, O noble seeker, listen,
Gold exists in the mine, but you must dig
in order to get it.

So you go deeper into yourself. You transcend yourself to find gold, and that is the light of God, the Truth. "Don't be deluded. Chant the name of God." Listen to the mantra. Don't be deluded. Understand these senses of perception that God has given you—eyes to behold His form; ears to hear about Him; a mouth to sing His praises; hands to serve Him, to serve Him fully, to serve Him with all your love.

Discipline in listening will give you the nectar of the Self. Whenever you want to hear something that is not beneficial for you, remember what Kabir said, "Don't be deluded." Don't be infatuated with words and with flattery. You must dig within in order to find gold. Listening is a very powerful process. So listen to the Truth. When someone is speaking, hear the Truth. Sometimes you can hear that ring in their voice, the ring of Truth. Listen to that Truth.

With great respect, with great love, I welcome you all with all my heart.

Sadgurunāth mahārāj kī jay!

July 9, 1995

Chapter Seven

Hear Only What Is Worthwhile

Discipline in Listening II

With great respect, with great love, I welcome you all with all my heart.

This is a very quiet morning, a soft morning. As the rays of the sun pierce through the mist every morning, you can experience the gentleness of nature. Within the heat of the sun is great tenderness, great love. The rays of the sun give life to all living beings; the heat of the sun is energizing. It removes all kinds of ailments. When the rays of the sun are absorbed in the right measure, the right amount, they have healing power. They give health to people whose minds are sick and whose bodies are sick. They also give health to seekers of the Truth, to Siddha students who want to know God, who want to walk the spiritual path. The heat of the sun is significant. To walk on the spiritual path, you need the full support of the sun.

In each of these satsangs, we have been focusing on one aspect of this great wonder, the yoga of discipline. Recently, we have been practicing discipline in listening. To choose what you should hear and what you should not hear provokes a great deal of subtle contemplation. It is not a simple, reflex action: "I'll take this in. I'll shut this out. Yes, I like this; I'll listen. No, I don't like this; I won't listen." Although it takes practice for this discipline to become spontaneous, even a little effort bears fruit quickly. It becomes clear that by making the right choices, you are able to take delight in the song of the Self. The benefits of this discipline are vast.

In his book *I Have Become Alive*, Baba Muktananda said: "A life of discipline is nectar; it is filled with joy. The scriptures say that in the beginning, a disciplined life may seem very strenuous and painful but that as you pursue it, it soon becomes joyful. On the other hand, the pleasures that give you momentary joy bring sorrow and trouble in the future. The joys of the senses are short-lived, but the joy you attain through discipline lasts a lifetime."

You may not believe in different lifetimes, in reincarnation, so just think about this particular life. When you have sincerely followed a certain discipline, notice how the fruits of this discipline lasted for a long time instead of just an hour, a week, or a month. The fruits of discipline are vast. Once you have followed a certain discipline, it stays with you. Even if you become lax, the good effects of that discipline do stay with you.

Consider those who do hatha yoga religiously. Say they do their hatha yoga postures for two years, day after day, week after week. Of course, they take a few breaks, but they are quite consistent for two years. Then they forget all about it for five or six years. And then one day, the longing for hatha yoga postures, for those *āsanas*, is rekindled, and they begin again. Of course, they re-experience tightness in the body, tightness in the ligaments. They can hear their joints crack. Nonetheless, within a few days they are back into the postures; once again, they are easy. What happened? The benefits of the discipline they followed for those two years are still with them. The fruits of discipline never go to waste. They stay with you forever. Whatever discipline you have followed, it will stay with you.

We are talking about discipline as nectar. No one is dragging us toward discipline; no one is holding a club over our heads and saying, "If you don't follow discipline, that's it; that's the end of you." We want to follow discipline joyfully, not out of fear. In fact, Baba Muktananda used to say very vehemently, "Follow discipline for your own sake. Don't follow it out of fear of me. Don't think, 'Baba won't like it if I don't follow discipline.'" He would say, "Do it for yourself. Experience your own joy." You don't follow discipline because you think the Guru will be angry if you don't. Nor should you follow discipline because you think others will be displeased with you. There shouldn't be any of these motives filled with fear, agony, and judgment. The discipline that you follow must arise from within yourself. That is when you can taste the nectar.

Now in this modern age, many people start out resisting discipline. They think, "Discipline comes from religion and we don't follow any religion; we are free people." They flinch at the very mention of the word *discipline.* But sooner or later, most of them discover that life without discipline is flat and confusing. There are teenagers, for example, who resist discipline, who want to live their lives in a haphazard way, who want to live a licentious life. When they finally come to their senses, they spend the rest of their lives improving their bodies, their lifestyles. They spend thousands of dollars in rectifying the damage done in those teenage years when they thought they had the freedom to eat five pieces of pizza and ten *dosas* and five hamburgers in an hour. They do all kinds of health practices to detoxify themselves, to remove the toxins that they collected in the name of freedom, in the name of rebelliousness. Most people want to reject rules and "do their own thing."

It doesn't matter what field you work in, or even if you stay home all day, discipline is what gives you the power to attain your goals. It is what makes your days pass productively. It is what creates the space for your daily duties to be performed with ease. Discipline makes life interesting, as well as manageable. When there is discipline in your life, you can attend to many great things, you can achieve more. Discipline saves time; it saves energy. It gives you a boost to do the things you really want to do.

Discipline in listening is one of the most challenging practices. How do you control what flows into your ears? You hear people speak, you hear many different sounds. How can you avoid them? As long as you are awake, you hear everything going on around you. Even when you are asleep, you hear traffic; you hear neighbors; you hear people moving around in the house.

It is not easy to filter what is rushing into your ears. All the more reason why this discipline is crucial to your sadhana on the spiritual path. Since you cannot stop yourself from hearing, you have to teach your ears to zero in on what is uplifting, on what enhances your vitality, on what relaxes your mind—on what is healthy in every respect.

Baba Muktananda said: "If you wish to listen to anything, don't listen to the terms of abuse used by other people. You should listen only to the name of Rama. You should listen only to the inner music that arises during meditation. If somebody abuses you, you are under no obligation to accept his abuse."[1] This is what is meant by training the ears to hear only what is worthwhile. Almost everyone on earth is afraid of being verbally attacked. A verbal attack can be so destructive. It can scorch the heart to such a degree that one may never again feel strong enough to live confidently in this world. It can turn aspiration to cinders and dust. Yet what obliges a person to absorb such an attack? And what happens when he does?

So many people embrace abusive terms that are thrown at them. The trouble is that once these things get inside you, they turn into grudges. Grudges are a particularly active form of ill will. They smolder away like secret passions. Grudge bearers always keep an eye on their target, waiting for the right moment to take revenge. So the nastiness goes on and on. If you have been affected by someone's verbal abuse, your heart becomes a stone, and then you wait for God-knows-how-long to get back at that person. In the meantime, you fire the same harsh words that wounded you at someone else. You treat others with the same kind of animosity, and then you are surprised that they too harbor grudges. This is what makes you say, "It's a dog-eat-dog world."

Resentments, grudges, desires to take revenge—all these things do poison the atmosphere. By attacking the person who has offended you, you make it even more difficult for yourself. As time goes by, and your heart grows harder and colder, it becomes impossible to love another, to forgive another, and to feel your own goodness within.

Baba was adamant about this. In his spiritual autobiography, *Play of Consciousness*, he said: "You should not undermine your sadhana by listening to the opinions of evil, leering types of people whose minds are perverted and whose habits are bad."

It is very important that you understand the value of your own sadhana. You have spent so many hours repeating the mantra, purifying your mind, and purifying your body. You have spent so much time in contemplation. You have spent hours doing seva to overcome the inner obstacles and to offer your gratitude. You have worked very hard to keep your mind in balance, to walk the spiritual path. You have made great efforts to seek good company. Therefore, you must value that sadhana—all the hard work you have done, all the times you have thought of God, all the experiences of the Self you have had, all the times your mind has been at peace. You must value your sadhana; it is your hard-earned spiritual wealth. You must not destroy your sadhana just because you have listened to hurtful words.

If you do not practice discipline in listening, you allow the arrows of other people's anger to pierce your heart. And then you want to retaliate. Once you buy into this sort of interaction, your choices are limited: you get stuck. It is a very strange phenomenon. Either you become the nasty attacker who is always ready to strike out. Or else you act so helpless that you are a victim in search of sympathy. What is the way out? Where is the saving grace? How do you protect yourself? How will you see the light? How do you clean your heart? How do you create armor for your hearing?

All the saints and great beings give us one remedy, one answer—saturate your power to listen in the golden name of God, in the mantra. Then you can learn to hear only those things that are good for you. Anoint your hearing with the lotion of God's name. You will be surprised at the results. When you do not waste your energy, it accumulates inside you. Baba Muktananda placed great emphasis on conserving the power of the senses. He would say: "If you keep listening to things that are not necessary to hear, then the power of your hearing becomes weaker." [2]

This is great advice for seekers. If you keep listening to things that are not necessary to hear, then it weakens your ability to hear the Truth. If you fill your ears with all kinds of things, then when you must hear the Truth, you don't have the power to hear it; you are too weak to take it in.

What does Baba mean, "things that are not necessary to hear"? This will mean different things to different people. For some of you, it may mean listening to things that don't apply to you, that are not uplifting, or that are none of your business. For others, it may mean things that are simply a waste of time, that are untrue, or that will lead you astray. It may mean things that will eat you up, things that are devoid of God's presence, things that are not steeped in the truth of the scriptures.

By listening to unnecessary things, you deplete your sense of hearing. You weaken the energy of your sense of hearing. There is only so much a person can take in. When someone is babbling away, have you ever wanted to say, "Please, stop! I can't take it!" It is important to understand how sensitive the faculties of perception are. The senses of perception are so delicate, yet we misuse them constantly; we abuse them all the time. We see whatever comes before us; we hear whatever comes along; we taste anything that appears before us. And we touch anything; we grab anything. We constantly overload the senses of perception. But they are so delicate, so sensitive. It is very difficult for them to process all the things that come at them continually.

Although human beings utilize the senses to derive pleasure, what the senses need is to be supported by divine feelings. If you do not allow divine feelings to arise within yourself, then the senses become weaker. What gives power to the senses of perception? It is your own divine awareness, your own inner experience of the Truth.

When your ears are overloaded by things that weaken your perception, it is only a matter of time until your whole system breaks down. Then the body becomes more and more receptive to ailments; it doesn't have enough strength to fight off germs. Of course, ailments come from different sources. There are certain things beyond our control, and there are other things we can control. Here we are talking about things that we can gradually bring under our control. And one of these is listening. If you continually allow your sense of hearing to be overloaded, your energy level is lowered. Then your thoughts and your feelings are affected and you cannot uplift yourself.

You do not experience stamina just from eating good food. You also experience stamina and good energy in the body when you have good feelings. When someone says something positive to you, when someone is gracious to you, when someone is loving toward you, suddenly you experience the lotuses of all the chakras in your body blossoming; you experience expansion. When you have good feelings and stamina, you are able to contribute much more to humanity.

The Indian scriptures recommend ways of strengthening a human being's innate ability to listen. One of the many techniques they give is to listen with great absorption to musical sounds, particularly those produced by classical Indian instruments. These sounds have the power to purify the sense of hearing and also to strengthen the cells and subtle nerves of the auditory system.

Baba Muktananda was quite emphatic about the importance of the instruments that are played during the *ārati* in the temple: the drums, conches, cymbals, and bells that resound while the lights are waved before the statue of Bhagawan Nityananda every morning and evening. Baba spoke about how these particular sounds touch different chakras in the body. "While listening to them," he said, "have you ever tried to find out which centers these instruments touch? The sound of the gong reaches the center where inner bells ring. It begins to resound there. If you listen to that with attention, you will find all your thoughts melting away. If your mind happens to be weak, you may even be scared when you hear these sounds. But they are very purifying; they purify the five elements within us." [3]

When you listen with great absorption to the sounds of the conch, the bell, the drum, or the cymbals, they purify different centers in the body. Baba used to say that the sound of the drum is good medicine for the heart. If your heart is weak, you should listen to this sound. Sooner or later, the sound of the drum strengthens the cells around the heart. The sounds of these musical instruments reach places in the body where even medicine cannot reach.

Many people who suffer from low back pain and joint pain say that when they hear modern instruments, like synthesizers and electric guitars, it makes the pain worse. Anything that is unnatural does affect the body somehow. And then, when they hear a classical instrument like the flute, they experience a very soothing energy. And of course the source of that sound is the breath.

The instruments that accompany the *ārati* and the chants produce sounds that echo the sounds of the universe. The conch is the ocean. The rumbling drums are the earth. The bells evoke the wind. And the ringing of the cymbals is like sparks of fire. Listening to these sounds makes your heart strong. It is also true that focusing your attention on natural sounds—earth, ocean, fire, wind, and ether—cleanses your mind of worldly concerns. It dissolves the age-old fears that cluster in the corners of your mind like cobwebs waiting to entangle you. Listening to these sounds increases your capacity to bear the turmoil of the world. In fact, it is possible through the discipline of listening alone to experience perfect attunement with God. You feel there is always a divine power sustaining and supporting you in your life. You can hear it all around you —the sounds of the natural world, the voices of nature. And in the same way, when you hear the words of the sages and Siddhas, your entire being is purified.

Then, brimming with this kind of experience, you remember Baba's comment, "A life of discipline is nectar; it is filled with joy," and these words delight you. You know from your own experience that they are true. The sounds of nature truly do heal the sense of hearing. In fact, this is the easiest way to practice discipline in listening. Listening to the sound of a mountain brook, the sound of leaves fluttering in the wind, the sound of singing birds, the haunting hollow sound of the wind blowing through bamboo trees—these are beautiful ways to practice absorbing your attention in sound. The *Sāma Veda* tells us that all this is God's intention. It says:

> Listen to the melodious music of the divine poet.
> He plays upon the flute of love —
>   the notes soar to heaven
>   and reach the distant stars
> and dance on the raging waves of the sea.

The earth, the sea, the sky, the stars
are all woven together
by the soft strains of the divine music.
Its vibrations echo through the corridors of time
in the endless canopy of the sky. [4]

Recently, a Siddha student who is staying in the *gurukula* shared her daughter's experience with me. One morning the daughter, who knows nothing about Siddha Yoga, was driving along a very beautiful stretch of highway on the Hawaiian coastline. It was after dawn and the surf was high. Huge gusts of wind were blowing off the ocean; they were singing a name she had never heard before, *Muktananda, Muktananda.* It was so mysterious. Later, she telephoned to ask her mother if she knew who Muktananda was!

The pure sounds of nature clear the mind, and a quiet mind is able to hear the divine Name. If you practice discipline in listening, it will bestow upon you such grace that you will be able to hear the word of God in all its purity and glory.

This is what happens often during a chant. You are chanting away, your thoughts are scattered, your feelings may be shallow at times, but you are chanting. Then, all of a sudden, you hear an ethereal voice. Your attention comes into clear focus. You hear this angelic voice singing, and you begin tasting nectar. Your mind has become absorbed in the chant in a way that you didn't know was possible. An instant before, your mind was thinking scattered thoughts, your feelings were shallow, your body was aching. But, suddenly, you are transported to another world. Your heart weeps with love. Your eyes long for a vision because you are hearing such melodious inner music. You are astounded at this boon, this unexpected gift. What else can you do but let your heart overflow with gratitude?

In a question-and-answer satsang, Baba once said: "Continue to recite the *Vishnu Sahasranām* or the *Guru Gītā* until the very end, with great reverence. What happens to your mind in this state of reverence is known as *shravana samādhi*, the kind of *samādhi* that comes through reading or listening to holy texts. While you are reciting holy texts, you are likely to pass into this state." [5]

By listening to the sounds of sacred texts, your sense of hearing gets cleansed and strengthened, and the mind naturally becomes calmer and calmer until it is completely absorbed in the sweet vibrations of the Truth. Such a mind is very slow to anger. It becomes a serene lake. It acquires such steadiness and power that going through life is as simple and graceful as water flowing, cascading through high mountains and meandering through green meadows.

When the auditory system is purified and strengthened by listening to sacred texts and the sounds of chanting, it develops clairaudience. You are able to hear things from a great distance. Although this may be called a supernatural power, a *siddhi*, all that matters to seekers of the Truth is to hear the voice of God. It is said that God is as distant as the galaxies of space and yet as close as the sound of your own breath. Therefore, the only reason a seeker aspires to the power of clairaudience is so that he may be able to hear the voice of God.

If you master the discipline of listening, you acquire the power to hear the inaudible sound of the Lord, the unstruck sound, the divine sound within. As Baba said: "You should listen only to the name of Rama, the Lord. You should listen only to the inner music that arises during meditation."

Discipline in listening bestows such grace upon you that you are able to hear God speaking within you. So practice this discipline in listening: what you hear, what you don't hear, what you want to let in, and what you want to keep out. Saturate your power to hear in the golden name of God, in the mantra. Listen to the soft strains of the mantra resounding within you. If you hear ethereal sounds within, respect them and let your mind become absorbed in them. For this, you have to speak less and listen more. Even while other people are speaking to you, listen for the sound of God in their speech. Whatever worldly noise you hear, listen for the ethereal sound in that noise. Practice discipline in listening, and see how quickly your mind becomes calmer and your patience increases and you are slow to anger.

With great respect, with great love, once again I welcome you all with all my heart

Sadgurunāth mahārāj kī jay!

July 22, 1995

Chapter Eight

Value Your Hunger

Discipline in Eating I

With great respect, with great love, I welcome you all with all my heart.

I hope you all had a good breakfast this morning. Sometimes when we talk about eating, people get very hungry.

Of all the yogic disciplines we have discussed so far, the one we are about to contemplate hits closest to home—discipline in eating. Of all the things a seeker willingly renounces in his yearning for the goal, bad eating habits are usually the last to go, the hardest to give up. You can turn away from other bad habits completely, but eating is something you do every day. You are exposed to temptation all the time, so you cannot simply renounce eating—you must overcome your bad eating habits. You have to transcend the desire for food that makes you ill. You must develop new habits and practice them at least three times a day.

Food is not something you can live without; eating is something everyone has to do. Of course, when you read the Puranas and other scriptural stories, you hear about yogis and great sages who lived on air or fire or water. They lived on the elements alone and could do without food altogether. Nevertheless, they performed great austerities to attain that state. Also it is said that in those days they could live for thousands of years, so they had plenty of time to overcome their tendencies and to perform austerities. However, it isn't so in this age, in Kali Yuga.

As important as the act of eating is in order to sustain life, it can also be quite deadly. In one of his songs, the great saint Sundardas sums up the seeker's situation. He said:

> God gave us feet to walk here and there.
> He gave us hands to perform good deeds for Him.
> He gave us ears to listen to His glory,
> and He gave us eyes
> so that we could see the path to Him.
> He gave us a nose to adorn our face
> and a tongue to sing His praises.
> Sundardas says, God gave us all these things
> for a good purpose;
> but this stomach, which He also gave us,
> is a cause of great sin.

There are idioms about the stomach in the Indian languages. It is said that the stomach is a place where you hoard sins. People say, "What do you hold in your stomach about me? What is it that you're carrying in your stomach?" Many sins are committed because of the stomach. When people are hungry they will do anything—even commit murder—to feed themselves and their families. In fact, before Valmiki became a sage and wrote the *Rāmāyana*, one of the great epics of India, he was a murderer. That was his livelihood, the way he earned money so he could feed his family. When a person is very hungry, he will do anything. He loses his mind; he loses his senses. So the stomach is said to be a cause of sin, the graveyard of sins.

When the stomach is upset, your thoughts become very negative. You can't even make an effort to have positive thoughts because you are so influenced by the stomach. Even when you feel a tiny bit off in your stomach, the color of your face changes, the color of your eyes changes, your mouth has a bitter metallic taste. When this happens, you don't have enough energy to move through the day. Even if you lie down to rest, an upset stomach still gives you so much trouble.

Once the stomach is in a bad state, usually your mental state is terrible too. Many times people come up in darshan and say to me, "Gurumayi, my mind is very weak. I can't hold on to good thoughts. I'm always thinking negative thoughts."

When I ask how their digestion is, often they say that it's not good. This is what Baba would ask people too, and that's where I learned it. He would ask, "How is your digestion? Can you digest your food? Can you eat well?" Over and over again, people would say, "No. My digestion isn't good. I get stomachaches. I'm allergic to certain foods."

Once the stomach is in a bad state, your mind will be weakened too, unless you have a tremendous amount of merit, of *punya karma* from past lifetimes, unless you have a lot of grace and a very strong will. These will help you overcome the effects of a bad stomach. Unless that much power is there, you will be under the influence of your stomach.

Food plays a vitally important role in the lives of all beings. The very fact that there is life means there is food. It is almost as though *life* and *food* are synonyms. However, when discipline is left out of the equation, *death* and *food* become synonyms. The very food that gives life can also become the source of death when there is no discipline in eating.

For this reason, the sages and seers have placed great emphasis on discipline in eating. This means controlling the insatiable desire of the taste buds for sensation and controlling the impulse to keep the stomach full at all times.

Have you ever noticed that for a yogi every part of life is an opportunity to come closer to God? This is the way we try to live in the ashram, in the *gurukula*. Every celebration, every program, every chant, every session of meditation is another step to take us closer to God. Even the food we eat is meant to bring us closer to the experience of God.

Improper eating habits put a heavy burden on the nervous system. The body can neither assimilate nor expel certain foods that come into it. Most people think about what to put in the mouth, what to put into the body, but they forget to pay attention to what comes out. It is very important in yogic life that what goes in, after it is assimilated properly, should also come out properly. Both eating and eliminating are important. They have a high importance in yogic life.

In ancient times, Gurus would not give initiation until the disciples were cleansed completely. Disciples would have to fast for days on end; they would have to cleanse themselves through *neti* and *dhauti* and other techniques. It was only after their bodies were completely purified that they could receive initiation. Baba Muktananda was very compassionate in giving initiation without requiring such intense purification.

One of the greatest pitfalls in sadhana, in spiritual practice, is laziness, *ālasya*. Believe it or not, laziness is caused mainly by a lack of discipline in eating. When eating is undisciplined, all the internal organs become sluggish from overwork. The consequences of this are listlessness and apathy. Laziness of the body, laziness of the mind, laziness of the heart—these things can often be traced to foolish, destructive eating.

Destructive eating is very subtle. It doesn't just mean eating junk food; it also means eating the wrong combinations of food. When you eat the wrong combinations of food, no matter how nourishing and delicious they are, your whole system can go haywire. All the internal organs become stressed. If you think your mind gets stressed, it is nothing compared to the stress of your internal organs.

When foods are combined improperly, toxins are created. It can take two or three weeks for the body to eliminate the poison completely and to return to its normal state. During that time the body is working very hard. It spends an immense amount of energy cleaning this machine, this temple, this body. If you think your mind works hard—let me tell you, your body works much harder.

Even when you are just sitting down, the scientists say your body is working hard. The heart is pumping and the other organs are doing their work of cleaning, maintaining, and nourishing every cell in the body. So your body is not just sitting quietly. It is actually working very hard, and this is why it is so important that you make time for rest, for relaxation, for meditation. When you do that, you are cooperating with the system; you are helping the body do what it needs to do. When you sit for meditation, even when you think you are not getting meditation, you are actually helping the body.

This is why Baba Muktananda never chided people who said they couldn't meditate. He would say, "Just sit for meditation every day anyway. It's all right. Just sit." Of course, he didn't always go into a complete explanation of why you must do that. Nevertheless, there is a reason: he knew that when people sat for meditation every day, even if they thought they weren't meditating, still a great process was taking place. Meditation really helps your body. When you sit for meditation, the body is able to return to its proper functioning. It is able to breathe well. All the cells can regroup themselves, so to speak—as if they have a chance to meet and discuss what they should be doing.

Once again, disciplined eating does not refer only to what you eat. It also refers to when you eat, how you combine your foods, and choosing the foods that are good for your body. A particular food may be very good for someone else, but not for you.

There is so much controversy about what food is good and what food is not. There are so many different food traditions. Every country, every culture has its own way of understanding food. What it boils down to is that you have to pay attention to your own body. You need to find out what is good for you. There are certain foods that you know are good for meditation because after eating them, your meditation is very good. Whenever you get very good meditation, you should think about what you ate because food does have an effect. It is not just what you read or whom you were speaking to or how much silence you have been observing. It also depends on what you have eaten. Whenever your stomach feels good, you should also consider, "Hmmm, what did I eat?" In this way, you learn about your body. What food you should eat and how you should combine food is different for each individual.

If you are not paying attention to what is happening to the internal organs, if you allow laziness to breed, then understand that your life span becomes much shorter. Over time, this leads to all kinds of ailments, making it impossible for a seeker to do spiritual practices or to focus his attention on the higher goal. When your way of eating becomes unnatural, then instead of being medicine for the body, food turns into poison. Food is supposed to be medicine for the body. When I say medicine, I don't mean the bitter pills you had to swallow at the doctor's office or the medicine your mother thrust into your mouth that made you gag. I'm talking about healing qualities. Food is supposed to be healing, to have medicinal properties. But when eating habits become unnatural, then food turns into poison. What is meant to be life-sustaining becomes life-threatening.

According to Ayurveda, the system of health described in the ancient scriptures of India, there are six flavors that are necessary for the body. They must be taken in moderation and in the right proportions. They are sweet, sour, bitter, salty, astringent, and pungent. These six flavors occur naturally in food. As soon as there is an imbalance of these six flavors, the body undergoes a negative reaction. There should not be too much or too little of any of these *rasas*, these flavors. A lack of balance puts the body under tremendous pressure. So from the most ancient times, the great values of yoga have also been applied to eating—harmony, moderation, and equipoise. In other words, discipline.

Food addictions are very hard to overcome. This is well known, particularly in the West, where scientists have done a great deal of research on the subject. These addictions exist everywhere. A lack of knowledge about eating creates a lack of respect for food. And this lack of respect lies at the core of food addiction, which abuses the body, the heart, and the mind. These three things go together: the body, heart, and mind. When there is no balance in eating, the heart has to work so hard, the mind has to put forth so much effort to have one good thought, and of course the body is also undergoing its own suffering.

When there is no respect for food, your body becomes a kind of haunted house. All sorts of fears and insecurities breed inside you, and you try to smother them with food, food, and more food. Whenever you experience fear, think about what you have eaten. Whenever you are indulging in insecurities, try to understand what you have eaten recently—not just that day, but the entire week or two preceding. You can keep a journal. In the beginning it may seem tedious or useless to keep a journal of what you have eaten, but if you do this, and then look at it at the end of the week, it will give you a very clear picture of how you treat food and how you treat your own body.

The other day someone said to me, "Gurumayi, I'm so afraid. I'm just so afraid."

As he said that, it was clear that there was weakness in the solar plexus, in the area of his stomach. So I asked, "Are you not eating well?"

Immediately, he answered, "No, I eat very well. I eat very well. Everything is fine. Just fine."

Now it's natural to want to protect the stomach. It's a sensitive area, and it's not easy to talk about it in public. So if someone asks a direct question, it's easy to say, "Everything is fine. Just fine."

When people respond like that, there isn't much you can say at the moment. On the other hand, when they ask a question and they have made up their minds to be open to whatever the advice or the instruction may be, they respond in a different way.

Baba Muktananda went to great pains to make seekers aware of the significance of discipline in eating. For example, in a question-and-answer session he said, "When you become too attached to your body, you lose your self-control. Then you begin to eat all sorts of things at all hours and you find it impossible to observe your discipline. Even when you go to sleep, you like to have a snack in your hand."

That's news to me. But Baba said it, so he must have seen someone about to go to sleep with a snack in his hand. He went on to say: "Even though you may not need it at night, so great is your attachment to your body that you like to have some food in your hand. You like the feel of it. . . . If you keep on feeding yourself all the time, your visceral organs will be constantly at work and they will lose their power. If you overwork a machine, you shouldn't be surprised if it meets with an accident one day. Some of the nuts and bolts may give way, or the boiler may burst. It is not good to eat too little, either. One should be able to digest fully what one has eaten, and the stomach should be left empty for a while. Everyone should take great care of his health because health is great wealth."[1]

Some people hide food in cupboards or under their beds. Of course, you can say they have a disease or some kind of imbalance in their system. But many people have overcome this tendency to hide food, this feeling that there won't be enough food if they don't hoard it. This is something you can work on, slowly but surely, particularly if you want to make progress on the spiritual path. You should try to overcome these things that keep you feeling ashamed about yourself.

Why cultivate discipline in eating? Discipline in eating

brings you good health. And good health is called great wealth. Why? Because it allows you to experience heaven in this very body. Health is of the utmost importance if you want to experience the inner worlds. In their songs, in their poetry, the poet-saints said, "God is the greatest wealth. Ram, the name of God, is the greatest wealth." Mirabai said:

> I have attained this great wealth, Ram, the Name.
> And this wealth is so great.
> No matter how much I spend it, it never becomes less.
> No thief can ever steal it.
> I have attained this great wealth.

Wealth represents the Lord, the name of God. When you have health, you have great wealth. It is easier to experience the presence of God inside your being all the time; you can experience that presence in the environment, in your surroundings. A seeker always needs to pay attention to how he spends the energy of his body. It is so valuable. The more a seeker spends it uselessly, the more he becomes a target for all kinds of ailments. The more he conserves his energy, the more able he is to experience the supreme Reality, the great wealth.

In India, people who are trying to please God and win His favor fast on different days, and each day is attributed to a different aspect of God. There was once a woman who decided to observe a particular fast in hopes of receiving a boon. She vowed not to take any meals and not to drink even water. But after several hours, she began to feel hungry. When she could no longer bear the pangs of hunger, she said to herself, "Well, it's mainly water that is forbidden. I can certainly eat some sweets—that's not a regular meal."

So she ate one sweet after another until she had emptied several boxes. Then she began to feel thirsty. She told herself, "It is only water that is forbidden." So she drank the juice of twenty oranges, but still she wasn't satisfied. Then she roasted a huge bag of peanuts and munched on them because she had heard that during a fast it is all right to eat food that grows under the ground. Of course, she could not digest all this, and her stomach began to ache. Terribly.

As she lay moaning in bed, a doctor was called. He examined her and said, "You must have eaten too much."

She sat up outraged. "Doctor, what do you mean? I've been observing a waterless fast!"

This is why Baba Muktananda advised most seekers not to fast. During his own sadhana days, Baba had fasted quite a lot. He used to go without solid food for months on end. There is a particular kind of fast called *ekānna*, in which you eat only one kind of food for weeks, and Baba had often done that kind of fast as well. So Baba knew a great deal about fasting. Nevertheless, when seekers asked him about it, he would say, "Don't fast. Just eat in moderation. Eat in a disciplined way, and when you're not hungry, don't eat. That is the best fast." Because otherwise you see what happens— the waterless fast.

The *Kulārnava Tantra* says, "The mantra does not bear fruit where there is excessive eating." [2] That alone should be a good enough incentive to eat in moderation.

Disciplined eating has nothing to do with being fat or thin. We are not talking about the way the body looks— whether it is big or small, whether it is lean or fat. Once there is discipline in eating, your body will naturally and automatically look and feel the way it should. You don't want to force your body to look the way you think it should. Depending on the structure of the body, the genes in the body, and the way your mother ate when she was pregnant, you are going to have a certain kind of body. You cannot change that. You don't really have much control over the body you receive. Different people have different reasons why their bodies look the way they do. You should not be critical of how people look.

You do not need to watch what other people eat; you do not need to be their supervisor in eating. Let people eat what they want to eat. Don't point your finger at them, saying, "No, no, no!" That kind of behavior is not good. In fact, it is regarded as a sin in India—unless it's a doctor who has prescribed a particular diet, or a nutritionist who is advising you, or your parents who are still guiding you. Otherwise, no one has the right to point his finger at someone else's plate and say, "You shouldn't be eating that," or "That's bad for you." You should never judge what another person eats.

For your spiritual practices to bear fruit, discipline in eating is crucial. When you don't care about how you eat, when you eat, what you eat, and with whom you eat, then your practices too become futile. Excessive eating has caused the downfall of many yogis. Lack of discipline in eating becomes a breeding ground of sins.

A seeker in whom the Kundalini energy is awakened needs to be extremely careful about how he utilizes the divine energy. If you continually burn incense sticks at the garbage dump, it will not make any great difference. In the same way, if the Kundalini energy is used just to digest the food that you have inflicted upon this body, then you will never reach the supreme goal. Baba often used to speak about this. In one satsang, he said: "The divine power of Kundalini should not be compelled to digest all sorts of things. Her entire energy should not be spent on trying to digest the filth that you put in your system by eating all sorts of fried things from the neighboring cafe, or by filling your stomach with endless sweets." [3]

Discipline in eating is important. If you understand what food is all about, it will give you a clear frame of reference. How did the ancient sages deal with the subject of food and eating? The Upanishads have preserved their words in praise of the sacred nature of food. The *Taittirīya Upanishad* says:

> All creatures whatsoever that dwell on earth
> are born of food and live through food.

Food is the first-born of all beings.
Food is the healing herb that nourishes all.
Whoever worships Brahman as food wants for nothing.
[2.2.1][4]

Food is Brahman. Food is God. Food is the healing herb. This is one reason why you would not want to hide food—because it is sacred. You want to give food its proper place. When you recognize food as scintillating Consciousness, then your whole relationship with it is altered. Once you see food as Brahman, once you understand that food *is* Brahman, the Absolute, then just as you would not think of grabbing particles of shimmering light, similarly, you will not grab food carelessly.

When gentle drops of rain fall upon your being, you simply let yourself soak up the beauty and refreshing energy of these showers. You don't try to grab the raindrops. Similarly, having realized that food is Brahman, the Absolute, you will not try to grab food. When a gentle breeze blows across your face, you simply surrender your being to its caress. You don't try to grab the wind. In the same way, once you know that food is Brahman, the Absolute, you will just let it nourish your being.

Just as you let your eyes feast on the radiant beams of the full moon because you know that these luminous particles are healing for your mind and body, similarly, knowing that food is Brahman, the Absolute, you let the energy of food nourish you. You don't try to grab moonbeams, and you don't grab food either.

Therefore, with a deeper understanding of what food is all about, with the understanding that it is the blessed gift of the Lord—that it is, in fact, a form of the Lord—you are able to have great respect for food. You are able to embrace it gracefully. As you receive food, your heart becomes humble. Baba Muktananda was always concerned that seekers grasp this point clearly. He would say: "There is a popular saying that people attribute to Tukaram Maharaj, but they often misinterpret it. The saying is, 'Your stomach comes first and then the Lord.' People take it to mean that first you must fill your stomach and then the Lord can take care of Himself. But the meaning of the saying is that you must first take good care of your stomach and keep it in order. If your stomach is in good order, the Lord will come and dwell there Himself. Therefore, food, your digestive system, and meditation are very closely interrelated." [5] Those who long to have profound meditation need to keep their digestive tract as clean as possible. Good meditation and a good digestive system depend on each other.

Discipline in eating is a sadhana in itself. Therefore, Baba said: "Food is your very *prāna*, your very life. Eat with discipline. Eat with regularity. If you are not regular and disciplined in your food, you cannot be regular and disciplined in any other field either. Your eating habits are of prime importance." [6]

You all know very well that a person's moods are related to the condition of his digestive system. If the digestive system is functioning at its best, then your mood is also pleasant and rewarding. You are a happy person. On the other hand, if the digestive system is in constant disrepair, then your mood is as terrible as that of a wolf with bleeding gums.

Discipline in eating is very relevant to a person's progress on the spiritual path. A seeker should keep contemplating these questions: Who is it that eats the food? Who is it that digests the food inside? Who is it that assimilates this food? Why am I eating? Who provides the food for me? Due to what good fortune have I received this food today? What is the deeper purpose of eating food?

When this new understanding about the sacred nature of food becomes strong, you can begin to bring about a positive change in your eating habits.

In the *Bhagavad Gītā*, Lord Krishna explains the divine origin of the digestive fire. He says:

Having become the digestive fire of all men,
I abide in the body of all living beings;
and joining with the *prāna* and *apāna*,
I digest the four kinds of food. [15.14] [7]

Jnaneshwar Maharaj explained that these four kinds of food are dry, juicy, well-cooked, and burned. It is the Lord Himself who has become the digestive fire. He is the *prāna* and *apāna*, the in-breath and the out-breath. In the Brahmanic tradition, the brahmins first pray to the *prānas*, the vital forces. They offer the food to each of the five *prānas*, saying, *Prānāya Svāhā* and so on. In this way they perform worship to the *prānas* because the *prānas* are needed to digest the food and to carry the nutrients to different parts of the body, as well as to eliminate waste matter properly.

Discipline in eating becomes natural to you once you realize that it is the Lord Himself who is digesting the food. The digestive fire is the Lord too. And the food itself is also the Lord. It is scintillating light; shimmering Consciousness. Eating food is so much more than a sense pleasure. Partaking of food should become worship. When food is eaten as a sacred ritual, the effect it has on you is quite extraordinary. When you eat, it should become a *pūjā*, worship.

To follow discipline in eating, to make it a sacred ritual, you can consider the following steps.

Make sure you are hungry before you eat. Make sure the digestive fire is blazing. When you are really hungry, there is a kind of joy, a certain divine sensation in the stomach area. Then you know the fire is blazing high. Of course, if you become too hungry, then the stomach starts to hurt.

When you sit before your food, offer a prayer to the Lord.

Offer your gratitude to the earth that has produced this food.

Offer your gratitude to all the people who have made it possible for you to have this food today.

Look at your food, respecting it as Brahman, the Absolute. See it as filled with the light of God. See it as filled with *prāna*, the life-force.

Consider the food as prasad, a gift from God.

Reflect on the value of food, and why you want to eat it—to sustain your body so you can pursue your sadhana with vigor, so you can offer your service to God, to humanity.

Familiarize yourself with your stomach, and offer your homage to the divine inner fire that will digest your food.

Repeat your mantra so your food will be infused with its power.

Put your mind and heart in a very happy state, a pleasant state, a blissful state, by remembering good things in your life, by counting all the blessings in your life, by remembering happy stories. Let there be laughter.

Offer the food to God with the feeling that with every bite you will be feeding the Lord.

Then begin to eat the food as if it were nectar.

Every morsel of food that you put in your mouth should be chewed and chewed until it becomes pastelike; then you swallow it. As you chew, let the fire of love, devotion, and faith in God be mixed with each mouthful. In this way, partaking of food becomes worship.

There are some other guidelines that are worth following with great care. The food you eat must be light enough to digest easily, beautiful to look at, and nourishing in its effect. You do not drink water with your food unless it is absolutely necessary to wash down what you are swallowing. You don't want to throw water on the great fire of the Lord; you want that fire for digestion.

Also, it is much better, when you are able, to eat in silence so the energies of the body are not scattered. In this way, your body knows it is performing the act of eating. If there is no silence during a meal, the body gets confused. It doesn't understand that it is supposed to be eating and digesting food, that all its energies need to be engaged in that. When there is still a little bit of hunger left in the stomach, you stop eating. In this way, you keep the digestive fire active instead of smothering it.

This is how a yogi eats, one who is longing for the experience of God.

How do you know that you will be left with only a little hunger and not too much? Once again, it requires practice. Each person needs to recognize the state of his or her own stomach. You should not feel heavy after you have eaten. If you do, that means you have eaten too much. You should still be feeling light; your hunger is satiated, but you are feeling light. You can still feel a little space in the stomach—and that's when you stop eating and get up from the table. If it is a very strong hunger, you will need to eat a little more so that you won't be inclined to eat again within an hour or two.

Seekers who sincerely practice this discipline in eating sometimes ask what to do when they feel hungry between meals. Just as it is important to understand food as God, in the same way, it is crucial to develop a new awareness about hunger. A healthy amount of hunger is very good. You should learn to recognize that it is actually hunger for God. This is why the Sufis say, "Place hunger in the soul; do not regard it with contempt." If you dampen your hunger by eating every time you feel it, you will kill your hunger for God. You don't want to extinguish the fire of hunger for God. That is priceless. If you are hungry for God, cherish that. You are very fortunate. If you let it blaze, it will become a hunger for Truth. This is what the Sufis call "the alchemy of hunger." This hunger is very fulfilling; this hunger is what keeps your heart in God's heart. It is this hunger for God that actually sustains you even more than food.

Once a disciple asked permission to take part in the ecstatic prayer dance of the Sufis. The sheikh told him, "First, fast completely for three days. Then we will have a delicious meal cooked and placed before you. In that moment, if you would rather dance for God than eat to appease your stomach, then you may join the circle of the lovers of God."

Hunger for God has been highly praised, and you need to recognize your own hunger for God. Just as you must pay close attention to your stomach and treat it with respect, in the same way, you must value your hunger for God. You should worship your hunger for God. It is your hunger for God that has brought you here today. The great mystic poet Rumi prayed to his beloved Lord saying:

> Separation from Thee destroys me! Thy image has become my food: For my heart has gained a stomach, full of insatiable hunger for Thee! [8]

Hunger for God is actually something everyone knows. Yesterday after darshan, we were walking up the road when all of a sudden I realized that one of the little girls had sat for darshan the whole time. It was 2:15, and she had not yet gone for lunch. She had been sitting without moving during the entire program, like a great yogini. It was amazing. I said to her, "You haven't had your lunch yet, have you?" She was very quiet and just shook her head a little, as if to let me know that she hadn't had her lunch and she wasn't really bothered by it either. She knew she would have her lunch later. Another young girl, standing nearby, pulled on my shawl and said, "You see, Gurumayi, the *shakti* filled her up so she doesn't have to eat!" So even children recognize that deeper hunger for God. It is very important for seekers in general to recognize the power of this hunger for God.

In the words of Baba Muktananda: "For one who has intense longing to attain That, for one who is thirsty to attain that supreme Truth, it reveals itself in his own heart." [9]

We have touched only the tip of the iceberg on this topic. Discipline in eating is a vast subject, something you will explore and pursue as you continue your sadhana. Maintain the awareness of food as God. Remember that your hunger for

God is valuable.

With rapt attention you have been listening to this talk about discipline in eating. Let there be the same concentration and deep awareness as you go about the other activities of your life today, tomorrow, and the rest of your life.

With great respect, with great love, I welcome you all with all my heart.

Sadgurunāth mahārāj kī jay!

July 23, 1995

Chapter Nine

A Cause for Celebration

Discipline in Eating II

With great respect, with great love, I welcome you all with all my heart.

In this fast-moving world, yogic discipline is a great blessing. The steady hand of yogic discipline supports your sadhana and allows you to go deeper and deeper. It is the anchor that keeps you connected to the teachings you value most. The ancient sages of India verified the importance of discipline for themselves first. Then they exhorted others to follow discipline too. Although they lived thousands of years ago, their teachings apply just as much to our lives and our world as to theirs. That is quite extraordinary. In their day, people did not rush around the way they do now. Nevertheless, discipline was just as important then.

Discipline is built into the universal law. Where there is no discipline, there is no true life. As long as one is breathing and moving and engaging in action, discipline must become the foundation of one's life. All activities must have discipline at their core. When it comes to the experience of the highest Truth, serenity of mind is essential. And that serenity is the fruit of consistent discipline. It cannot be sustained any other way. Without discipline, a person goes round and round and never drinks the elixir of the Truth. Yet a life of discipline is a life of nectar.

The yoga of discipline is a vast and deep subject. We have been studying it methodically, using as a framework the senses, and taking one sense at a time. When the senses are turned outward and allowed to go anywhere they want, they take a person reeling into an abyss of exhaustion and despair. Therefore, it is essential to bring them into the safe harbor of discipline.

We will continue to look at discipline in eating. The sense of taste holds everyone in its thrall. For the sake of the tongue, there is no telling what a person will do. Everything that lives must eat. But this very process of eating can take you to heaven or hell. It can make you a wonderful person or an evil one. Eating can make you ignorant or it can help you realize the Truth. Depending on what food you eat, you will have a mind filled with agitation or with tranquillity. Depending on what food you eat, you will have good relationships with people or terrible relationships. The food you eat determines what you feel, what you think, and what you do. Understanding the value and the nature of food itself is just as important as the process of eating. Discipline in eating must be practiced with every bite.

In his book of aphorisms *Mukteshwari*, Baba Muktananda says:

> As you take medicine in a measured dose,
> take food in a measured, frugal quantity.
> Eat with restraint and reverence — to live.
> Food is your heaven. [190]

There are two key words to remember in this verse of Baba's — restraint and reverence. As long as you use your intelligence about what you eat, as long as you exercise restraint and self-control, then food becomes heaven for you. Along with this restraint, there must be reverence. Food is a gift from God. Food is the giver of life. Food nourishes. Food is God. Food is Dhanya Lakshmi, a form of Lakshmi, the goddess of abundance and beauty.

When restraint and reverence become part of your daily eating, then your life is filled with happiness and worship. If you were sick, you would not take too much medicine. In the same way, to maintain a healthy body, you must not take too much food. Restraint is something you must constantly remember. In time, it becomes something you will be able to do very naturally, as many of you must have already experienced. By applying a little bit of discipline in eating, a little bit of self-control, you experience such good health.

As Baba Muktananda once said: "There is no harm in partially starving yourself, but overeating is positively harmful."[1] Please understand that Baba is not talking about continually starving yourself for the sake of keeping your weight down or because of shame, family pressure, tension at work, or mental problems. Or just because you forgot to eat. What Baba is referring to is maintaining a pleasant hunger in the stomach. This will support your physical health. This pleasant hunger is called yogic hunger, maintaining a lightness in the stomach, keeping the yogic fire blazing in the stomach. He means that you should not extinguish the digestive fire by overloading it.

Sometimes, after you have eaten, you feel hungry again within a couple of hours. It is important to question this hunger because it is false hunger. It takes at least four hours for a full meal to be digested, so if you eat again within that time, the undigested food piles up and it can cause many ailments.

Of course, the body is kind and compassionate. Sometimes I wonder if it's because the body is so compassionate that we treat it poorly and don't recognize its needs, its cries, its weeping. The stomach is kind—it expands and expands and expands. The more you put in, the more it takes. It just goes on taking whatever you give it. But still the undigested food piles up.

If restraint is difficult for you, if you have a tendency to go toward foods that are detrimental to your health, then you must learn to exercise great vigilance about food. Take Baba's advice: add reverence to restraint. Then discipline in eating becomes much more palatable. When it comes to a lack of discipline in eating, one thing is clear: you have no one to blame but yourself. Baba said: "Food is health, and food is disease. If you take food with regularity, then it is pure nectar, but if you take the same food irregularly, it turns into poison." [2]

So food can be heaven; food can be hell. Food can be nectar; food can be poison. Baba went on to say: "If one cannot resist the tendency to overeat because of one's sheer greed for food, and if an illness comes as a result of overeating, how can you attribute it to the will of God?" How can you say, "It must be my karma to be sick; it must be God's will"? To say this is to misuse the teachings. You are using them to cover up your own mistakes and your own lack of discipline, your own lack of restraint, your lack of reverence for food.

Many of you have been contemplating discipline in eating for a while now. You have been observing your relationship with food. Have you noticed that every time you overeat, it brings about a feeling of sluggishness? You can make yourself sluggish by eating too much, by eating more than your gentle and compassionate stomach can handle.

When you give in to your craving for food, have you noticed that it sometimes makes you feel sick afterward? Even if you don't feel sick after you eat too much, still you need to be very careful. Understand that the body is affected by your mistakes, and eventually you will have to pay a very high price. Just because you don't get sick right away after you eat the wrong foods or too much food, it does not mean that everything is all right. It may be all right for a week or a month, but it may not be all right in a few years. Many people say when they become ill, "All my life I was feeling so good, so healthy. I don't know where this sickness came from." They really shouldn't be surprised. Undigested food is a breeding ground for illnesses. It is one of the main things that lowers the natural resistance of the body to disease and makes it break down.

Two weeks ago there was a newcomer here, the husband of a woman who has been practicing Siddha Yoga for a long time. Someone asked him what he thought of the topic, and he said he found it especially interesting because he was a farmer. But he wanted to take it one step further. When it comes to food, he said, it is not just the final product on the table that must be taken into consideration, but also the soil from which that food is produced. The soil must be healthy, and the amount of water and nutrients that are added to the soil are important too. The amount of sunshine, the kind of weather, the breeze—all the elements play a great role in how healthy and nourishing the food will be. Also what kinds of chemicals and compost and fertilizers are added to the soil—all this has a great effect on our bodies.

The earth plays an essential role in the lives of all beings. We are so closely related to the earth; we are made of earth. Without the earth, we couldn't exist. This is something the ancient sages always took into account. The Vedas are filled with praise and glorification of Earth, of Nature—her beauty, her generosity, her compassion. There is a beautiful hymn to the Earth called the *Bhūmi Sūkta* in the *Atharva Veda.* It says:

> Untrammeled in the midst of men, the Earth, adorned with heights and gentle slopes and plains, bears plants and herbs of various healing powers. May she lay out her treasures for us and afford us joy!
>
> The Earth—on whom are oceans, rivers, and all waters, on whom have sprung up food and plowman's crops, on whom moves all that breathes and stirs abroad—may she grant to us the long first drink! [12.1.2-3] [3]

In times gone by, farmers used to worship the land. Before

they began any work with the soil, they would propitiate the land. They would ask for her permission and blessings. Only then would they touch her. While they tilled the ground and planted seeds, they recited mantras and chanted. When the crops were ready to be harvested, once again they chanted and repeated the name of God as they worked. In Indian villages, at harvest time, you could hear the farmers singing as they worked. It was a very happy time. The first crops of the harvest were carried to a temple and offered on the altar with hymns of gratitude before they were taken to market.

The preparation of food was also a great ritual. Women took care to dress in clean clothes, and the first thing they did was *pūjā*, worship. Before they lit the fire and began to cook, they would pray. Then when the meal was ready, they would first offer a portion to God, placing it on the altar as they chanted mantras. Next the food was offered to a guest. Only then did the people of the household eat. Those who did not believe in God still followed the practice of cleanliness in preparing food. They, too, would offer food to a guest first, and then they would eat. In fact, people would go looking for guests to feed. In those days there were many travelers, pilgrims visiting holy places.

In this way, eating, like all sacred things in life, was part of an elaborate ceremony. There was never any question of gulping food down. Eating was like an intricate dance, a great symphony in which every passage was refined and accorded due respect. Everything to do with food was regarded as a form of meditation. From farming the land to harvesting the grains, to taking them to market, to preparing the food, to eating it—everything was a pure form of meditation. People would become intoxicated as they performed these acts. Every part was played meticulously and efficiently. Every job was done with great joy, as sacrifice. It was a *yajña*, a fire ritual.

Performing each action was a way of coming closer to the Truth. Each meal, each ritual associated with food was an experience of the Truth. Having eaten food meant that you soared—not just in the satisfaction of a full stomach, but in the ecstasy of God's life-sustaining grace. Eating was a sublime experience. Your heart overflowed with gratitude. Eating was a sacred act, a ceremony, a ritual.

Baba Muktananda spoke a great deal about the proper manner of eating food. One of the passages that he liked most came from Ayurveda, the traditional Indian system of health, which taught people to remain conscious of three criteria: *hitabhuk*, *mitabhuk*, and *ritabhuk*. Baba loved to explain these three rhyming principles. Once he said: "*Hitabhuk* means to eat that which is good for one's blood, one's health, one's mind, one's brain, and one's general well-being. It will not spoil one's mind or brain or health. *Mitabhuk* means to eat frugally, to eat only as much as one needs and as much as one can digest without any difficulty. It means to eat only as much as will not burden the stomach and to get up from eating while one is still a little hungry. That is *mitabhuk*. *Ritabhuk* means to eat that which is appropriate in a particular season. For instance, if it is cool and raining, yogurt is not at all suitable; one who eats yogurt at that time is only inviting trouble. One who eats a food out of season and then eats it again after four days and yet again after five or six days, all the while suffering its bad effects, is not observing *ritabhuk*; he is violating that principle." [4]

These three principles are wonderful guidelines. Of course, in this modern age, food is flown in from everywhere in the world, so we are not always able to follow the rule about seasonal foods. Nevertheless, you can follow the other two. You can certainly eat only as much as your body needs and only that kind of food that is beneficial for your well-being.

Baba concluded, "Only those who follow these three principles will be free from disease, and they alone will be living for their own happiness and bliss. All others exist only for the sake of doctors."

Discipline in eating should be a joyous act; it should be a celebration. It should not be fraught with fear, anxiety, and nervousness. There is no need to behave as if every bit of food you eat should be weighed on a scale. All the wisdom you receive from the scriptures and the sages, or even from nutritionists and dieticians, should be put to good use. It is for your benefit. Their advice should not make you feel that you can't do anything right, that everything is forbidden, that every morsel of food you eat will be dangerous for your system. Thinking in that way defeats the entire purpose of discipline in eating.

So remember, it should be a joyous act; it should be a cause for celebration. "Yes! I'm going to eat now!" If you don't have this attitude of celebration when it comes to eating, if you are nervous, if you think every morsel of food you eat is sinful, then it's like throwing ink all over fine paper, instead of writing with a beautiful pen. When we have Siddha Yoga celebrations, we are not just eating and drinking and chanting and meditating and meeting people. Much more is going on. There is a constant awareness of the individual soul merging into the supreme Soul, a human being merging into God. There is this great awareness of the Truth—and that is what we are celebrating. As Jnaneshwar Maharaj says:

> Then in the palace of oneness with the Eternal,
> the world sees the festival of supreme bliss.

The point of discipline in eating is to increase your awareness of food, of your eating habits, and of the greatness of living. You have to eat because you are alive. You are alive to achieve a higher aim, to bring you to your true destination — and that is to know God, to love God, to be aware of the divine presence, to experience the Shakti in your own body, to live in the Truth. You are alive to activate the cells in the brain, to activate the consciousness in the mind, to activate the purity of the heart so that you can listen to other people, so that you can be with others without feeling burdened by their presence, so that you can experience ecstasy flowing through your veins.

All this is the real purpose of discipline in eating. If you become obsessed with discipline in eating, it is no better than overeating or becoming obsessed with not eating at all. Then, instead of a great remedy, discipline in eating will turn into a malady, an obsession rather than a practice of yoga. So relax, and allow yourself to follow the instincts that arise in the pure space of your own heart.

In the *Chāndogya Upanishad*, the sage Uddalaka gave his son Shvetaketu this teaching:

> When food is eaten, its grossest portion is expelled as waste matter; its intermediate portion becomes flesh; and its subtlest portion becomes mind. [6.5.1] [5]

The subtlest portion of food consists of the highest nutrients—and to discover that this is what becomes the mind is staggering. It is a revelation to know that your mind, which is the most important asset you have on the spiritual path and for life in general, is to a great extent the product of the food you eat. So the saying "You are what you eat" turns out to be as old as civilization. To find scriptural evidence for this is exhilarating.

It is as though you are walking down the road of life quite casually. All of a sudden, someone stops you and says, "Guess what! You are on the road to paradise." How do you feel at that moment? Jubilant! Your hopes are high, your energy is fresh, and your enthusiasm is bright because you have just discovered that the very food you are eating is the raw material of the mind. Therefore, you actually have the power to cultivate a good mind, a strong mind, a healthy mind, a noble mind, an intelligent mind, a mind that will bring you to the feet of the Guru, a mind that will inspire you, a mind that will fill you with tremendous love for God.

All this is so purifying and uplifting. Discipline in eating! What a great discovery! The mind is made of the subtlest part of the food, so you are in control. It's a cause for jubilation.

In another dialogue of the *Chāndogya Upanishad*, the sage Sanatkumar instructs Narada:

> If your food is pure, your whole nature will be pure. When your whole nature is pure, memory becomes firm. When memory remains strong and unbroken, then there is release from the knots of the heart. [7.26.2] [6]

"Then there is release from the knots of the heart." Ideally, the purity of food is passed intact from the soil to the farmer, to the cook, to the one who eats it. However, not all of us can influence the way our food is cultivated. What *is* within our power is the ability to choose from what is before us. And we should feel very fortunate, because there are thousands of people on earth who don't have this privilege. They can't even get enough food to nourish themselves, let alone have some choice about what they eat. Keeping this in mind, with gratitude for our good fortune, we should take full advantage of this gift of abundance and use it wisely.

The Upanishad says that if your food is pure, it will make your mind pure. With a pure mind, your character, your personality, and your higher understanding will all evolve. When at last your whole nature is pure, then your memory becomes firm. In Vedic times, all knowledge was passed on through the oral tradition, rather than in written form. So the preservation of wisdom depended entirely on the strength and purity of each student's memory. It was crucial to have a perfect memory of what was heard from the teacher, from the Guru. Also the sages, who heard divine mantras in meditation, had to remember their experiences accurately, so they could pass them on to others, so the teachings could be transmitted from generation to generation. Only then could they maintain the purity of the *shrutis*, which are the revealed scriptures, the words of God that were heard, and of the *smritis*, the scriptures that were composed by sages and memorized by their students. All these treasures were preserved intact in a purely oral tradition.

This memory that the *Chāndogya Upanishad* refers to entails constant remembrance of the supreme Self, constant remembrance of each glimpse one is shown of the inner world. Remembering in this way also implies gratitude, which is kindled naturally by the recollection of the experiences one has received. Therefore, it is said that when memory becomes unshakable, the knots of the heart are released and the experience of the Self becomes more and more evident.

When you eat food of great purity, you can soar in ecstasy. You feel so light, you feel lighthearted. This happens because the knots of the heart are being released. Sustained by good nourishment, you are able to perform all your actions with equipoise, and your entire being dances with joy. Then life itself becomes prasad, a great boon that carries God's blessings.

Discipline in eating—there is another essential point to make about this discipline, and it is explained in the *Bhagavad Gītā* by Lord Krishna to Arjuna. He said:

> Good people, who eat the remainder of the sacrifice,
> are released from all evils;
> but the wicked, who cook only for their own sake,
> eat their own impurity. [3.13][7]

Jnaneshwar Maharaj comments on this, saying:

> Ignorant of any act of sacrifice, they seek only the selfish enjoyment of pleasure.
>
> Preparing dishes to satisfy their senses, these sinful people nourish themselves on evil.
>
> You should regard all worldly wealth as material for offerings, and dutifully pour it out as an oblation to the Supreme.

> The food with which a sacrifice is performed and which is pleasing to the Highest is not ordinary food.
>
> Don't think of it as ordinary food, but rather as a form of God, for it is the means of life for all creation.
>
> [3.128-30,132-33]

Whatever is offered to the deity, whatever is offered to God in a temple—that becomes prasad. Whatever is offered on the altar—that becomes prasad. And when you eat food as prasad, you can easily digest it.

Of course, these days, not everyone has the ability, the knowledge, or the means to perform a *yajña*, a Vedic ritual of sacrifice. Not everyone is an *agni hotri*, in whose house the ritual fire burns brilliantly. An *agni hotri* maintains five fires in his house and dedicates himself to feeding them with offerings and mantras every day of his life. This spirit of sacrifice has taken a different form in our modern age: the act of giving in charity.

As Jnaneshwar Maharaj explained in his commentary, "You should regard all worldly wealth as material for offerings, and dutifully pour it out as an oblation to the Supreme." Think of everything you have as an offering to the Lord. Everything you have is a gift from God and must be returned to God. If you give food in charity, you become free from impurities. Then when you partake of your own food and share it with others, you get rid of the tenacious negative consequences of karma. It is almost like dipping food in nectar before you eat. It has the same power as repeating the mantra before you put a morsel of food in your mouth.

If your body is ill for a long time, it is said that giving food in charity is a way to become free from that illness. During your illness, if you desire a certain food very strongly, but you know it's not at all good for your body, then you should give that food away in charity to others. This helps you become well. The same thing is true if you are greedy about a certain food, and you don't know how to overcome this addiction. If you give away that food in charity, then you are freed from its grip.

Once again, not everyone can actually give food away; instead, they give money in charity. Charity may take the form of giving to places where seekers worship God, or giving to the needy, to guests, to brahmins, or to children. Giving to children is considered a great charity. During celebrations, people who practice Siddha Yoga offer donations for special meals. This is one way of becoming free from food karma, and it is also a way of serving humanity. Both parties truly benefit from this sacred act, this sacred charity.

Discipline in eating takes on new dimensions when you investigate it in depth. What you come back to, again and again, are the two words Baba Muktananda used—restraint and reverence. If you just apply these two profound concepts to the way you deal with food, new worlds will open before you. If you find yourself going in the wrong direction—toward the wrong food, or down the road of excess, or up the road of deprivation—exercise restraint. Remember to respect food, remember that food is God. Each time you do, you will find yourself crowned with grace. Then, in this grace-filled state, you make your choice of food.

Discipline in eating is not just about the food on your own table. It is also thinking about others, doing good things for others as well. Every time you are filled with reverence toward food, toward any aspect of God's creation, you experience such lightheartedness. Then, when you perform your actions in this state, it is as though the world you inhabit is continually being filled with love. You are in control; you can allow your world to become filled with love.

In this way, discipline in eating becomes a sacred act, an act of worship offered to the Lord within the heart. In his spiritual autobiography, *Play of Consciousness*, Baba said, "Respect your body as the temple of a deity. Become a priest, offering it the right food and the right relaxation. Let there be only one desire in the body—the desire for love; one wish—to attain the vision of inner light that comes through meditation; one hope—for a body that is moderate and disciplined and radiates inner love."

Discipline in eating fills you with spiritual radiance. The whole purpose of this, as of all yogic disciplines, is to know God, to become established in the awareness of God. That is why the saints use the image of hunger so vividly. They speak of the hunger for God's love, hunger for knowledge of the scriptures, hunger for the wisdom of the sages, hunger to behold the face of God and spend their lives at His feet. *Hunger* is a sublime word, a sacred term. Hunger is a deep longing for the Truth, a hunger to know God. You could say all seekers are hungry, all devotees are hungry. You want God's love. You want to swim in God's ecstasy. You want to eat God's love, to imbibe God's love, to touch God's love. You are hungry to know God, to be in His presence. You are hungry to merge into God. This hunger for God, for God's love, has a very high place on the spiritual path. When you are deeply hungry for God, God appears in your own heart.

By following discipline, you are cooperating with God, you are cooperating with grace. Discipline in eating *is* a cause for celebration; therefore, accept it wholeheartedly, a little at a time. Make it yours. Let the word *discipline* become a fragrant flower for you, so that every time you hear this word you think, "Ahhhh. Intoxicating! It is so wonderful!" Instead of cringing and contracting at the idea of discipline, let your being expand, let your heart run to embrace it.

Revere food as God. Revere your own body as a temple. Observe restraint and practice reverence. There are so many great treasures and miracles within you, so many magical possibilities hidden inside you. Through discipline, you can make them manifest for you, and in this way, you can make the earth a greater paradise. Give this earth the opportunity to feel that she is blessed, that she is happy to have you, that she is grateful for your presence on this planet.

With great respect, with great love, I welcome you all with all my heart.

Sadgurunāth mahārāj kī jay!

August 5, 1995

Chapter Ten

WITHIN THE WORD DWELLS THE RADIANT LORD

Discipline in Speaking

With great respect, with great love, I welcome you all with all my heart.

In this yoga of discipline, we are continually pondering the nectar of disciplining the senses. We have been focusing on one aspect of this discipline at a time and practicing it with great attention, with great fervor. In this way, the vast and deep yogic understanding of life can become part of every action. By looking at each aspect of discipline so closely, it becomes crystal clear. Little by little, it becomes clear that discipline is not only a way to cherish life, it is also a straight road to God. Where there is discipline, you experience the presence of God.

Recently, we have been examining discipline in eating. Have you been watching your eating habits? Were you able to decide how much food you really wanted? As you know, the body is very kind. If you help the body even just a little, it will give you an immense amount of support.

All the disciplines of yoga can be brought to bear on any one of the senses. Discipline in eating primarily has to do with the tongue, with the taste buds. Before we move on, it is worth taking a good look at another function that the tongue performs.

Our topic today is discipline in speaking. In the Indian

tradition, whenever one is pursuing knowledge or the arts, it is considered highly auspicious to begin by invoking Saraswati, the goddess of eloquence, wisdom, and learning, the goddess of speech. It is through her power that language and writing are revealed to mankind. To experience the flowing river of her blessings is indispensable. One of the most frequently recited verses invoking her grace is this:

> O goddess Saraswati, white as snow,
> as the moon, as *kunda* flowers,
> clothed in white garments,
>   holding a magnificent *vīnā*,
> seated on a white lotus,
> ever glorified with offerings
>   from the gods Brahma, Vishnu, and Shiva,
> protect us from all forms of ignorance
>   and mental lethargy. [1]

The Vedas refer to the goddess of speech as Vak, and what they say about her is deeply meaningful. Vak is described as the principle of pure affirmation. In her, everything is glorious, everything is splendid. She is bountiful with good energy. She emerges out of pure nothingness. "O goddess Saraswati, white as snow, as the moon, clothed in white garments." Purity is without any color as such; nevertheless, to give some symbol, to have something for the mind to hold on to, it is said that she is white as snow.

The *Aitareya Brāhmana* invokes Vak as the Mother, saying Vak is truly "the womb of the universe." [2] She is the Mother of all sounds, the Mother of all words. The *Rig Veda* speaks of how Vak, the Word, is discovered, saying:

> O Lord of the holy Word!
> That was the first beginning of the Word
> when the seers fell to naming each object.
> That which was best and purest, deeply hidden

within their hearts,
they revealed as the Word
by the power of their love. [10.71.1] [3]

It was out of love that the sages named each object. Out of love, out of pure nothingness, she emerged. The *Brihadāranyaka Upanishad* defines the relationship between the inner Self and Vak in these words:

He who dwells in speech,
who is different from speech
and yet within it,
He whom speech does not know,
yet whose body is speech,
who inspires speech from within,
He is the Self,
the inner Inspirer, the Immortal. [3.7.17] [4]

Speech is the body of the great Self. These magnificent verses are an indication of the high place accorded to speech in the Vedas and other scriptures. Within the Word dwells the radiant Lord. Speech is the body of the Truth. Speech is the great communicator. In the form of mantras, Vak is the connection between heaven and earth. With the support of Vak, brahmin priests establish a relationship between the mortal world and the immortal world, between the living and the dead. Vak is the link, the great mediator. She also links the inner and the outer worlds of a human being. Through words, you know what is happening inside, and you know what is happening outside. When you feel something through the words of another, when you communicate through words your feelings, your emotions, your thoughts, your concepts, this is the power of Vak, the power of speech.

Although it is said that the Truth is unspeakable, indescribable, beyond the realm of language, still it is through speech that the teachings are delivered, that the heart speaks to God, and that the unspeakable is attained. Prayer has great significance. Mantra has great power. Chanting has great power. *Swādhyāya*, the recitation of holy texts, is filled with great power. What is the source of this great power? For the answer to that, we turn to the scriptures.

The Indian scriptures say that out of the silence, the Word sprang into being. Therefore, speech in its original form is divine; it is a saving grace. However, as a person becomes more and more disconnected from the great Self within him, as he becomes more extroverted in his preoccupations and cravings, he begins to lose touch with the power of Vak, the power of speech. This being so, gradually his communication with the inner Self breaks down.

So the first communication breakdown happens with your own Self. Then you are like a wheel stuck in the mud. The wheel spins furiously, but carries the vehicle nowhere. This is the first breakdown in communication—with your own Self.

The *Rig Veda* speaks of such people saying:

> Certain ones, though seeing, may not see her,
> and other ones, though hearing, may not hear her.
> But to some, the Word reveals herself quite freely,
> like a fair-robed bride surrendering to her husband.
> [10.71.4] [5]

Speech, Vak, originates in the Divine out of the supreme silence. That is her abode. Out of pure nothingness, she arises, she emerges. Speech, Vak, is also capable of reuniting a seeker with his or her own inner glory. Because of misuse, though, her power diminishes, and the impact of words becomes weaker and fainter.

However, this power can be regained; it is not lost forever. Through discipline in speaking, we can once again regather the power of speech, the power of words. One of the most effective ways to do this is through cultivating discipline in speech. Just as a farmer cultivates his field carefully so he can grow proper food, in the same way, you carefully cultivate discipline in speaking.

Though everyone pays lip service to the virtue of picking and choosing his words, few people actually practice it. As the poet-saint Sundardas sings:

> Some people speak like animals;
>   their words have no meaning.
> They chatter day and night like frogs in a well.
> People have their own ways of talking,
>   and they are all different.
> Sundardas says, You should think carefully
>   before you speak.
> Words should be uttered with great discrimination.

It is no coincidence that Sundardas recommends thinking before you speak: there is an intimate relationship between the mind and the word. In the ancient *Shatapatha Brāhmana* it is said:

> The cosmic mind was said to be neither existent nor non-existent. Once created, this mind desired to become manifest. . . . The cosmic mind then created the word.
>
> [10.5.3.2-4] [6]

Speech is at the very root of this manifest world: it is the force through which forms vibrate into existence. It is the first creation of the cosmic mind.

In worship, both the mind and the word play major roles. Without them, sacrifice, *yajña*, is not possible. If mantras are uttered mindlessly, they do not carry the heart's intention, and their ability to invoke the divine presence remains unmanifest. If those who recite the mantras make mistakes, that can nullify the power of the *yajña*.

Therefore, pure brahmin priests are very careful. They protect themselves from hearing ordinary songs, those not created by sages and great beings. They do not want to water down their power of thought and speech, their power to recite Vedic mantras. The brahmins have to carefully maintain this power of speech. They have to continually propitiate the goddess of speech, Saraswati. They must have presence of mind when they repeat mantras. The scriptural texts say that the mantra, the repeater of the mantra, and the goal of the mantra are one and the same; and therefore, your awareness must be present when you repeat the mantra. The goal of the mantra—which is the deity of the mantra—should be present in your mind, and you should be totally focused on the mantra as you repeat it. Then if you repeat the mantra even once, it bears great fruit.

For that reason, you must not speak without having your mind fully present. So many people say, "I didn't think," when their words cause trouble. If you speak mindlessly, what are your words worth? Frogs chatter; stray dogs bark. Is that all the divine gift of speech means to you? Just chattering and barking? Think about it. When you speak, how does your voice sound? What do your words mean? How carefully do you choose your words? How much do you contemplate before you say something?

To realize the power of words, Sundardas says great discrimination is necessary. First of all, it takes great concentration to discover what you really think. That is the basic issue. Often, you don't even know what your mind contains. Before you speak, you have to sort through everything the mind has collected to get to what is really meaningful. Secondly, it takes great contemplation to discriminate between what must be said and what is better left unsaid. It is like walking on the sharp edge of a sword. How do you know what should be said and what should not?

Concentration and contemplation are two essential qualities that you must develop before you speak. This does not mean you will never speak again—you learn from your mistakes, you take the advice of others. When you say something inappropriate, and someone points it out to you, you learn from it. Most of the time, people tend to become defensive. "No, I didn't say that! Me! No, I would never say such a thing. No one else ever mentioned that. You must have a problem. Maybe you need therapy."

People can be defensive in obvious ways, like that, or in ways that are not so obvious. Sometimes you just wrap your brains in leather. Nothing can penetrate. You have just enough patience to listen to the person's advice, which you think is condescending. But you don't imbibe any of it and you can't learn from it.

So it's not that you will never speak again because you haven't practiced enough contemplation and concentration. No. You keep learning from childhood until you die. As you accept the advice of others, as you listen to their feedback, you make greater and greater improvements. If you just speak without concentration and contemplation, you are wasting your energy, squandering your *shakti*. If you don't include others' good advice, their helpful feedback, their constructive criticism, you are just wasting energy because you will be saying the same things and making the same mistakes. You won't improve. In this way, you literally lose *shakti*. This is also an invitation to misfortune. You begin to lose your friends. They no longer want to be with you because of your refusal to change the way you speak, to change the abrasive quality in your voice. Then you begin to regard the whole world as negative, and you become very critical.

If you are not disciplined in speaking, it also widens the gap between your heart and your words. Therefore, take the words of wisdom that the poet-saint Sundardas offers and consider them thoroughly. Sundardas says, "You should think carefully before you speak." This is a great discipline. Discrimination makes you pause before you utter a word. Pausing is a great technique. This pausing helps, not only in the discipline of speaking, but in every action. If you can just pause—even before you take another step. If you can pause before a second thought arises, if you can pause before you go into another feeling, you will have more control over your thoughts and feelings. Just by pausing, you can save yourself from great troubles.

We talk about the breath coming in and the breath going out. Although the in-breath and the out-breath make a circle, and it is truly one breath, still, there is a split second, a pause, that takes place. For a split second, the breath pauses within, and for a split second, it pauses without. It is in this pause that the breath regathers its energy. If you carefully watch the dance of the breath as it comes in and goes out, there is a distinct pause, both inside and outside. Meditators actually rest their minds in this space where the in-breath pauses and where the out-breath pauses. In this way, they create *kumbhaka*, the retention of breath; they are able to go deeper and deeper into meditation and stay in the *samādhi* state, the state of total absorption, for long periods of time.

Discrimination makes you pause before you utter a word. The poet-saints emphasized discipline in speaking. Tulsidas said:

> Complications are created by talking.
> Problems are solved by talking.
> By talking discriminately,
>   one may gain blessings.
> By talking senselessly, one may go crazy.

Tulsidas wants you to see how talking and talking makes everything very complicated. The more you talk, the worse it gets. Situations can go from bad to worse, simply because of the words we use to describe them. Haven't you noticed? It is no exaggeration to say that you can dig your own grave by incessant talking. It has been done. A writer once said, speaking about discipline in eating, "Don't dig your grave with a knife and fork." In the same way, we can say, "Don't dig your grave with too many words."

Vain, empty talk indicates that there is no respect for Vak, for the power of speech. It also implies that the link with the mind, which is the source of all words, has been disconnected. And it definitely proves that a person has never experienced the world of deep silence.

On the other hand, the words of great beings arise from that deep silence and are divinely inspired. They break the boundaries of past, present, and future. They are eternally true. They apply to everyone's life, regardless of religion, nationality, class, or creed. According to Tulsidas, there is a kind of speech through which problems are solved. This kind of speech has a foundation in the Truth. It is the natural outcome of mature understanding. A person who speaks in this way has cultivated virtues like humility, patience, sensitivity, and egolessness. Therefore, his words can turn even a whole mountain range of problems into dust.

When words have their foundation in the Truth, they attract blessings, they attract grace, they attract good fortune. But by talking senselessly, as Tulsidas says, you can actually drive yourself crazy, not to mention the people around you. When there is no discipline in speaking, your talk swirls through the day like a tornado. You never know where you will wind up or what damage you will do. Uncontrolled speech is totally out of touch with the knowledge of the Self. It drowns out the inner voice. When there is senseless talking, you cannot hear the voice of your own Self.

The other day someone in darshan asked how to tell the difference between her voice inside and Gurumayi's voice inside. She said she hears Gurumayi's voice inside, and when she follows that, it is very beneficial. But then, there are times when she hears a voice inside that she thinks is Gurumayi's—and things really don't go well. After a while, she discovers that she was following her own voice.

Truly, we all have one voice, and that is the voice of God, the voice of the Truth. It is within each one of us. So what you want to do is learn more about this one voice, the voice of the Truth, the voice of God. Then you must bring what you think is your own voice into the voice of the Truth, make it merge with the voice of the Truth. And you do that by contemplation. You want to purify what you think is your own voice, the voice that has not led you in a good direction. You do not want to discriminate between your voice and the voice of the Truth—you want to bring about unity between them. Speech has emerged from pure nothingness, from deep silence, and you want to re-experience this deep silence. In this silence abides the voice of the Truth. So when you meditate, when you contemplate, when you concentrate, you get in touch with the source. That is what you truly want to do: get in touch with the source, the deepest part of your being.

Sometimes you say, "I had a great vision. I was not quite asleep; I was not quite awake. In between these two states, I had this great vision, I heard something." And you experience such divinity when you remember that vision, when you remember the voice you heard. You are still in deep silence—not in the lethargic state of sleep, nor in the busy activity of the waking state. Here, in this pause, you experience great ecstasy, great bliss.

So you want to bring about unity between the voices. You don't want to continually debate: "Is this the voice of God? Or the voice of the ego? Is this the voice of my mind? Is this the voice of my feelings? Is this the voice of the Guru?" You will get caught up in many complications with no way out. So just transcend what you think is the level of your voice and get in touch with the deep silence of your own being. Once again, it is right within yourself.

Speaking in itself is all right. Speech itself is absolutely pure. However, if your words are not harnessed to purity of mind, they wander from door to door like orphans, and you never know what will become of them. So bring about discipline in the way you speak; speak in such a way that you welcome blessings into your life. If you practice discipline in speaking, you will find that you have very little cleaning up to do. Then you won't have to take refuge in apologies or waste time in regrets. "I'm sorry. I didn't mean it. I'm really sorry."

Or, "Oh my goodness. I always speak like that. I just don't know why the words come out of my mouth like that. I can't believe how I always say the wrong thing. I know it's not right. I just know it."

Or, "Maybe I should fast for a few days. Maybe I'll go and sit on top of a mountain and just make myself suffer. Maybe I'll tell my boss to reduce my salary. I just feel so bad. What can I do? I just . . . I just can't get it right. Maybe in my next life."

Now all this drama arose only because you didn't contemplate your words before you spoke. It's so simple. Baba Muktananda often spoke against social chitchat, especially in the ashram. In Gurudev Siddha Peeth, he frequently asked people to stop chitchatting. In a satsang once he said, "Don't talk compulsively all the time. Don't behave like a man suffering from an unbearable itch, who is scratching all the time. Talk only when it is necessary. To talk only when necessary and to remain silent otherwise—that is good." [7]

Chanting is a form of silence. *Swādhyāya* is a form of silence. Prayer is a form of silence. The repetition of the mantra is a form of silence. And if you speak only when it is necessary, that too is a form of silence. When people used to ask Baba if they could wear a badge saying *Silence* to remind themselves as well as others about silence, Baba would say, "You don't have to go to that extreme. If you just speak when it's necessary, then that is considered silence." Sometimes, however, Baba did give permission to wear such a badge because it heightened people's awareness of silence.

From the image Baba paints, it is clear that compulsive

talking is a disease. When you are not comfortable with yourself, you go on babbling as if you were trying to hide behind a river of words. But your words have no purpose. This river of words is not the Ganges. Your words have no intention and no proper target either. They just fly out of your mouth like a swarm of disturbed hornets. Did you ever poke at a hornets' nest with a long pole? There is a man here who did that by accident and hundreds of hornets came buzzing out. They landed on him and he had to hose himself down to get rid of them. He had to destroy them. If you speak compulsively, if the words come out of your mouth like hornets, it is quite destructive, and you lose *punya*, you lose merits. In this case, the man destroyed the hornets, but when your words come out of you like hornets, then they turn on you and destroy you.

Therefore, the wise seeker will follow Baba's advice: "To talk only when necessary, and to remain silent otherwise— that is good." Putting this into practice requires great concentration and contemplation. Otherwise, how can you tell what is necessary and what is not? How do you know which words are appropriate and which are not? How can you tell who is the right person to speak to? Or whether he has time to listen? If you take everything into consideration, it is really a very difficult choice to make. All this sounds like too much to think about. When should you speak up? And when should you be silent?

Now this was Sheikh Nasruddin's dilemma. Once Nasruddin was working for a millionaire who had a fight with his wife. Later, the millionaire wanted to make up with her, so he sent Nasruddin to get a beautiful gift for her. Nasruddin shouted at everyone he met, "Step aside! My boss and his wife had a big fight, and now he wants me to bring a beautiful gift for her. He really wants to make up with her. Step aside! Step aside!"

Naturally, that got back to the boss, who got very red in

the face and scolded Nasruddin, saying, "Don't you have any brains? You should have been more discreet. From now on, just keep quiet! This is my order! Nasruddin, keep quiet!"

A few days later, the millionaire's house caught on fire. Nasruddin whispered, "Help. The house is on fire. Everyone! Everyone," he whispered softly, "please bring a bucket of water." Of course, no one heard him, and the house burned to the ground.

Discrimination plays a key role when it comes to discipline in speaking. Without it, the same thing could happen to you. In the *Nīti Shataka*, the great sage Bhartrihari said this:

> To give charity in secret, to honor a guest,
> to be silent after doing good work,
> to speak openly of the good done by others,
> to be free from vanity in spite of wealth,
> and to speak well of others —
> these are the virtues generally possessed
> by good people.
> I wonder who has taught these good people
> to observe such a difficult vow,
> which is as sharp as the edge of a sword? [64] [8]

Bhartrihari maintains that these vows are difficult to follow. It does take a tremendous amount of effort to keep your pride from erupting after you have done something good for others. It is said that if you speak about your good deeds, you lose the good karma, the *punya* or merit, they brought you. But it is very difficult not to mention all the good works you have done for other people. It takes great discipline.

It is equally difficult to speak about others without making a single innuendo about their characters, their actions, or their words. To refuse to find fault with other people—this is a practice for a lifetime. Haven't you ever caught yourself saying, "She did a fabulous job, but her manner is so abrasive." Or, "He's such a marvelous person, but he is so stingy." "It's delightful to work with Beverly, if only she were not so self-centered." Or, "She's got such a sense of humor, but her taste in clothes!" "He's really shaping up and exercising a great deal. I can't wait till he gets around to cleaning his room." "She is so devoted. Too bad she's not more efficient."

Refusing to find fault with other people is truly a practice for a lifetime. Take as much time as God gives you—you will need it. As positive as you may think you are about people and situations, when you begin to watch your words—or even your impulse to speak—you discover what you really think. It is as though the words on the tip of your tongue reveal the secret contents of your mind. As we learn from the Vedas, there is a very strong correlation between the mind and speech. The same connection exists between the mind and writing. This is why we encourage people to write their experiences down. Also when you keep a journal, you can affirm the good experiences that you haven't yet allowed yourself to express. But most importantly, you want to be clear about what your words convey.

The other day in a course, one of the scholars did a beautiful exercise. He asked people to contemplate their experiences deeply and then speak about them. He said that true research comes from this kind of contemplated speaking and listening, that just going to the library was not real research. Of course, people exercised great discipline: they thought about their experiences, they pondered them, and then they spoke. And as they spoke, they were able to see that they had not recognized that those experiences had in fact happened to them. They were very surprised. When you speak with such discipline, things become much clearer for you. Speaking in this way is very valuable.

To attain discipline in speaking requires great discrimination. Bhartrihari knew very well what a difficult vow it is. With all your heart, you must want to follow the path of the Truth. Empty words and careless speech are a great danger.

Saint Francis of Assisi spoke out against them in no uncertain terms. He said:

> I consider it no less a virtue to know how to keep silent well, than to know how to speak well. A man ought to have a long neck like a crane so that whenever he wished to speak, his words would have to pass through many joints before they reached his mouth.

What a spellbinding image. When I read this quote, I thought about it for hours and days. Of course, in the Indian scriptures they talk about the four levels of speech, and the words actually travel through these different levels. But when Saint Francis says there should be joints, you can understand how the words also have to pass through the knots, the different *granthis*, in the *sushumnā nādī*, the central channel. And each syllable that arises from the unspoken word, from the unstruck sound, each syllable that arises from pure nothingness, from pure silence, purifies each center in the body. In deep meditation, that is what you experience.

Just as eating is a necessary function of the body, speaking is something that comes naturally to all human beings. Luckily, there are many great spiritual practices to purify the speech and to strengthen its connection to the supreme Self. In this way a seeker is able to experience the Truth even as the words manifest through his mouth. In the *Viveka Chūdāmani*, "The Crest Jewel of Discrimination," Shri Shankaracharya says:

> The first door of unity with the Self is control of speech. [367] [9]

Discipline in speaking. What are the practices that purify the speech and help one attain this discipline? There are many great practices, but we'll consider just a few for now.

One of the most beautiful ways is through prayer. As you pray, you begin to notice that the words come from a place far beyond ordinary thought. True prayers arise from deep inside you. Because of prayer, you begin to recognize this pure place within, and you begin to feel deep respect for the words that issue from it.

Sometimes people come in darshan and they read out a prayer that they have written during the program. These pure words had emerged from the pure silence during meditation or chanting. Sometimes they do not want to just put the prayer in the basket—they want to read it aloud. And it is amazing to see people who usually speak in a very different way saying these beautiful words. So in each person there is such a pure place, and through meditation you get in touch with it.

Do you know what else happens through the practice of prayer? You begin to absolve yourself from the impurities you have collected through indiscriminate, senseless speech and gossip. Through prayer, you free yourself from these impurities. When you begin to understand the ill effects that your words have had, prayer helps you overcome the tendency to use your tongue recklessly. Prayer is a bridge that takes you across the swamp of sense pleasures to the imperishable world and gives you the darshan of the Truth.

Take a moment now. Sit comfortably with a straight back. Allow your spine to elongate. Become aware of your breath. Become aware of the space where the in-breath rests for a moment. And become aware of the space where the out-breath rests for a moment. Allow the mind to relax with the breath. Let the mind settle into the relaxation of the breath.

All your life you have used many words. You know all the letters and syllables. You have used many words in conversations, in reading and writing. And now, with your eyes closed and your mind relaxed, write a prayer in your own heart. Write a prayer to the Lord, to your chosen deity, to the true Friend, to God. Don't worry about which word should be first and which word should be second. Don't edit your prayer.

Let it be simple and pure. Whether it's a full sentence or a few words, don't be concerned with how it looks. Allow the prayer to be written in your heart. Then just sit quietly for a few moments.

When you stop like this to write a prayer in your heart and to sit quietly with it, you are able to see how beautiful your heart is; what great silence exists inside your being. It is wonderful to reconnect with your own Truth over and over again. Remember this prayer that you have written in your heart. If you can't remember the entire prayer, just recall a few words of it. Cherish these words. They spring from the Truth. They will guide you.

Another great practice that is part of discipline in speaking is reciting sacred texts, *swādhyāya*, which literally means "studying one's own Self." *Swādhyāya* trains the tongue to formulate and utter sweet words, beneficial words, words filled with the presence of God. This is why in the tradition of the brahmin priests, they begin teaching Vedic recitations at the age of seven to train the tongue. In olden days, young children spoke quite purely; they were in touch with their own Self. Of course, in those days there was no television or radio, and the adults were very careful not to use abusive terms in front of children. But after the age of seven, children have their own society, and they begin learning things that are not appropriate. So at the age of seven, speech training begins. In the beginning it is not reciting the Vedas as such; instead, the tongue is trained with pure vowels, pure syllables. Because the tongue has a way of slipping here and there, a great deal of exercise is done to bring firmness to the tongue. And *swādhyāya* is a great exercise.

Baba Muktananda praised the practice of *swādhyāya* in many ways. He saw it as the cure for all ills, including careless speech. In a satsang, he once said, "*Swādhyāya* saves you from the habit of fault-finding, from the habit of imagining sins where they do not exist, from the habit of indulging in silly gossip, from the habit of wasting time." [10]

When you recite the scriptures or study the texts of the Siddhas, you build up a reserve of positive energy. You create a very uplifting atmosphere. You purify all the cells in your being. Daily recitation of the holy texts is like bathing in holy rivers. It refreshes the mind, it cleanses the speech, and it fills you with *shakti.*

Another great practice is to recollect your experiences. If you have chanted holy texts in special places, like beside flowing rivers, these are great experiences to recall. Once when we were on tour and we were visiting Maui, we chanted the *Guru Gītā* at Haleakala. To this day, people come in darshan and remind me of that; they say, "That *Guru Gītā* was so sublime." And it has sustained them throughout the years—whether they had difficulties with their friends, whether they went through the dark night of the soul in their sadhana. Whatever happened, as soon as they remembered that *Guru Gītā* on that mountain, it would wash away all their negativities.

Some people talk about chanting the *Guru Gītā* silently on the subway. When they go to work, they may have a long subway ride, so they do their chanting there. And they remember those moments. So if you think that your *swādhyāya* has become a bit stale, that your recitation of the *Guru Gītā* doesn't have any more *rasa*, then choose another spot, find another place, or get together with other Siddha Yoga students.

I remember some of the *Guru Gītās* that we have chanted in various Siddha Yoga Meditation centers around the world. They were very powerful. When we were in Ganeshpuri at Gurudev Siddha Peeth, Baba sometimes used to take us to Bade Baba's *samādhi* shrine, which is a mile away from the ashram, and we would chant there. Even though it was the same chant, with the same Guru, and the same person chanting, still the experience would be so exalted.

So you can make your own practice divine. You don't ever have to think your sadhana has dried up. Sadhana doesn't dry up — it's your attitude toward sadhana, your attitude toward what's happening with you. Sadhana is always very juicy, and you should continually extract that juice.

It is not only in the Brahmanic tradition that they train the tongue; this is done in all Indian schools. When you first go to school at the age of six, the teachers make you say the vowels and consonants over and over again. For example, *ka kā, ki kī, ku kū* and so on. This goes on for almost a year. You just recite the vowels and consonants. In this way, the tongue becomes very firm; it acquires the ability to recognize the syllables. In one of the courses here at the *gurukula*, many of you went deeper into this knowledge — the knowledge of the vowels and consonants, and where they actually emerge from.

Chanting is part of the discipline of speaking. Chanting focuses the mind on God's glory, it burns up all sins, it redirects the tongue and teaches it how to speak wisely. Chanting saturates the tongue inside and out with the nectar of the name of God. Almost every one of you has experienced the power of chanting.

Tukaram Maharaj often sang about the glory of chanting. He said:

> If one repeats the name of God all the time,
> one's body becomes pure and one's speech
> is filled with virtue.

The other practice that purifies the speech, that gives us the ability to follow discipline in speaking, is mantra repetition. When the mantra is repeated silently, it pulsates in the mind. You can recognize this pulsation of the mantra within the mind. Mantra repetition also teaches the tongue to be active in silence. As the tongue recognizes its silent movements, its oneness with the mantra, the mind becomes free from agitation and falsehood. It becomes filled with the luminous sparks of the mantra. The mind acquires sweetness and a new awareness of its nature. It realizes that its purpose is to convey God's message, to console a wounded heart, to give assurance to the downtrodden. So the tongue, as it moves silently with the repetition of the mantra, acquires sweetness. The tongue also acquires, just like the mind, a new awareness of its nature.

So many of the *bhajans* by the poet-saint Kabir were about repeating God's name. It was advice that he couldn't give often enough. He spoke about it very strongly. He said:

> The mouth that is not repeating
>   the name of Rama, the Lord,
> this mouth is full of dust.

When mantra repetition becomes more noticeable, the mind becomes purer, the tongue becomes purer.

Discipline in speaking leads you into the presence of God. It helps you to acquire good company. It is like a good investment—and what it yields is merit, greater merit than you could ever imagine. Discipline in speaking conserves the good energy of the mind and body. And little by little, it dissolves the impulse to engage in loose talk. When you use words with discrimination, concentration, and contemplation, you attract grace. You also gain the respect of others. Your words may be fewer in number, but they ring with the heart's true intention; they resonate with the word of God. So discipline in speaking has many great benefits. Not only does it allow you to attain liberation from your daily agitation, not only does it bring you closer to God, not only does it reveal God's form, but also you receive the respect of others. Very naturally, others have good feelings for you. Then wherever you go, the door is open, people smile, and amazing things just happen—all from discipline in speaking.

Of course, the greatest merit is to become attuned to the presence of the Lord within. It is very important to hear the voice of God within at all times. Kabir said:

In every heart the Lord speaks.
Like a bird singing the sweetest songs,
the Self is always speaking in everyone's heart.

"The Self is always speaking in everyone's heart." Allow yourself to become anchored more and more in the deep silence of your own being and to hear the words that emerge from this great silence.

With great respect, with great love, I welcome you all with all my heart.

Sadgurunāth mahārāj kī jay!

August 6, 1995

Chapter Eleven

THE STATE OF SHIMMERING CONSCIOUSNESS

The Discipline of Silence

With great respect, with great love, I welcome you all with all my heart.

Yoga is vast and deep. The only way we can imbibe yoga, which is divine, is by looking at it and imbibing it a little at a time. This morning we will look at and imbibe the discipline of silence.

On the spiritual path, silence is one of the most essential practices. Only a seeker who has been able to silence all his senses is worthy of beholding the splendor of God. And when it comes to sustaining the vision of God's splendor, silence is even more important. Through this discipline, the vision is not just a haphazard experience but a continuous state of being. When the discipline of silence becomes natural to a seeker, he is on his way to attaining liberation, *moksha.* The discipline of silence should become natural to you if you want to have the constant experience of God's splendor.

Disciplined silence is not at all the same as shutting down the system. Being cold, brooding, or sulking because of anger, jealousy, pride, or any of the other inner enemies has nothing to do with the discipline of silence. Silence is not what happens when you choke back an insult, or swallow someone else's harsh words with tears stinging your eyes. The discipline of silence is not a way of retaliating for things you don't get.

It isn't about getting your own way; it isn't blackmail. The discipline of silence is an austerity on the spiritual path, a practice full of merit.

The *Ashtavakra Samhitā* takes a very interesting approach to this discipline. It says:

> First, one should become detached from physical action, then from talking, then from thinking. In this way, one abides in the Self. [12.1] [1]

Here the sage is talking about silence as detachment in three stages: detachment from physical action, then from talking, and finally from thinking. Right away, you understand from this verse why you should observe silence—so that you can experience the Self, so that you can abide in the Self, so that you can see the face of God and know God, so that you can experience that great love. The sage Ashtavakra defines these three levels of silence, giving a seeker very clearly defined steps to follow. The first step is detachment from physical action.

Most physical action occurs because of the influence of ego. The yogic scriptures say the reason your physical body cannot sit still is because of *ahamkāra*, or ego. As long as the ego is in control, the physical body cannot become still, no matter how much you try. Therefore, the sage talks about becoming detached from physical action. He doesn't tell you to put a stop to action, but rather to develop a new relationship with action, one that gives the great Self the upper hand.

Becoming detached from physical action means you let the body know very clearly that you cannot be subjugated by its activities. You let the ego know that you are not going to be influenced by its games and tricks. You are free from the illusions that physical action creates. You are not going to be dragged down by the cravings of the physical body, either.

Applying the discipline of silence to physical action is a great form of *tapasya*, austerity. It is a spiritual practice that does not come easily. As the scriptures explain, no human being can live without performing actions; they are part of our nature. Therefore, a seeker must develop the awareness of silence in relation to his actions. This is an extraordinary process—applying the discipline of silence to every move you make. This is not a matter of putting actions to death: rather, it is extracting silence from each action. It is not a matter of making your body rigid or austere or inactive. It is a process that happens slowly and systematically.

What does it mean to apply the discipline of silence to physical action? Let's take it step by step. As the scriptures point out, physical actions happen due to ego. Every physical action is prompted by one desire or another. If there is no desire, there is no movement. And so a seeker has to recognize the value or the uselessness of each desire as it comes up. This is where we use self-inquiry, *ātma vichāra*. A seeker has to go to the source of each desire if he really wants to learn the discipline of silence. Once again, the point of this discipline is to rise above disturbance and attachment, and to abide in the higher Self.

Many of you practice hatha yoga. In the yogic world, hatha yoga has its own importance. The postures of hatha yoga are a form of physical action, yet they lead to detachment from physical action. Outer movements are taking place, of course—the physical body is becoming stronger and more supple—yet the whole purpose of hatha yoga is to draw the attention inward. As you move the body with every breath, as you still the body with every breath, you bring it into perfect alignment. The fruit of hatha yoga is *pratyāhāra*, the withdrawal of the senses from outward attention.

In *ashtānga yoga*, outlined by Patanjali in his *Yoga Sūtras*, there are eight limbs of yoga. One of them is *pratyāhāra*. In this practice, you draw all the senses inward. In this way, you become tranquil and completely free from the pull of the senses. This is how you apply the discipline of silence to the senses. Hatha yoga is really the best example of the principle of detachment in physical action. When it is achieved, the experience is so liberating; the physical body is no longer an impediment to sadhana, no longer an obstacle. Your entire body becomes a temple of God, and all its movements are a joyful expression of the Lord. You actually experience a great joy from each physical action. And in each action, you are aware of silence. In each hatha yoga movement, there is an air of silence, a pool of silence.

The body has a natural ability to adapt to its environment and circumstances. This is a positive quality. It is very fortunate that most of the time the body is able to adapt itself naturally to changes in climate. In this way, the body can go on living, can go on serving God. But if the body is given no discipline, then it becomes like a river without any banks, and the water—its energy—spills out everywhere.

You must teach your body the discipline of silence so you can experience tranquillity in all your actions. As Ashtavakra said, "Become detached from physical action." The truth is you can cultivate anything you want in this body. You can let it go to waste, or you can use it as a vehicle to carry you to God. The body is a gift from God. You can do anything with this body, but the purpose of the body is to help you know God, to help you reach God.

Many of you have participated in seva projects. The practice of seva, selfless service, is designed to create an environment of silence within and without. There is a person here who used to find it difficult to get into meditation or chanting. Recently, she has focused on seva, nothing but seva. She was feeling a bit guilty that she did not take an interest in meditation or chanting or the workshops and courses. However, whenever she came to the morning program and chanted, immediately she would go deep into the intoxication of chanting. And during the ten-minute meditations that were given during these programs, she would notice, all of a sudden, that she was deep in meditation. She did not realize that these were the fruits of her seva. She has been busy applying herself to her seva, and quite naturally, as a beautiful boon, she was receiving the intoxication of chanting and of meditation.

It is amazing how we don't connect things; how we don't relate things to each other. Even though great things are happening in our lives, often we are not able to see them, not able to recognize them. We attach more importance to our negative thoughts or to the things we think we should be doing but are not. In the meantime, so many great things are happening. Even spiritual experiences are taking place, and we neglect them totally. We don't recognize them and we feel deprived. Then we think the whole world owes us something. God owes us something. Everyone else owes us something too.

Think about this—how many great things happen in your life that you let go by without ever noticing them. Yet you pay attention to things you regard as negative. If you want to experience silence, it is very good to watch your own mind and to notice what it thinks about. We will come to that a little later on.

Let's look again at this detachment from physical action that Ashtavakra spoke about. Another great way to attain detachment from physical action is through meditation. Even though meditation requires you to sit quietly, it is still a physical activity. You are exercising the discipline of silence in your actions by holding your body still, by diluting the power of ego, by removing the power of ego. During meditation, the body is completely alert, yet all the senses have been drawn inside.

There are two images you can use to envision meditation. One is the image of a boulder falling into the ocean. Once it breaks the surface of the water, its movements are slow and sure. It just goes down, down, down, and down until it reaches the bottom. It sinks steadily through the layers of light into the darkness of deep water. Finally, it reaches the absolute stillness at the bottom of the ocean. The other image is of something flying higher, higher, and higher into the ether until it finally disappears from view. Through this steady act of rising, this calm ascending, there finally comes a point where everything is nothing but universal Consciousness.

The discipline of silence does not mean bringing the body and mind to a sudden halt in a jerky manner. It means developing detachment through steadiness—this is what frees you from physical action and gives you the experience of the supreme Self. You abide in the Self, and that is the goal. The discipline of silence is not meant to torture the spirit by harnessing it to certain demanding physical actions. The object is to experience the nectar of the Self. You utilize physical actions as the path to supreme silence. You cannot create the atmosphere in which silence is possible without performing the proper actions.

Think what a silent dance is like. Although movements are taking place and physical actions are happening, they are creating silence. You begin to notice how your mind becomes quieter and calmer. You enter the state of meditation. This silence is not an inert state of the body but the state of shimmering Consciousness, the state of supreme bliss, the bubbling of ecstasy. When you see the birch trees with the wind blowing through the leaves, they shimmer. They shake tenderly yet fiercely. Nevertheless, as you watch this shimmering Consciousness, your mind becomes very still. It becomes ecstatic. It experiences silence.

The great poet-saint Kabir describes this experience magnificently. In one of his *bhajans* he says:

> My heart is so intoxicated with love
>   that I have no wish to speak.
> Your Lord dwells within you,
>   so turn your gaze within.
> What will you find outside?

Kabir says, Listen, brother!
I met the Lord in a tiny seed within me.

My heart is so intoxicated with love
 that I have no wish to speak.
I found a diamond. I wrapped it
 securely in my cloak.
Why take the risk of opening it again and again?
When I was being tested and weighed,
 I was still empty and worthless.
Now I am full. Where is the need for weighing?
I look like a person who has just drunk too much.
But actually it was the wine of God's love
 that I drank without measure.
Once a swan has flown to the heavenly lake
 beyond the mountains,
why should it bother to drink from ditches
 and tiny pools?
Your Lord dwells within you,
 so turn your gaze within.
What will you find outside?
Kabir says: Listen, brother!
I met the Lord in a tiny seed within me.

The tiny seed that Kabir refers to is the Blue Pearl, exquisite and most brilliant. How can you possibly perceive it if your body is distracted by endless activity? It is only in deep silence, when all physical action has been suspended, that the splendor of the Blue Pearl can be seen—the *nīla bindu.* When you become detached from all physical action, when you experience great silence, there is also great fruit. You have the vision of the Lord.

After detachment from physical action, Ashtavakra speaks about becoming detached from talking: One should become detached from action, and then from talking, in order to abide in the Self.

Most people are quite familiar with this one. This is how we usually think of silence. As great as words are, they can also be quite detrimental. Sometimes you have to eat your own words. Used properly, language inspires, instructs, and opens the heart. But when words are used irrationally or for base motives, what then? A Chinese philosopher said, "A dog is not considered a good dog because he is a good barker. A man is not considered a good man because he is a good talker."

Most people are aware of this aspect of the discipline of silence. In fact, in the *gurukula*, there are two distinct groups: one group vigorously advocates silence, and the other goes right on talking. This division has a long tradition. In the early days in Gurudev Siddha Peeth, there were two groups: one was called the yogi group, those who embraced the discipline; the other one, the *bhogī* group, those who loved worldly pleasure and reminded others that Consciousness pervades everything—including talking at meals. Similarly, here in Shree Muktananda Ashram, we have a silent group and a talking group. This dilemma has been going on for many years, particularly in the dining hall. One group wants the signs that call for silence on every table, so that they can eat their meals surrounded by an absence of noise.

The other group keeps taking the silence signs off the table or turning them face down, so that they can season their food with the sweet and sour spices of conversation. When questioned, they insist that talking with seekers and lovers of God is satsang—whatever the subject matter may be, it's satsang!

The management receives hundreds of suggestions about the silent tables in the dining hall. You see, although these tables have been silent, their advocates have been quite noisy. Anyway, it is very apparent that both groups—the silence group and the satsang group—understand the discipline of silence, whether or not they choose to follow it. It is difficult to say which group has a stronger case—the group that demands silence and grumbles at others for not agreeing, or the group that has never felt the need for silence, and doesn't notice any kind of sign, unless they have to move it to reach for the salt. It's a very interesting phenomenon—silence or no silence—and it depends on which group you belong to. You may not belong to the same group every day. You might skip from one group to another.

Once upon a time, the full moon rose in the clear night sky above a little town in the country. All the dogs in town began to bark. Only one dog did not bark. He spoke to the others in a grave voice full of authority. "Do not awaken Stillness from her sleep, nor bring the moon down to earth with all your barking." All the dogs were impressed and stopped barking. But the dog who had spoken out continued to bark for silence the rest of the night.

So it's a dilemma. If you ask for silence, you are the one who is making the noise. And if you don't ask for silence, no one seems to take any notice of it.

Practiced as a yogic discipline, silence is a high road to liberation. We need to raise our awareness of silence. If you think silence means just shutting up, closing your mouth, then you want to rebel. You want to talk a mile a minute just to get on someone's nerves, just to irritate someone, because all through school, people have told you that you talk too much. Every time you opened your mouth, people walked away, and so you think of silence as punishment. In this case, you need to raise your awareness of silence: what silence can do for you, what silence is from the yogic point of view.

Silence does have a wonderful effect on your physical state. The benefits of silence are tremendous and the penalties for avoiding silence are equally heavy. If the tongue is not given rest from talking and talking, the energy of the body is depleted. The talking tongue is filled with tension that permeates your whole system: your shoulders get tight, your stomach gets upset, and your toes wriggle under the desk. If the tongue is not given some time off, if it engages incessantly in talking, then the body panics. In deep yogic meditation, there is a special *mudrā* that happens, the *khecharī mudrā*, in which the tongue curls upward and tries to pierce the soft palate so it can go above it. *Khe* means "the space," the space of Consciousness, the sky of Consciousness; and *charī*, "movement, moving, or roaming." Your awareness wants to roam in the sky of Consciousness. When the *khecharī mudrā* happens, it relaxes the entire body. It actually draws the entire body into the state of deep silence. In hatha yoga, the instructor always says you should let the tongue rest on the floor of the mouth, let it melt into the floor of the mouth. When you relax the tongue, it relaxes the entire body.

The discipline of silence doesn't mean just taking a short vacation from the spoken word. It also means giving complete relaxation to the muscles, the tissues, and the tongue itself. A modern writer once said, "Knowledge has never been known to enter the head via an open mouth."

It's a beautiful statement! In the Spanish language they say, "Flies never enter a closed mouth." So, hygienically, it is good to keep the mouth closed, and if you want to attain higher knowledge, it is also good to keep the mouth closed. It is when you become completely silent that you are able to absorb knowledge. In silence you hear the songs of the birds. In silence you hear the message of the Truth. In silence you hear the sounds of the stars and the voice of the inner Self. It is in silence that you hear the voice of the earth. God speaks in silence.

This absence of distraction, this freedom from noise is a sure sign that the ego has stopped its tricks for once and shed its defensiveness. When you are able to observe silence in this way, when you become aware of silence, you are surrendering your small will to God's will, the great Will. Your heart becomes full of humility, patience, and steadfastness. When you apply the discipline of silence to the words you speak, they carry the power of the heart's intention, and you can be heard.

Silence is, after all, a form of self-respect. When even your speech carries the quality of silence, then you gain the respect of others as well. Sometimes you hear someone speak, and you could listen to them for hours on end. Whether it's a child or an adult, it doesn't matter—you want to hear them speak, you don't get tired of their speaking. That means they have cultivated the power of silence in their speech.

Baba Muktananda wrote *Ashram Dharma* to help seekers derive the greatest benefit from their time in the *gurukula*, no matter how long or short their stay might be. He said, "The residents of an ashram must not fritter away their calm and silence by indulging in futile arguments and idle chatter. If you earn only fifty paisa daily but spend ten rupees, what can you save?" You waste your energy, not just by talking, but also in arguments and idle chatter. When you can't come to any conclusion, you go on arguing even though you know no one is going to back down. But you still keep at it, and in this way you lose your yogic energy.

Baba constantly pointed out the need for a seeker to conserve energy for sadhana. How can you do sadhana with a depleted body, a weakened mind, or a loose tongue? No one with a loose tongue can ever do sadhana. That is impossible. That's like trying to carry water in a bucket full of holes. How far will you go? Conserving your energy for the good of your sadhana is vitally important. Only then can the seed of your devotion sprout and grow into the tree of spiritual attainment. This was always one of Baba's main teachings: Conserve energy through discipline, through silence.

Let's say you meet your friend for twenty minutes. Just for twenty minutes to get a couple of things off your chest. Now, if you were to write down word for word everything you and your friend said, you would find that the transcript would run to ten or twelve densely typed pages. And that one conversation is just a small sample of the huge department store of thoughts in your mind. If you experiment with this, you will be amazed how much you speak and think throughout the day.

Therefore, the third point that Ashtavakra makes is about becoming detached from thinking. "Then one should become detached from thinking. In this way one abides in the Self."

This is where our subject becomes very delicate—applying the discipline of silence to the chatterbox of the mind. You see a frog sitting quietly on a rock by the pond waiting for flies. Do you suppose its mind is very still? You see a vulture perched very quietly on a branch. Do you suppose its mind is completely still? You see a cat sitting very quietly on a window sill. Do you suppose its mind is still? You see a fox sitting in the forest without moving a muscle, gazing at the chicken yard. Do you suppose its mind is completely still? You see a lizard clinging to the wall behind the curtain. Do you suppose its mind is still? You see a thief sitting quietly in a parking lot. Do you suppose his mind is still? Do you suppose *your* mind is still?

Could you say all these creatures have been following the discipline of silence because they look so quiet on the outside? Outwardly, one can look so quiet and still, while inside, one's mind is traveling a thousand miles a minute, racing around the past and future, networking, leaping from one desire to another. True silence must take its seat in the mind. It must emerge from there.

The discipline of silence is essential on the path. And it is also part of what you find at the goal. When you realize the Supreme, you melt into silence. This is the most wonderful experience—to melt into silence, just as butter melts in the presence of heat. It is the ultimate experience, the end of sadhana, to just melt into silence. This is the experience we used to have every day in Shree Gurudev Siddha Peeth when the ashram was very small. In fact, Baba created the ashram from silence. And that silence shimmered with Consciousness.

Even now, if I want to experience true silence, I visualize my time in Ganeshpuri in those days. The entire ashram was filled with the fragrance of silence. No one had to teach us to be silent. The whole place spoke of silence; it echoed with silence. And this silence of the ashram was not like the silence of the forest or the silence of the deep ocean or the silence of the mountaintop. It was its own silence, suffused with the energy of the Siddhas. It was tangible and sweet and profound.

So the silence we are talking about is not a flat state of mind; it is very full. You dwell in the golden womb of the cosmic energy. The scriptures talk about the sound *Om* emanating from the golden womb, *hiranya garbha.* That is what we experienced in the ashram in the early days.

In those days, we did not have stainless steel plates for our meals. We used leaf plates, and their soft sound was very musical. When someone did speak, it was like chanting, like music. Even footsteps didn't bother us. We were able to experience the sound *Om,* we were able to experience silence even in the sound of people's footsteps. And people became so tender and quiet within themselves. They would respect silence. It was as though you were seeing the deity of silence everywhere. To this day in Gurudev Siddha Peeth, this divine silence draws seekers into its embrace.

As you walk the spiritual path, it is possible to make this silence a reality. And if you ever want to take a vow of silence, remember that chanting is considered to be a form of silence. You can always include chanting as part of the discipline of silence. It is when the mind can taste the nectar of the Self that it lets go and melts into silence.

Even the knowledge that this is possible, that such a divine experience lies in store for it enables the mind to bring itself to a very quiet space. You have to let your mind know that this awareness of silence is actually a great state, a state in which you experience inner miracles, inner treasures. Then the mind will accept it; it will allow itself to become quieter. It will not think of it as punishment.

In the *Viveka Chūdāmani*, "The Crest Jewel of Discrimination," Shri Shankaracharya describes the experience of plunging into the Absolute. He says:

The ocean of Brahman is full of nectar—
  the joy of the Self.
The treasure I have found there
  cannot be described in words.
It is inconceivable.
My mind fell like a hailstone
into the vast expanse of that ocean of Brahman.
Touching one drop of it, I melted away
  and became one with Brahman.
And now I abide in the joy of the Self. [482] [2]

Silence. Allow yourself to experience the deity of silence, to receive the pleasure of the god of silence. Applying the discipline of silence throughout your sadhana may sometimes seem like an arduous task. Yet all the scriptures say silence is the state that overcomes the mind at that moment when it encounters the vision of the Truth. When the mind has the vision of the Truth, it falls into deep silence, it melts into silence.

This silence does not render the body or the mind inert. Just the opposite—your entire being scintillates with Consciousness. Your entire being is immersed in the ecstasy of the Self. In this state, you are all-knowing, you are free.

So the discipline of silence can take you on an adventure that is greater than climbing every mountain in the world. Experiencing the silence that lies behind every action, within every word, and at the center of every thought is a sublime form of sadhana. Silence is the sadhana of the Siddhas.

Watch your physical actions; see if they induce the power of silence. Watch your words; see if your words induce the power of silence. Watch your thoughts; see if they induce the power of silence.

With great respect, with great love, I welcome you all with all my heart.

Sadgurunāth mahārāj kī jay!

August 19, 1995

III. How Does a True Seeker View the World?

True seekers long to see the face of God
in everyone they meet,
to feel God's presence everywhere they go,
to see the divine light sparkling in all directions,
to experience oneness with every particle of the universe.
No matter what circumstances they encounter,
true seekers want to experience
each situation as God's blessing —
God's ever-new way of revealing Himself
and of deepening their sadhana.
They want to see God's hand
in everything in their lives.

Chapter Twelve

Acknowledge Your Own Goodness Every Step of the Way

Discipline in Thinking I

With great respect, with great love, I welcome you all with all my heart.

In the ancient hymns of the *Rig Veda*, the sages transmitted wisdom that is immortal. They said:

> The wise and true seekers realize God
> through meditation on their own Self;
> they see Him as vividly
> as the eye ranges over the sky.
> By deep meditation and pious acts,
> the vigilant seeker of Truth realizes
> the all-pervading God
> within the innermost cave of the heart,
> the supreme abode of the Lord. [1.22.20-21] [1]

As the sages point out, wise and true seekers realize God through meditation on their own Self. This is what we do in Siddha Yoga—we meditate on the great Self to realize God.

And the sages also speak about pious acts. These are actions done according to dharma, actions that lead to complete satisfaction, satisfaction beyond the mind and senses. Through these actions, you feel absorbed in the Self. By performing these actions, you feel you are in meditation, you feel very happy to be living in God's creation.

It is in the innermost cave of the heart that you realize the Lord. Within each person, the divine spark dwells. Baba Muktananda said, "Perceive the divine spark within your own heart." A true seeker comes to the *gurukula* longing for the knowledge of God and for the awakening of his inner being through the grace of the Guru. In addition to this longing, what matters most is that the seeker undertake spiritual practices so he can contain the *shakti.*

It is through sadhana that a seeker imbibes yogic discipline. Baba Muktananda used to say that in the beginning, sadhana seems to be a practice to attain God. However, this very practice is also *sādhya,* the object of practice. So within sadhana dwells the object of sadhana — the attainment of God, the state of enlightenment. Baba also used to say that even after he had completed his sadhana, still he continued to meditate and chant because it had become pure worship. When you attain that state, sadhana is no longer an arduous process of putting your body and mind through great austerity. It becomes pure worship; it is for glorifying God. Sadhana is what gives a seeker access to that divine inner world.

How does a true seeker view the world? It is so important as a seeker on the spiritual path that you never give up the notion of attaining God, the highest wish, the greatest longing to know God. Always have that wish in the foreground of your mind. Then, as Baba said, even after you experience the Truth, after you have become anchored in that divine state, you continue the practices because to do so is in keeping with universal laws.

When a seeker turns his energy within, through practices that open the heart and quiet the mind, he is able to experience God's presence in his own being, as well as in the material world. What is important is that you experience God's presence in everything. No moment should pass when you haven't thought of God's presence, when you haven't contemplated why you are performing an action. Is this action a service to God? When you are taking care of your body, ask yourself: Is this a service to God? When you are entertaining all kinds of thoughts: Is this a service to God? Will I experience the light of God in these actions? Sadhana gives a seeker the true vision of the world around him and the world within.

Some seekers are so disgusted with the world that they see it as a forest of illusion, a whirlpool of lies. They see it as a fatal trap of infatuation and ignorance, like a river infested with crocodiles. They denounce the world in no uncertain terms. But as a genuine seeker's understanding ripens through the Guru's grace and the purifying power of sadhana, he yearns to see the world through the eyes of the enlightened Master, through the eyes of the great Self within.

Everyone has understanding. No one is devoid of knowledge as such, but some seekers' understanding is not yet ripe and other seekers' understanding is genuinely ripe. Depending on how well your understanding has ripened, you will experience the Truth within accordingly. Although some people have been doing sadhana for many years, they may not be acting as you think seekers should. But then, you can't really judge: some people progress very slowly and others very quickly.

Often, when you first begin to walk the spiritual path, you are so open, so ready to receive, that your entire being blazes with the fire of great knowledge. You are completely open to inner knowledge. You are able to see things no one else can see. You are able to feel things no one else can feel. You are very fortunate if you have this kind of destiny to accept the energy immediately, to be open to grace from the beginning. This is a matter of great fortune, and with it comes a greater responsibility. You must cultivate this fire, this energy. You must not ignore its great effects. When you ignore them, you are in the same boat as seekers who have been on the spiritual path for a long time, whose progress is very slow.

True seekers long to see the face of God in everyone they

meet, to feel God's presence everywhere they go, to see the divine light sparkling in all directions, to experience oneness with every particle of the universe. No matter what circumstances they encounter, true seekers want to experience each situation as God's blessing—God's ever-new way of revealing Himself and of deepening their sadhana. They want to see God's hand in everything in their lives.

Once a true seeker, who had accomplished his quest, who had fulfilled his purpose, spoke of the world, saying:

> Because your own heart is narrow,
> you think that God is alone somewhere,
>   separate from you.
> Find God in every garden, acting through every hand.
> See Him in everyone you meet.
> See Him in bright colors, in fading colors,
>   in that which has no color at all.
> See Him in your journey and in your goal.
> See Him in everyone you greet.
>
> In every street, in every dealing,
> see Him in everyone you meet.
> He is in your resolve and in your determination.
> Recognize Him in everyone you meet.

This is the goal of sadhana, the purpose of sadhana—to know God in everything and in everyone; to understand that God is doing everything. Not to use this as an excuse for your mistakes, but truly to become anchored in the presence of God all the time.

Think of what happens when the moon is waning. You can still see its fullness; you can still see its circle. The lighted portion of the moon becomes smaller and smaller, just a sliver, yet the moon itself is always full. In the same way, at times you may feel very good; at times, you may not. At times you may have wonderful thoughts; at other times, you may not. The saint says, "See Him in bright colors, in fading colors, in that which has no color at all." You don't have to think of sadhana as always a peak experience, always a festival. Sadhana is an ongoing process. There is much to learn, much to imbibe, much to accept in God's creation.

"See Him in bright colors, in fading colors." These words also imply life and death. Life is filled with bright colors; then comes death, and the fading colors of this world. See God in life as well as death. Everyone has to face life; everyone has to face death. Death is not something unnatural, not something that should happen quickly and be forgotten. See God even in the pain of losing someone. See God even in that moment of great loss, in profound pain, just as you visualize God in profound ecstasy.

What stands between sublime vision and an ordinary seeker's view of the world? Only one thing. Every seeker's constant companion on his spiritual journey is his own mind, *manas*. The mind is always pestering a seeker, trying to tell him how to view the world, and then coloring the seeker's world according to its advice. People think fearful thoughts: "If I come to the Guru, will the Guru control my life? What will happen to my life?" At least that's what they have heard from others or read somewhere. Let me tell you: no one controls your life but your mind. No one. No matter how much you think you have surrendered, your mind is always there, until it has become completely one with God—like the minds of the saints.

The mind is intriguing. It can be so great—it can achieve the impossible. The mind can also be downright horrendous—it can create the impossible. In his book *From the Finite to the Infinite*, Baba Muktananda told a wonderful story about this. He said, "When I became a monk, I traveled all over India by foot. I was very fond of traveling and walking. This was my habit—just to walk and walk and walk. During that time I met many great beings. I would visit them and hear what they had to say. One of these great beings said to me, 'God's creation is so beautiful and everything is fine. Do you ever wish that it had been created differently?'

"I replied, 'Everything that God has created is just fine. But it would have been so great if He hadn't created the mind.'

"This great being said, 'Oh no, no, no! It's only because of the mind that you have become a monk. If you didn't have a mind, you wouldn't even come close to God. If the mind didn't trouble you, you wouldn't think of getting closer to God.'"

When you meditate, be aware of your own breath. If you notice your breathing is becoming a little fast or uneven, then understand that your mind is wandering quite a bit. You are restless about something. You cannot remove all the problems and worries of the mind just by using your intellect. The mind needs to have a focus, so when you are meditating, watch your breath. As much as possible, allow the breath to come in deep and go out long. Of course, if you do too much deep breathing, you may feel dizzy, and therefore, there has to be moderation. Each time you notice your breath becoming very uneven, breathe in deep and breathe out long just for a few seconds, and then breathe naturally. You will notice how the breath settles into itself. And the mind, too, settles into this quiet breath.

Make some time every day to sit for meditation in order to quiet your mind, to quiet your tongue, to quiet your body. Make some time every day to go inside and to travel in your own inner world. The only way to meditate, to become a meditator is by doing it every day. If you just meditate every few months, then you are a shopper, not a meditator. You are just shopping when you feel a need for something. But a true meditator will cultivate experiencing the presence of God all the time.

So travel inside your own world and begin to recognize the inner treasures, the inner miracles. Also, acknowledge yourself for becoming stronger, becoming more courageous, becoming more peaceful. Acknowledge these great things that happen to you all the time. Don't wait for the world to give you a reward. Acknowledge your own goodness, your own divinity every step of the way. By sitting for meditation, not only are you surrendering your small will to God's will, you are also acknowledging the fact that divinity exists within you. Baba's message is that God dwells within you, as you. So become anchored in your meditation practice. Even if you think you don't have deep meditations, you should still make the effort. We see over and over again that when people make the effort of learning to quiet the mind and body, that very effort becomes sweet.

Everything in the world can be handled by a person, provided his mind is healthy and gives him full support. As long as you have the full support of your own mind, you can face any challenge. But as soon as the mind weakens, everything else falls apart. Things don't go wrong in this world because nothing is working — things go wrong for you only when your mind has become weaker, when your mind has turned against you, when your own mind has become your enemy.

If the mind is experiencing its well-being, then even if your body is ailing, you may actually feel all right. If the mind is unwell, no matter what shape your body is in, you see disease wherever you look. By conquering the tendencies of the mind, you experience your own divine strength. That strength is inside you. The awakened Kundalini energy purifies the tendencies of the mind, the modifications of the mind. In this way, you are able to experience the true nature of the mind, which is supreme Consciousness, or as Baba says, the supreme Being.

The *Maitri Upanishad* suggests a reason why a seeker is not in touch with his own strength. It says:

> If people thought of God as much as they think of the

world, who would not attain liberation? [6.34.5] [2]

If you are truly doing sadhana, if you have embraced a spiritual path, you will not run here and there asking others what the future holds for you. You will extract strength from your own sadhana. What can a psychic or an astrologer do for you? *You* have to do the work. *You* have to experience your own strength. There is nothing wrong in going to a psychic; there is nothing wrong in going to an astrologer. They, too, have knowledge. But if you are dependent on them, that means you are neglecting the strength of your own mind, the divinity of your own Self.

When do things go wrong? When there is dependency on something that will not give you full strength and support. Therefore, ask yourself if you have truly embraced a spiritual path. In the Sanskrit language, a spiritual path is called *paramārtha*, "the supreme means, the supreme aim." Where you place your mind is of the utmost importance.

People talk about relationships not working, about not having enough support from their relatives, not having a good job, not having a proper life. When you look into this closely, you will notice they have placed their focus on shaky ground. Life is temporary, it is transitory. If you place your trust in the life you know, it will be very shaky. But if your focus is on the supreme Being, the highest Truth, then it doesn't matter how many storms come and go in your life. You know where you have invested your energy, and that will never go to waste. "If people thought of God as much as they think of the world, who would not attain liberation?"

The great Maharashtrian poet-saint and yogi Samartha Ramdas sang about the same theme. He said:

Although the Lord has been within
throughout many births,
I did not see Him.

The Lord of the three worlds pervades everywhere,
but the eyes of the world have missed Him.

The mind acts like a veil of illusion; it obstructs the vision of the Truth. Who controls the mind? Is it wise to shift all the responsibility onto the mind and behave as though you were helpless? Why should you act as if you have no choice? Why should you give so much power to the mind and say, "There is nothing I can do about this. My mind is out of control." Do you think you can cross *samsāra*, the ocean of birth and death, like that? Is this how a true seeker views the world? What should you be doing instead?

A poet-saint from Karnataka sang about the challenge of controlling the reckless mind. He said:

A person always experiences anxiety
until his mind becomes one with the Lord,
  one with Krishna.
If you have a wife, you worry.
If you don't have a wife, you also worry.
If your wife is a fool, you worry.
If your wife is very intelligent
  and very beautiful, you also worry.

And vice versa—if your husband is smart and handsome—boy, do you worry!

If you have children, you worry.
If you don't have children, you also worry.
If your children ask for food, you worry.
If they don't ask for food, you worry.
If you have no relatives, you worry.

If you have no income, you worry.
If you loan money, you worry.
If you borrow money, you also worry.

O brother, in all these three worlds,

there is nothing but anxiety.

By "all three worlds," he means heaven, hell, and earth.

If you have a house, you worry.
If you don't have a house, you also worry.
If your household doesn't run well, you worry.
If your household runs very well, you still worry.
In this world, there is nothing but anxiety.

If you are poor, you worry.
If you have enough, you also worry.
Even if you are wealthy, you still worry.
In this world, everyone is filled with anxiety.

The only way to dissolve your anxiety, says the saint, is to remember the Lord constantly. Only then, will you find peace. The saints are so compassionate. They say that when it comes to focusing your mind on the Lord, it doesn't really matter how you focus. You don't have to find the auspicious time, you don't have to find the right people, you don't have to be in a special place either. Just focus your mind on the Lord. And if you can't focus your mind on the Lord in His entirety, then just focus your mind on any of His attributes, and then see what happens.

As Jnaneshwar Maharaj sang in a most beautiful *abhanga*:

On the bed of the formless Absolute,
a mattress of forms and qualities has been spread,
and upon it rests the beautiful blue form
  of Lord Krishna.

When my mind was lost in meditation,
my eyes perceived nothing but this beautiful,
  deep blue form,
and every moment was like a festival,
  filled with His ecstasy.

In the region of the heart
    and in the temple of my mind,
there is only Krishna,
and He alone is reflected in every corner
    of my heart, of all hearts.

By the grace of his Guru, Nivritti,
Jnaneshwar has found the path to the real heaven,
this unending experience of supreme bliss.

How does a true seeker view the world? A true seeker sees the world with the vision of equality, with equality-consciousness. A true seeker sees the One everywhere; he sees the world through God's eyes. A true seeker maintains *samatā*, the balanced state of mind in which his focus is on the highest. This is how someone who is a true seeker views the world. And the only way to attain this equality-consciousness is by focusing your mind on the Truth, on God, over and over again.

With great respect, with great love, I welcome you all with all my heart.

Sadgurunāth mahārāj kī jay!

August 12, 1995

Chapter Thirteen

Sweep the Path Clean Every Day

Discipline in Thinking II

With great respect, with great love, I welcome you all with all my heart.

Yesterday during darshan, people shared many wondrous experiences. One person said, "I love God tremendously." It was so good to hear—someone acknowledging his love for God without any doubt.

A woman came up in darshan, a very sweet person who was here for the first time. When I asked her how she was doing, she said, "Very sad. Really, very sad." As she walked away, her daughter confided in me that her mother had been struck by something in the program, and she was contemplating it; she was doing a lot of self-inquiry. I told her what was happening was very good.

Contemplation is the sign of a true seeker. True seekers do not let anything go by without examining it. True seekers take things to heart. They try to understand how something relates to them, and how to apply the truth of the scriptures to their own lives. Sometimes when you hear quotations from the scriptures, they ring a bell of truth immediately. At other times, you have to look deep within to understand the meaning of the scriptures.

As I listened to everyone in the darshan line, it was very clear that each one of you has been contemplating what it is to be a true seeker. Even though some of you might not describe your experience in that way, it was apparent that you were immersed in that place of true seeking.

One of the prayers of the *Yajur Veda* says:

> May this mind of mine, which travels too far,
> which is the light of lights,
> the source of all wisdom,
> and which wanders to far-off places
> whether I am asleep or awake —
> may this mind of mine resolve
> on what is noble. [34.1] [1]

Praying to the Lord, praying to the *shakti* of the mind, the sage asks that his mind be resolved on what is noble. May his mind always entertain good thoughts.

The *Maitri Upanishad* gives us another great insight into the nature of the mind and how it affects the way a seeker views the world.

> The mind has been declared to be of two kinds: pure and impure (*shuddha* and *ashuddha*). It becomes impure when it is touched by desire and pure when it is freed from desire. [6.34.6] [2]

When the mind is pure and free from desires, it rises to a higher level. When there is purity, there is also lightness. And when there is lightness, then the mind can rise higher. It can create auspiciousness. It can be the source of impeccable virtues. It enables a seeker to see the world with the vision of equality, *samadrishti.*

However, when the mind is impure, it can bring about a seeker's downfall. It can create hell. An impure mind loves to concoct complications that are hard to overcome. Then a veil of confusion drops over a person's vision of life until all he is looking at is a thick web of desires. That's all he can see — the web of desires.

So this verse from the Upanishads clarifies another important matter. It says the mind becomes impure when it is associated with desire. The question is, of course, how can anyone live without desires? For example, the desire for food is a matter of survival for the physical body. If you don't have a desire to eat, how will you survive? The desire for shelter, the desire to serve humanity, the desire to have a family—there are so many desires. And these desires give a shape to life; they make your life what it is now. How can you live without desires?

If the mind becomes impure at the slightest brush with desire, and if an impure mind means you are being misled, how can you live your life? How can you do away with basic desires? Is that possible? What will support your existence then? What will keep you going? What will your motivation be? This is not a new question. It's been around for centuries; it's very well preserved.

The sages are referring here to people who use their desires only to fulfill the cravings of their senses, people who don't make use of their desires to achieve a higher goal, a higher awareness. The sages are not putting down desires; they are pointing to our actions, to how you use your desires. For example, if you have a desire to eat, that is naturally all right, and the pure mind will want to eat food that is beneficial for the body. But the impure mind wants to eat only food that will satisfy the senses, the taste buds. Such a mind will not consider whether this food is beneficial for health. The impure mind eats almost without thinking—just for the sake of eating. This is what the sages mean by saying that when the mind is touched by desire, it becomes impure.

When desires are not used properly, they become impure. The mind on its own is neutral. It is neither this nor that; it is pure Consciousness. And the entire universe is like that. The universe is beautiful if you leave it as it is, if it is not tainted by impure desires, by an impure mind. The mind itself is pure energy, a neutral power.

It is what you fill the mind with that determines how it reacts. All your reactions come from what you have stored in your mind, from how you have treated your mind. If you have treated your mind with compassion, then that is how you will react to a situation or to a person. If you have filled your mind with anger, then every circumstance will spark that anger. So what you put in the mind determines how the mind reacts.

These days people talk about organic crops—those that have flourished purely on the natural elements of the earth, as opposed to crops that have been treated with pesticides and artificial fertilizers. On the one hand, you have fruits and vegetables that may look terrific—bigger, more colorful, and, of course, more marketable than other produce. But as for taste and nutritional value—that's another story. Is it any different when it comes to the care and nourishment of the mind? Think about it. Like plants that bend toward the sun, the mind is naturally attracted to the Truth. It wants to know God. It wants to experience God's love. It wants to rest in its own nature. The mind wants to relish its own nectar. That is its organic inclination. But so much depends on how it has been treated and how its desires have been expressed and conveyed.

By nature, the mind is pliable. It is almost like soft clay that you can turn into anything you want. You can shape it in any way you choose. If the mind has been entertained by certain ideas and desires, it gets used to their company. That is the mind's nonorganic inclination. So it all depends on what types of desires you present to the mind.

Understand one thing: good thoughts don't come easily. They are the result of hard work, great austerity. They are precious. Protect your thoughts constantly. Like a miser, be alert and protect your thoughts. Every good thought is worth a million dollars. It uplifts not only you—your entire world will benefit from it.

By teaching the mind to pause between thoughts, by practicing this in a disciplined manner, you will be able to watch your mind become purer and healthier and stronger. Your mind will recognize that its true nature is pure Consciousness, and you will live in the presence of God, in the energy of God.

Good thoughts don't come easily. This is why Baba said that you are fortunate when you have a good mind. When people expressed good thoughts from their good minds, he would say, "You are so fortunate, you are so lucky."

Recently, someone said to me, "I thank God every day for giving me a mind that can think of God, a mind that can function properly." Now this is a person whose body lacks strength—although he works very hard. Nevertheless, every day he says, "I thank God for my mind that can think about the Truth, my mind that can function properly. This mind is a gift."

If you ever think God is displeased with you, that God has not given you what you should have in your life, then just look at your mind. If you have a mind that can function properly and think clearly, you should be very grateful. That is the highest gift you can receive in this life.

In an Intensive recently, a man from a nearby town gave a beautiful sharing. He said: "This is my first Intensive, and when I came here yesterday I was a little disappointed. I was uncomfortable with many little things. Today I saw I was carrying a lot of judgments around. In the last meditation, I realized that I had to accept this fact and make peace with it. Only then could I give it up. This realization was followed by a wonderful vision. Toward the end of meditation, I saw white light rise from the base of my spine and then flow out into the sky. As it went out into the sky over my head, there was a flash of lightning very similar to the blue lights you see here in the hall. And it spread; that blue light covered the world. It was a very moving experience. I will never forget it."

What created such an exquisite experience for this man?

It was the sacred atmosphere of the Intensive, where everyone's focus is on the highest Truth. In that environment, he couldn't help but focus on what is great. He couldn't help but let his barriers down. This experience illustrates what the sages say: if everyone practices having good and noble thoughts, beneficial thoughts, uplifting thoughts, elevating thoughts, then the atmosphere also becomes pure, both within and without. This man was able to let go of his judgments with the power of everyone's good thoughts, with the power of the great Shakti. So good thoughts are precious. The power of one good thought can carry you across. The mantra is a good thought—just the mantra alone. Even if you have many uncomfortable and negative thoughts, if you repeat the mantra, it nullifies their negative effects. The mantra *Om Namah Shivāya* is a very powerful good thought.

When you hear the mantra *Om Namah Shivāya* being chanted, you can experience how natural and easy it is to chant the mantra, to be in the body of sound. It is so easy for the mind to relax and let go. You feel that you could continue chanting *Om Namah Shivāya* for hours. You have no desire to do anything else because chanting this mantra will purify you, will give you meditation, will give you the experience of God, will give you just about everything.

As true seekers, you constantly examine the state of your mind. Spiritual experiences abound; they are great in number. However, whether we ourselves have such experiences depends on how we cultivate the thinking process of the mind. Many times you mistakenly think a desire is innocent.

Let's take just one example. Suppose you are one of the people who has a strong desire to sit in the front of the hall for a program. Now you may think this is quite innocent—a sign of interest or even devotion. Or you want to be close to the speaker. But if you analyze this apparently innocent desire, if you put it under a microscope, so to speak, you see that it is crawling with millions of germs. For instance, perhaps you want to prove to someone that you have a good bond with the speaker, a good relationship. Or you want to show the hall monitors that you can get your own way. You want to reassure yourself that you are *someone*; you want to impress your friends. You want everyone to know that you are important in this organization. You want the speaker to know that you are a very serious student, a very dedicated yogi. It's just that you have a tiny little tendency to step on everyone's toes.

Now, you may come up with a hundred very reasonable excuses for your desire: you are a little hard of hearing, you can't see from the back, there is a draft in the rear of the hall. Just a few minor discomforts that make you feel you *should* sit in front. After all!

However, since you really do know that the Shakti is very strong in the back of the hall, in the front of the hall, and also in the middle of the hall, your desire to fight, beg, and wriggle your way into a front seat does indicate a little pollution in the area of the mind. This is something that has gone on for years and years. Even after all these years, you have not been able to deal with the manifestation of this desire or resist it when it comes up. So when you have a desire, think about what that desire really contains.

To renounce something is not easy. Nor should you renounce something without examining it. Renunciation is very good. Letting go is very good, but you should not let go of something unless you have truly understood it. Otherwise, it's a mockery, and you will do the same thing over and again. This is why you must contemplate something before you let go of it—even if it seems to be a small matter.

Many times you think that what's bothering you is a small issue. You may say, "Oh, it's nothing. It doesn't matter." But when you say something doesn't matter, when you dismiss something in that way, it doesn't disappear. It waits. And then, those little issues can turn into a monster that's very difficult to deal with. Therefore, it is vital that you take care of every little issue right away, particularly when you want to focus your attention on the highest Truth, on God. You want to clean up all the particles of dust that collect on the path. You want to keep the path very clean.

When we were in Japan, we visited the monasteries in Kyoto. Every day the monks and the people who serve the monasteries would rake the gardens. They would make beautiful designs for concentration, for meditation. Every day they performed this task, whether there were tourists or not. Keeping the path clean every day is very important. Not only do you keep the path clean for yourself, but also for others who walk on the path. You may think these tiny issues do not matter, but they do.

A seeker once asked Baba Muktananda: "If God wants man to recover his inner energy and know himself, why has He placed this material world as an obstacle that is so hard to overcome?" Baba replied: "From God's point of view the world is not an obstacle. From your point of view, it may be an obstacle; however, it is your attitude that is the obstacle and not God's attitude. Shaivism says that according to God, everything from Shiva to the earth is Consciousness." [3]

How will you experience this? How will you experience that everything from the highest Lord to the tiniest ant is Consciousness? You must contemplate the state of your own mind. This is the lens through which you see the world, through which you see each man and each woman, through which you examine every circumstance. How do you truly see what goes on in your own mind?

The sages make it very clear. When the mind is freed from its notorious desires, it experiences its pure nature. The pure nature of the mind, once again, is Consciousness. It is filled with the high vibrations of virtues. You want your mind to be filled with these high vibrations. It is said that when there is plenty of oxygen, certain germs don't breed. In the same way, when the mind has high vibrations, then negative thoughts don't make nests there. They come and they go. A pure mind is healthy and strong with positive elements.

Keeping your mind active, bounding from one thought to another, does not necessarily make you rich in knowledge. This is not how to experience the Truth, nor is it how to make your mind become pure. The best thing to do is to eliminate the useless thoughts and give power to the beneficial ones.

When we were very young, Baba used to give us a particular exercise when he saw us looking upset or sad. He would ask us why we were unhappy, but we could never really put our finger on the cause. We were too young to have the capacity to contemplate and discover the true reason for our unhappiness.

So he would give us a very simple exercise: "Every time you have a good thought, write it down. Every time you have a sweet thought, write it down. Every time you have a loving thought, write it down. At the end of the day, read all the good thoughts you have had. Then you can see you have so many things to be happy about. After you finish reading the list, tear it up and throw it away. The next day, start again. Every time you have a good thought, write it down. Every time you have a sweet thought, write it down. Every time you have a loving thought, write it down."

As we did this exercise, it was amazing to see that, after all, we were good people! And we had many reasons to be happy. In fact, our life was filled with more happiness than unhappiness. Not realizing that, we had been parading our unhappiness much more than our joy. We had been going around showing our disappointments and our feelings of being upset and sad and negative. But then, when we looked at our notes, it was so clear that we had fewer negative thoughts and many more happy thoughts.

We just had to make a shift in awareness. We needed to be much more aware of our happy thoughts and allow the negative thoughts to be burnt away in the Shakti, knowing that they have their place for a limited time only, but then they must go. They come only to make us feel humble—because negative thoughts do make you feel humble. So their existence is all right. Up to a point they should be there, so you don't become egotistical about always having happy thoughts. On the other hand, you don't need to sink under the heavy burden of negative thoughts. You can rise higher with the support of happy thoughts, of good thoughts.

When you collect your thoughts, you are able to look at them very clearly and distinctly. You are able to understand what has formed each thought, what action has precipitated a thought, and what thought has created another action. You can decide which of your thoughts to keep, and which to discard. In this way, you are able to become a master of your senses. Of course, you have the help of grace. When you have the support of grace and the Shakti, it is much easier, and sadhana becomes much more enjoyable.

In this way, the mind becomes stronger. You are removing useless thoughts and making the mind stronger with good and noble thoughts. When you bring all the good thoughts together, you are able to see the whole picture. And that is very important. In sadhana, you must see the whole picture, and one of the most important points in this picture is your destination, your wanting to know God, wanting to live in the presence of God, wanting to live in the company of the Truth.

With great respect, with great love, I welcome you all with all my heart.

Sadgurunāth mahārāj kī jay!

August 13, 1995

Epilogue

There is so much to say. We have so much to talk about. I know you have many things to tell me. I too have many things to tell you. There is so much to express, so much to convey. Yet we can't go on indefinitely talking to one another in person. Nevertheless, we can communicate our love for one another abundantly at any time, at every time, at all times. And that is what will continue to happen. We will be experiencing our love for one another. And as you know, we never grow apart — we always come closer and closer and closer to divine love.

We are together in the Shakti at all levels of Consciousness — in the waking state, in the dream state, in the deep-sleep state, in the *turīya* or transcendental state. May you always experience the intoxication of the Shakti, of divine love. May it heal you all the time. May it support you. May it guide you.

The Shakti is so strong. It is the supreme Intelligence. When you close your eyes, when you open your eyes, the Shakti is totally aware of it. When you wake up in the morning, when you go to sleep at night, the Shakti is completely aware of these movements. When you speak to someone, when you are in silence, the Shakti is totally conscious of each movement of yours. When you are open, when you are hiding, the Shakti is completely aware of this. You must have this trust—that the divine eye is watching over you. Wherever you go, it is watching over you. Know that the Shakti is protecting you. Whenever you feel uneasy or restless in your heart, understand that the Shakti is completely aware of what you are going through. Have trust, have faith.

No matter how many words you say in person, you will still feel there is so much more to say. And because of this, Baba's message to meditate is so important. If you meditate every day, even for a few minutes, even for a few seconds, you will have this very strong experience of how much love is inside your heart, how much God loves you, how much the Guru's love permeates your entire life.

With great respect, with great love, I welcome you all with all my heart.

Sadgurunāth mahārāj kī jay!

September 4, 1995

Note on Sources

Most of the poetry from saints of the Indian tradition was newly translated for the series of talks from which this text was taken. Many of the scriptural quotations were freshly rendered, drawing from the following sources in English, in addition to the Sanskrit texts:

The Bhagavad Gītā, translated by Winthrop Sargeant (Albany, New York: State University of New York Press, 1984).

The Vedic Experience: Mantramañjarī, edited and translated by Raimundo Panikkar (Pondicherry, India: All India Press, 1977), ©1977 by editor. All passages cited in the Notes are reprinted by permission.

The Principal Upanishads, translated and edited by Swami Radhakrishnan (United States: Humanities Press, Inc., 1978).

Vasiṣṭha's Yoga, translated and edited by Swami Venkatesananda (Albany: State University of New York Press, 1993).

Kulārnava Tantra, translated by Ram Kumar Rai (Varanasi: Prachya Prakashay, 1983).

All quotations from Jnaneshwar's commentary on the *Bhagavad Gītā* are from *Jnaneshwar's Gita*, rendered by Swami Kripananda. Copyright © 1989 by State University of New York Press. Reprinted by permission of SUNY Press.

Guide to Sanskrit Pronunciation

Vowels

Sanskrit vowels are categorized as either long or short. In English transliteration, the long vowels are marked with a bar above the letter and are pronounced twice as long as the short vowels. The vowels *e* and *o* are always pronounced as long vowels.

Short:	Long:
a as in c*u*p	*ā* as in c*a*lm
i as in g*i*ve	*ī* as in s*ee*n
u as in f*u*ll	*ū* as in sch*oo*l
e as in s*a*ve	*ai* as in *ai*sle
o as in ph*o*ne	*au* as in c*ow*
ṛ as in w*ri*tten	

Consonants

The main difference between Sanskrit and English pronunciation of consonants is in the aspirated letters. In Sanskrit these are pronounced with a definite *h* sound. The following list covers variations of pronunciation for most of the Sanskrit consonants found in this book:

c as in su*ch*	*ṅ* as in si*ng*
ch as in *ch*ew	*ñ* as in ca*ny*on
jh as in he*dgeh*og	*ṇ* as in no*n*e
th as in boa*th*ouse	*n* as in s*n*ake
ṭh as in an*th*ill	*ś* as in bu*sh*
ḍh as in roa*dh*ouse	*ṣ* as in *sh*ine
dh as in a*dh*ere	*s* as in *s*upreme
ph as in loo*ph*ole	*kṣ* as in au*ct*ion
bh as in clu*bh*ouse	*ṃ* is a strong nasal *m*
ḥ as in *ha*	

The full transliteration for each Sanskrit term is given in brackets for glossary entries and in the Notes for quotations. For a detailed pronunciation guide, see *The Nectar of Chanting*, published by SYDA Foundation.

Notes

I. The Sunrise of Supreme Bliss

1. The title of the Siddha Yoga Meditation New Year's Intensive for 1995, from which the two talks in Part One were drawn, was inspired by a passage from Swami Muktananda's book *Light on the Path*, in which he says: "After the awakening of the divine Shakti, a yogi realizes that he is perfect, accomplished, nonattached, powerful, filled with love, and of divine nature. In the joy of his attainment he utters, 'I am bliss.' Drinking a fresh cup of joy every day, he remains in a state of deep intoxication. . . . Those whose divine Kundalini Shakti is awakened naturally . . . sip from the spontaneous fountain of bliss within."

Chapter One: The Foundation of Yoga

1. *Taittirīyopaniṣad 3.6.1*

   ānando brahmeti vyajānāt /
   ānandāddhy-eva khalv-imāni bhūtāni jāyante /
   ānandena jātāni jīvanti /
   ānandaṃ prayantyābhisaṃviśantīti . . . //

2. Swami Muktananda, *From the Finite to the Infinite*, (South Fallsburg, New York: SYDA Foundation, 1994).

3. *Kathopaniṣad 2.3.12*

   astīti bruvato 'nyatra kathaṃ tad-upalabhyate //

   English Translation: *The Upanishads*, translated by Alistair Shearer and Peter Russell (Great Britain: Unwin Paperbacks, 1989) © 1978 Peter Russell and Alistair Shearer.

4. *Śivasaṃhitā 2.41*

   yadā karmārjitaṃ dehaṃ nirvāṇe sādhanaṃ bhavet /
   tadā śarīra-vahanaṃ saphalaṃ syān-na cānyathā //

5. *Kathopaniṣad 2.1.1*

   parāñci khāni vyatṛṇat-svayambhūs-tasmāt-parāṅ paśyati nāntarātman /
   kaścid-dhīraḥpratyag-ātmānam-aikṣad-āvṛtta-cakṣur-
   amṛtatvam-icchan //

6. *Bhagavadgītā 18.39*

   yad-agre cānubandhe ca sukhaṃ mohanam-ātmanaḥ /
   nidrālasya-pramādotthaṃ tat-tāmasam-udāhṛtam //

7. *Bhagavadgītā 18.38*

   viṣayendriya-saṃyogād-yat-tad-agre 'mṛtopamam /
   pariṇāme viṣam-iva tat-sukhaṃ rājasaṃ smṛtam //

8. *Bhagavadgītā 18.37*

   yat-tad-agre viṣam-iva pariṇāme 'mṛtopamam /
   tat-sukhaṃ sāttvikaṃ proktam-ātma-buddhi-prasādajam //

Chapter Two: In Pursuit of a Great Goal

1. *Bhagavadgītā 6.3*

   ārurukṣor-muner-yogaṃ karma-kāraṇam-ucyate /
   yogārūḍhasya tasyaiva śamaḥ kāraṇam-ucyate //

2. *Bhagavadgītā 6.10*

   yogī yuñjīta satatam-ātmānaṃ rahasi sthitaḥ /
   ekākī yata-cittātmā nirāśīr-aparigrahaḥ //

3. Swami Muktananda, *Paramartha Katha Prasang* (Ganeshpuri, India: Gurudev Siddha Peeth, 1981).

4. *Yogavāsiṣṭha 2.13.6*

   parityakta-samasteha mano-madhura-vṛttimat /
   sarvataḥ sukham-abhyeti candra-bimba iva sthitam //

5. *Yogasūtra 1.14*

   sa tu dīrgha-kāla-nairantarya-satkārāsevito dṛḍha-bhūmiḥ /

6. *Chāndogyopaniṣad 1.1.10*

   yad-eva vidyayā karoti śraddhayopaniṣadā tad-eva
   vīryavattaraṃ bhavatīti . . . //

7. *Bhagavadgītā 6.26*

yato yato niścarati manaś-cañcalam-asthiram /
tatas-tato niyamyaitad-ātmany-eva vaśaṃ nayet //

8. *Yogasūtra 2.32*
   śauca-santoṣa-tapaḥ-svādhyāyeśvara-praṇidhānāni niyamāḥ //

9. The mindlessness of a yogi is not mental inertia but rather a state in which he is identified fully with the supreme Power that is the source of the mind.

10. Swami Hariharananda Aranya, *Yoga Philosophy of Patañjali* (Albany: State University of New York Press, 1983).

II. The Path of Discipline

Chapter Three: The Road to Liberation

1. *Ṛgveda 1.90.6*
   madhu vātā ṛtāyate madhu kṣaranti sindhavaḥ /
   mārdhvīrṇaḥ santvoṣadhīḥ madhumat pārvi rajaḥ //

2. *Ṛgveda 4.57.3*
   madhumatīr-oṣadhīr-dyāva āpo madhumān-no bhavatv-antarikṣam /
   kṣetrasya patir-madhumān-no astv-ariṣyanto anv-enaṃ carema //

   English translation: *The Vedic Experience: Mantramañjarī*, translated and edited by Raimundo Panikkar (Pondicherry: All India Books, 1977).

3. *Rudram, Camakam 11*
   pṛthivi mātar-mā mā hiṃsīr-madhu maniṣye madhu janiṣye madhu
   vakṣyāmi madhu vadiṣyāmi madhumatīṃ devebhyo vācamudyāsaṃ
   śuśrūṣeṇyāṃ manuṣyebhyas-taṃ mā devā avantu śobhāyai pitaro
   'numadantu //

4. *Yajurveda 19.9*
   tejo 'si tejo mayi dhehi vīryam-asi vīryaṃ mayi dhehi
   balamasi balaṃ mayi dhehyo /
   jo 'syojo mayi dhehi manyur-asi manyuṃ mayi dhehi saho
   'si saho mayi dhehi //

5. Muz Murray, *Seeking the Master: A Guide to the Ashrams of India* (Great Britain: Neville Spearman (Jersey) Ltd., 1980).

Chapter Four: Teach Your Eyes How to See

1. In this poem, a sage presents images from Indian tradition to illustrate

the dangerous lure of the senses. Both the male elephant and the male musk deer can become frenzied to the point of death, the elephant in search of a mate and the deer trying to locate the source of the intoxicating fragrance that issues from its own body. The snake and the fish are haplessly caught by hunters, the snake because it is mesmerized by the sound of a flute and the fish in being tempted to bite the fisherman's bait. The moth, drawn by light, flies to its death in a flame.

2. Swami Muktananda, *Satsang with Baba, Vol. Two* (Ganeshpuri, India: Gurudev Siddha Peeth, 1976).

3. From "The Upanishad Mantras," which are sung after the *Ārati* each morning in Siddha Yoga ashrams: (*sarve bhadrāṇi paśyantu*).

4. *Vivekacūḍāmaṇi 77*
   doṣeṇa tīvro viṣayaḥ kṛṣṇa-sarpa-viṣād-api /
   viṣaṃ nihanti bhoktāraṃ draṣṭāraṃ cakṣuṣāpyayam //

5. The swan is seen in the Indian tradition as a creature of great discrimination, selecting only the most sublime fare even in an earthly setting such as Lake Manasarova, a lake in the Himalayas that is sacred to Lord Shiva.

6. Swami Muktananda, *Selected Essays*, (South Fallsburg, New York: SYDA Foundation, 1995).

7. Swami Muktananda, *Sadgurunath Maharaj ki Jay* (New York, 1975).

8. Swami Muktananda, *Satsang with Baba, Vol. One* (Ganeshpuri, India: Gurudev Siddha Peeth, 1974).

9. *Sadgurunath Maharaj ki Jay.*

Chapter Five: Who Is Looking Through Your Eyes?

1. *Vivekacūḍāmaṇi 530*
   ghaṭo 'yam-iti vijñātuṃ niyamaḥ ko 'nvavekṣate /
   vinā pramāṇa-suṣṭhutvaṃ yasmin-sati padārtha-dhīḥ //

2. *Śvetāśvataropaniṣad 6.11*
   sākṣī cetāṃ kevalo nirguṇaś-ca

3. *Satsang with Baba, Vol. One.*

Chapter Six: What Enters Your Ears Goes Straight to Your Heart

1. *Bhagavadgītā 2.40*
   nehābhikramanāśo 'sti pratyavāyo na vidyate /

svalpam-apy-asya dharmasya trāyate mahato bhayāt //

2. *Ṛgveda 1.89.8*

   bhadraṃ karṇebhiḥ śṛṇuyāma devā

3. *Lalleshwari,* rendered by Swami Muktananda (South Fallsburg, New York: SYDA Foundation, 1981).

Chapter Seven: Hear Only What Is Worthwhile

1. Swami Muktananda, *Satsang with Baba, Vol. Four* (Ganeshpuri, India: Gurudev Siddha Peeth, 1978).
2. Baba Muktananda, "Answers to Your Questions," *Siddha Path,* April 1982 (Ganeshpuri, India: Gurudev Siddha Peeth).
3. *Satsang with Baba, Vol. One.*
4. English translation: *The Holy Vedas,* translated by Pandit Satyakam Vidyalankar (Delhi: Clarion Books). (*Sāmaveda: pra va indrāya vṛtra-hantamāya viprāya gāthaṃ gāyata yaṃ jujoṣate. . . .*)
5. *Satsang with Baba, Vol. Two.*

Chapter Eight: Value Your Hunger

1. Swami Muktananda, *Satsang with Baba, Vol. Three* (Ganeshpuri, India: Gurudev Siddha Peeth, 1977).
2. *Kulārṇavatantra 15.107*

   atyāhāraḥ . . . mantro na sidhyati //
3. *Satsang with Baba, Vol. Three.*
4. *Taittirīyopaniṣad 2.2.1*

   yāḥ kāśca pṛthivīgaṃśritāḥ / atho annenaiva jīvanti / . . . /
   annagaṃ hi bhūtānāṃ jyeṣṭham /
   tasmāt-sarvauṣadham-ucyate /
   sarvaṃ vai te 'nnam-āpnuvanti / ye 'nnaṃ brahmopāsate / . . . //
5. *Satsang with Baba, Vol. Three.*
6. *Satsang with Baba, Vol. Three.*
7. *Bhagavadgītā 15.14*

   ahaṃ vaiśvānaro bhūtvā prāṇināṃ deham-āśritaḥ /
   prāṇāpāna-samāyuktaḥ pacāmy-annaṃ caturvidham //

8. William C. Chittick, *The Sufi Path of Love: The Spiritual Teachings of Rumi* (Albany: State University of New York Press, 1983).

9. *From the Finite to the Infinite.*

Chapter Nine: A Cause for Celebration

1. *Satsang with Baba, Vol. Two.*

2. *Satsang with Baba, Vol. Two.*

3. *Atharvaveda 12.1.2-3*

   asaṃbādhaṃ madhyato mānavānāṃ yasyā udvataḥ pravataḥ samaṃ bahu /
   nānā-vīryā oṣadhīr-yā bibharti pṛthivī naḥ prathatāṃ rādhyatāṃ naḥ //
   yasyāṃ samudra uta sindhur-āpo yasyām-annaṃ kṛṣṭayaḥ sambabhūvuḥ /
   yasyām-idaṃ jinvati prāṇadejat sā no bhūmiḥ pūrvapeye dadhātu //

4. Swami Muktananda, *Satsang with Baba, Vol. Five* (Ganeshpuri, India: Gurudev Siddha Peeth, 1978).

5. *Chāndogyopaniṣad 6.5.1*

   annam-aśitaṃ tredhā vidhīyate tasya yaḥ sthaviṣṭho
   dhātus-tat-purīṣaṃ bhavati yo madhyamas-tan-māṃsaṃ yo 'ṇiṣṭhas-tan-manaḥ //

6. *Chāndogyopaniṣad 7.26.2*

   āhāra-śuddhau sattva-śuddhiḥ sattva-śuddhau dhrutvā smṛtiḥ
   smṛti-lambhe sarva-granthīnāṃ vipramokṣas-tasmai //

7. *Bhagavadgītā 3.13*

   yajña-śiṣṭāśinaḥ santo mucyante sarva-kilbiṣaiḥ /
   bhuñjate te tvaghaṃ pāpā ye pacanty-ātma-kāraṇāt //

Chapter Ten: Within the Word Dwells the Radiant Lord

1. *Purāṇas*

   yā kundendu-tuṣāra-hāra-dhavalā yā śubhra-vastrāvṛtā
   yā vīnā-varadaṇḍa-maṇḍita-karā yā śveta-padmāsanā /
   yā bhrahmācyuta-śaṅkara-prabhṛtibir-devaiḥ sadā vanditā
   sā māṃ pātu sarasvatī bhagavatī niḥśeṣa-jāḍyāpahā //

2. *The Vedic Experience.*

3. *Ṛgveda 10.71.1*

bṛhaspate prathamaṃ vāco agraṃ yat-prairata nāmadheyaṃ dadhānāḥ /
yadeṣāṃ śreṣṭhaṃ yadaripramāsīt-preṇā tadeṣāṃ nihitaṃ guhāviḥ //

English translation: *The Vedic Experience.*

4. *Bṛhadāraṇyakopaniṣad 3.7.17*

   yo vāci tiṣṭhan vāco 'ntaraḥ /
   yaṃ vāṇ na veda /
   yasya vāk śarīram /
   yo vācam-antaro yamayati eṣa ta ātmāntaryāmy-amṛtaḥ //

5. *Ṛgveda 10.71.4*

   uta tvaḥ paśyan-na dadarśa vācam-uta tvaḥ śṛṇvanna śṛṇoty-enām /
   uto tv-asmai tanvaṃ vi sasre jāyeva patya uśatī suvāsāḥ //

   English translation: *The Vedic Experience*, Panikkar.

6. *Śatapathabrāhmaṇa 10.5.3.2-4*

   neva hi sanmano nevāsat //
   tadidaṃ manaḥ sṛṣṭamāvirabubhūṣat . . . //
   tanmano vācam asṛjat . . . //

7. *Satsang with Baba, Vol. One.*

8. *Nītiśataka 64*

   pradānaṃ praccanaṃ gṛham-upagate sambhrama-vidhiḥ priyaṃ kṛtvā maunaṃ sadasi kathanaṃ cātyupakṛteḥ /
   anutseko lakṣyāṃ nirabhibhavasārāḥ parakathāḥ satāṃ kenoddiṣṭaṃ viṣamasidhārāvratam-idam //

9. *Vivekacūḍāmaṇi 367*

   yogasya prathamaṃ dvāraṃ vāṅnirodho 'parigrahaḥ //

10. *Satsang with Baba, Vol. Three.*

Chapter Eleven: The State of Shimmering Consciousness

1. *Aṣṭavakrasaṃhitā 12.1*

   kāya-kṛtyāsahaḥ pūrvaṃ tato vāg-vistarāsahaḥ /
   atha cintāsahas-tasmād-evam-evāham-āsthitaḥ //

2. *Vivekacūḍāmaṇi 482*

   vācā vaktum-aśakyam-eva manasā mantuṃ na vā śakyate svānandāmṛta-pūra-pūrita-para-brahmāmbudher-vaibhavam /
   ambho-rāśi-viśīrṇa-vārṣika-śilā-bhāvaṃ bhajan-me mano

yasyāṃśāṃśalave vilīna-madhunānandātmanā nirvṛtam //

III. How Does a True Seeker View the World?

Chapter Twelve: Acknowledge Your Own Goodness Every Step of the Way

1. *Ṛgveda 1.22.20-21*

   tad-viṣṇoḥ paramaṃ padaṃ sadā paśyanti sūrayaḥ /
   divīva cakṣurātatam //
   tad-viprāso vipanyavo jāgṛvāṃsaḥ samindhate /
   viṣṇor-yat-paramaṃ padam //

2. *Maitryupaniṣad 6.34.5*

   samāsaktaṃ yathā cittam jantor-viṣaya-gocare /
   yady-evaṃ brahmaṇi syāt-ko na mucyate bandhanāt //

Chapter Thirteen: Sweep the Path Clean Every Day

1. *Yajurveda 34.1*

   yaj-jāgrato dūram-udaiti daivaṃ tad-u suptasya tathaivaiti /
   dūraṅgamaṃ jyotiṣāṃ jyotir-ekaṃ tan-me manaḥ śiva-saṅkalpam-astu //

2. *Maitryupaniṣad 6.34.6*

   mano hi dvividhaṃ proktaṃ śuddham cāśuddham-eva ca /
   aśuddhaṃ kāma-samparkāc-chuddhaṃ kāma-vivarjitam //

3. Swami Muktananda, "Answers to Your Questions," *Siddha Path*, October/November 1980 (Ganeshpuri, India: Gurudev Siddha Peeth).

Glossary of Poets, Philosophers, and Sages

Amir Khusrau
(1255-1325) Court poet to seven of Delhi's sultans during the time of Moghul rule in India; the greatest disciple of the celebrated saint, Nizamuddin.

Ashtavakra
A crippled sage of the Indian epics whose teachings are contained in the *Ashtavakra Gītā*, also known as the *Ashtavakra Samhitā*. This work is a dialogue between the teacher and his most illustrious disciple, the legendary King Janaka.

Bhartrihari
A king from ancient times who gave up his throne to become a yogi, sage, and poet. The collection of Bhartrihari's poems is known as *Shatakatrāyam*.

Dhu al-Nun
(796-859) An Egyptian Sufi poet-saint. In 829 he was imprisoned for heresy at Baghdad, but during his trial, Dhu al-Nun so moved the caliph with his defense of Sufism that he was released unharmed. His tombstone is preserved in Cairo.

Eknath Maharaj
(1528-1609) A poet-saint who lived as a householder in the Maharashtrian village of Paithan. Eknath was the disciple of Janardan Swami and the author of several hundred *abhangas*, which he wrote in the Marathi language to foster a spiritual revival among the common people.

Francis of Assisi
(1181-1226) Founder of monastic orders for men and women, the Franciscans, and leader of a Christian reform movement that swept across Italy in the early thirteenth century. Saint Francis spent most of his life in the village of Assisi, yet the power and ecstasy of his dedication to God drew thousands of followers to him.

Jnaneshwar Maharaj
(1275-1296) Foremost among the poet-saints of Maharashtra; author of *Jñāneshwarī*, a radiant commentary on the *Bhagavad Gītā* that he composed in verse at the age of sixteen at the direction of his Guru, Nivrittinath. Jnaneshwar wrote in the Marathi language, making the scriptures available to the common people of his day, and he was one of the leaders of the revolutionary *bhakti* movement, which held that anyone could know God by chanting His name.

Kabir
(1440-1518) A poet-saint and mystic

who lived as a simple weaver in Benares. His followers included both Hindus and Muslims, and his influence was a powerful force in overcoming the fierce religious factionalism of his time. His poems, which describe the experience of the Self, the greatness of the Guru, and the nature of true spirituality, are still studied and sung all over the world.

Lalleshwari/Lalli
(Fourteenth century) A great yogini of Kashmir whose devotional poems were often quoted by Swami Muktananda. His rendering of her poetry is published in Hindi and English under the title *Lalleshwari.*

Mira/Mirabai
(1433-1468) A Rajasthani queen famous for her poems of devotion to Lord Krishna. She was so absorbed in love for Krishna that when she was given poison by vindictive relatives, Mirabai drank it as nectar and remained unharmed.

Muktananda, Swami
(1908-1982) Swami Chidvilasananda's Guru, often referred to as Baba. This great Siddha brought the powerful and rare initiation known as *shaktipāt* to the West on the command of his own Guru, Bhagawan Nityananda. As the inheritor of a great lineage of spiritual Masters, Baba Muktananda introduced the practice of Siddha Yoga Meditation all over the world, creating what he called a "meditation revolution." Baba made the scriptures come alive, teaching in words and actions, by example and by direct experience. His message to everyone was: "Honor your Self, worship your Self, meditate on your Self. Your God dwells within you as you."

Narsi Mehta
(1470-1566) A poet-saint whose eloquent supplication and celebration of the Lord throughout the many trials of his life continue to inspire devotees. A brahmin from Junagadh, a village in Gujarat, Narsi Mehta sacrificed his own reputation to sing his *kirtanas*, his songs, with people of every caste.

Nityananda, Bhagawan
(d. 1961) Baba Muktananda's Guru; also known as Bade Baba (Elder Baba). Very little is known of Bhagawan Nityananda's early life; he was a born Siddha, living his entire life in the highest state of consciousness. He was seen first in south India and later settled in Maharashtra, where the village of Ganeshpuri grew up around him. He spoke very little, yet thousands of people would stand in line for hours to experience the profound blessing of his presence. His *samādhi* shrine is located at the site of his original quarters in Ganeshpuri, about a mile from Gurudev Siddha Peeth, the principal ashram of Siddha Yoga. In both Gurudev Siddha Peeth and Shree Muktananda Ashram in South Fallsburg, New York, Swami Muktananda has dedicated a temple to honor this great saint.

Patanjali
(Fourth century) Often given the title *mahārishi*, great sage. Patanjali is the author of the *Yoga Sūtras*, the exposition of one of the six orthodox philosophies of India and the authoritative description of *ashtānga yoga*, the eight aspects of the path to liberation.

Rahim
(1556-1627) The best known of the poets in the court of the Moghul emperor Akbar. Though a Moghul general, in his poetry Rahim celebrated his devotion to Hari, Krishna, and Rama.

Ram Tirth
(1873-1906) A distinguished professor of mathematics who withdrew to the Himalayas to meditate in solitude. Renowned as a great being, Ram Tirth wrote inspiring poetry in the Urdu language, and in the latter years of his life, he lectured on Vedanta in Japan and the United States.

Ramanuja
(1017-1137) Born in south India, this philosopher-sage was the founder of the Qualified Nondualism School of Vedanta, which says that the human soul is separate from but dependent on the supreme Soul.

Ramdas, Samartha
(1608-1681) A saint who helped to protect the Hindu religion in Maharashtra when it was threatened with extinction through Moghul persecution. He was the Guru of Shivaji, the heroic king who freed Maharashtra from the Moghuls. Ramdas's teachings, both social and spiritual, are contained in the *Dāsabodha*.

Sa'di, Sheikh
(1200-1291) A renowned Persian Sufi poet and scholar from the Iranian city of Shiraz; author of the *Gulistān*, "Rose Garden," a collection of allegorical tales.

Shankaracharya
(788-820) The greatest proponent of Advaita Vedanta, absolute nondualism; a sage so venerated that the title *āchārya*, teacher, has become a part of his name. Shankaracharya established *maths*, ashrams, throughout India and founded four orders of *sannyāsins*, monks, including the Saraswati Order to which Swami Muktananda and Swami Chidvilasananda belong. His best known work is *Viveka Chūdāmani*, "The Crest Jewel of Discrimination."

Sundardas
(Sixteenth century) A poet-saint who lived in Delhi; a Vedantin who wrote eloquently about the significance of the spiritual Master and the requirements of discipleship.

Surdas
(1479-1584) Born blind, Surdas was devoted to Lord Krishna and spent his life at Vraja, the place where Krishna lived in his childhood. The songs of this poet-saint are collected in *Sursāgar*.

Tagore, Rabindranath
(1861-1941) Bengali poet, educator, and visionary, whose work helped to introduce Indian culture to the West. His English translations of the poetry of the saint Kabir were among the earliest published.

Tukaram Maharaj
(1608-1650) A poet-saint who lived as a grocer in the village of Dehu in Maharashtra. Though Tukaram's life was one of trial and challenge, his devotion to God never waivered. He wrote thousands of *abhangas*, describing his sadhana and spiritual experiences, his realization, and the glory of the divine Name.

Tulsidas
(1532-1623) The poet-saint of north India who wrote, in Hindi, the *Rāmcharitmānas* or *Tulsī Rāmāyana*, the life-story of Lord Rama and one of the most popular scriptures in India today.

Valmiki
An ancient sage and the author of the original *Rāmāyana*, the epic account of the adventures of Lord Rama. Valmiki, who began his life as a thief, performed great austerity along the path to sainthood.

Glossary of Texts and Terms

Abhanga
A devotional song composed in the Marathi language that expresses the longing of a devotee for God.

Abhyās [*abhyāsa*]
Continuous endeavor; constant practice or repetition. This constancy is cited by the sage Patanjali as the means of establishing a strong yogic practice.

Absolute, the
The highest Reality; supreme Consciousness; the pure, untainted, changeless Truth.

Āchārya [*ācārya*]
(*lit.*, one who leads toward) A teacher; often refers to a sage who leads his students toward the highest Truth.

Agni hotri [*agnihotṛ*]
A brahmin who performs a specific fire ritual, *agni hotra*, each day at the auspicious times for worship.

Ahamkāra [*ahaṃkāra*]
Ego; of the four psychic instruments, that which creates the experience of limited individuality. *See also* Four psychic instruments.

Aitareya Brāhmana [*aitareyabrāhmaṇa*]
Connected to the *Rig Veda*; the earliest writings on the meaning of the sacrificial prayers and on the performance of Vedic rites.

Ālasya [*ālasya*]
Idleness; apathy; sloth.

Apāna [*apāna*]
See Prāna.

Ārati
1) A ritual act of worship during which a flame, symbolic of the individual soul, is waved before the form of a deity, a respected being, or an image that embodies the divine light of Consciousness. 2) *Ārati* is the name of the morning and evening prayer that is sung in honor of Bhagawan Nityananda twice each day in Siddha Yoga ashrams. The *Ārati* chant is always accompanied by the waving of a flame.

Arjuna [*arjuna*]
One of the heroes of the epic *Mahābhārata*, considered to be the greatest of all warriors. He was the friend and devotee of Lord Krishna. It was to Arjuna that the Lord revealed the knowledge of the *Bhagavad Gītā*. *See also Bhagavad Gītā.*

Āsana [*āsana*]
1) A hatha yoga posture practiced to

strengthen the body, purify the nervous system, and develop one-pointedness of mind. 2) A seat or mat on which one sits for meditation. *See also Ashtānga yoga.*

Ashram [***āśrama***]
The dwelling place of a Guru or saint; a monastic retreat site where seekers engage in spiritual practices and study the sacred teachings of yoga. *See also Gurukula.*

Ashtānga yoga [***aṣṭāṅgayoga***]
(*lit.*, eight limbs of yoga) Eight aspects of yoga described by the sage Patanjali in his *Yoga Sūtras.* The eight limbs are self-restraint (*yama*), daily practices (*niyama*), steady posture (*āsana*), breath control (*prāṇāyāma*), withdrawal of the senses (*pratyāhāra*), concentration (*samyama*), meditation (*dhyāna*), and union with the Absolute (*samādhi*). *See also Yoga Sūtras.*

Ashtavakra Samhitā [***aṣṭavakrasaṃhitā***]
Also known as the *Ashtavakra Gītā*; verses in which the famous crippled sage Ashtavakra conveys the essential teachings of Advaita Vedanta. *See also* Vedanta.

Ashuddha [***aśuddha***]
Impure; incorrect.

Atharva Veda [***atharvaveda***]
One of the four primary scriptures of India, containing many mantras for protection and healing. *See also* Veda(s).

Ātma samyama [***ātmasaṃyama***]
Self-control, springing from an awareness of the highest Self. *See also* Self.

Ātma vichāra [***ātmavicāra***]
The practice of inquiring into the nature of one's innermost being, the Self. *See also* Self.

Ātma vishvāsa [***ātmaviśvāsa***]
(*lit.*, Self-confidence) A trust in the beneficence of the highest Being within.

Ayurveda [***āyurveda***]
(*lit.*, knowledge of life) The ancient Indian science of medicine, which teaches that good health depends on maintaining the even balance of one's constitutional principles.

Baba
(*lit.*, father) A term of affection and respect for a saint, holy man, or father.

Bade Baba
(*lit.*, elder father) An affectionate name for Bhagawan Nityananda, Swami Muktananda's Guru.

Bhagavad Gītā [***bhagavadgītā***]
(*lit.*, song of the Lord) One of the world's great spiritual texts and an essential scripture of India; a portion of the *Mahābhārata* in which Lord Krishna instructs his disciple Arjuna on the nature of the universe, God, and the supreme Self.

Bhagawan [***bhagavān***]
(*lit.*, the Lord) One who is endowed with the six attributes of infinity: spiritual power, righteousness, glory, splendor, knowledge, and renunciation. A term of highest respect. Swami Muktananda's Guru is known as Bhagawan Nityananda.

Bhajan
An Indian devotional song in praise of God.

Bhaktā [***bhaktā***]
A devotee, a lover of God; a follower of *bhakti yoga*, the path of love and devotion.

Bhāv [***bhāva***]
(*lit.*, becoming; being) Attitude; emotional state; a feeling of absorption or identification.

Bhogī [***bhogī***]
One who enjoys worldly experience.

Bhūmi Sūkta [***bhūmisūkta***]
(*lit.*, hymn to the earth) A prayer from the *Atharva Veda* that explicates in vivid detail the many blessings offered by the earth.

Brahma [***brahmā***]
The absolute Reality manifested as the

creator of the universe, who is personified as one of the three gods of the Hindu trinity. *See also* Shiva; Vishnu.

Brahman [*brahman*]
In Vedanta, the absolute Reality or all-pervasive supreme Principle of the universe.

Brahmanic tradition
The observance of rites and ceremonies prescribed in the Vedas, the most ancient scriptures of India. *See also* Veda(s).

Brahmin
The first caste of Hindu society, the members of which are by tradition priests and scholars.

Brihadāranyaka Upanishad [*bṛhadāraṇyakopaniṣad*]
Associated with the *Shatapatha Brāhmana* and containing the teachings of the sage Yajnavalkya; often described as one of the most significant of the Upanishads. *See also* Upanishad(s).

Chakra [*cakra*]
(*lit.*, wheel) A center of energy located in the subtle body where subtle channels called *nādīs* converge, giving the appearance of a lotus. Six major chakras lie within the *sushumnā nādī*, or central channel. They are: *mūlādhāra* at the base of the spine; *svādhishthāna* at the root of the reproductive organs; *manipūra* at the navel; *anāhata*, the "lotus of the heart," at the center of the chest; *vishuddha* at the throat; and *ājñā* between the eyebrows. Once awakened, Kundalini flows upward from the *mūlādhāra* to the seventh chakra, the *sahasrāra*, at the crown of the head. *See also* Kundalini; *Sahasrāra; Shaktipāt; Sushumnā nādī.*

Chāndogya Upanishad [*chāndogyopaniṣad*]
One of the main Upanishads, which illustrates through dialogue and legend many of the requisite qualities of a disciple.

Chitprakāsha [*citprakāśa*]
The light of supreme Consciousness.

Consciousness
The intelligent, supremely independent, divine Energy that creates, pervades, and supports the entire universe.

Darshan [*darśana*]
(*lit.*, to have the sight of) A glimpse or vision of a saint; seeing God or an image of God.

Dhanya Lakshmi [*dhanyalakṣmi*]
The goddess of grain, food, and prosperity; one of the eight forms of Mahalakshmi, the goddess of abundance.

Dhāranā [*dhāranā*]
Concentration; the sixth of the eight limbs of the path of *ashtānga yoga.* In this practice, the mind becomes stabilized by being fixed on an object. *See also Yoga Sūtras.*

Dharma [*dharma*]
(*lit.*, what holds together) Essential duty; righteousness; living in accordance with the divine Will. The highest dharma is to recognize the Truth in one's own heart.

Dhauti [*dhauti*]
A traditional method of cleansing the throat and stomach that is used by hatha yoga adepts.

Dhyāna [*dhyāna*]
Meditation; the seventh stage of yoga described by Patanjali in the *Yoga Sūtras. See also Ashtānga yoga.*

Dīkshā [*dīkṣā*]
Any religious initiation; initiation given by a Guru, often by imparting a mantra; in Siddha Yoga it means the spiritual awakening of the disciple by *shaktipāt. See also Shaktipāt*; Siddha Yoga.

Dosa
A large, thin Indian pancake, like a crepe, made from fermented urid dal and rice flour.

Drishti [*dṛṣṭi*]
Vision, usually in the context of seeing with the outlook of God.

***Ekāgra manas* [*ekāgramanas*]**
One-pointedness of mind.

***Ekānna* [*ekānna*]**
The discipline of eating only one food, usually undertaken for a limited length of time.

Four levels of speech
The sages of India identify four levels of speech within the human body: *parā*, the deepest level of unmanifest Consciousness, where sound originates; *pashyantī*, the *bījā* or seed mantras that are heard from within; *madhyamā*, subtle sound in the form of the thoughts; and *vaikarī*, articulated speech.

Four psychic instruments
The Indian philosophical systems delineate four functions of the mind: *manas*, the capacity to receive sense impressions; *chitta*, the subconscious mind; *ahamkāra*, the ego; and *buddhi*, the intellect. *See also Ahamkāra.*

Ganeshpuri
A village at the foot of Mandagni Mountain in Maharashtra, India. Bhagawan Nityananda settled in this region where yogis have performed spiritual practices for thousands of years. The ashram, founded by Swami Muktananda at his Guru's command, is built near this village. *See also* Gurudev Siddha Peeth.

Ganges
The most sacred river of India, which flows from its source in the Himalayas, across all of north India to the Bay of Bengal. The Ganges, often identified as the goddess Ganga, is said to wash away the sins of anyone who takes a dip in its holy waters.

***Granthi*(s) [*granthi*]**
(*lit.*, knot) A mass of karmic traces, occurring at several significant junctures in the subtle system along the *sushumnā nādī*: in the heart, at the nape of the neck, and at the point between the eyebrows. These knots are cut through the purifying work of the awakened Kundalini Shakti. *See also* Chakra; Kundalini.

Gujarat
A state along the western coast of India, bordering on Maharashtra.

***Guna*(s) [*guṇa*]**
The scriptures of India identify three essential qualities of nature, which determine the inherent characteristics of all created things. They are *sattva* (purity, light, harmony, and intelligence); *rajas* (activity and passion); and *tamas* (dullness, inertia, and ignorance).

Guru [*guru*]
A spiritual Master or teacher; one who has attained union with God, who is learned in the scriptures, and who has been empowered by his own Guru to initiate seekers and guide them on the path to liberation. *See also Sadguru.*

***Guru Gītā* [*gurugītā*]**
(*lit.*, song of the Master) A sacred Sanskrit text; a "garland" or series of mantras that describes the nature of the Guru, the Guru-disciple relationship, and meditation on the Guru. In Siddha Yoga ashrams, the *Guru Gītā* is chanted every morning.

Gurudev Siddha Peeth [*gurudevasiddhapīṭha*]
(*lit.*, abode of perfected beings) The main ashram of Siddha Yoga and the site of the *samādhi* shrine of Swami Muktananda. It was founded in 1956, when Bhagawan Nityananda instructed Swami Muktananda to remain on this site near Ganeshpuri, India. Charged with the power of divine Consciousness, the ashram is a world-renowned center for spiritual practice and study under the guidance of the living Master Swami Chidvilasananda. *See also* Ashram, *Gurukula.*

***Gurukula* [*gurukula*]**
(*lit.*, school of the Master) In Vedic times, spiritual aspirants would serve

the Guru at his house or ashram for a period of time, studying the scriptures and practicing self-inquiry and other spiritual disciplines under the guidance of the Master. In essence, Siddha Yoga ashrams follow the model of these *gurukulas* of old.

Gurumayi
A term of respect and endearment frequently used in addressing Swami Chidvilasananda.

Hatha yoga [*haṭhayoga*]
Yogic practices, both physical and mental, performed for the purpose of purifying and strengthening the physical and subtle bodies. *See also* Yoga.

Hiranya garbha [*hiraṇyagarbha*]
(*lit.*, the golden egg) The cosmic form of the Self; the seed from which the universe arises.

Intensive
A Siddha Yoga Meditation program designed by Swami Muktananda to give direct initiation through the awakening of the Kundalini energy. *See also* Kundalini; *Shaktipāt.*

Japa [*japa*]
(*lit.*, prayer uttered in a low voice) Repetition of a mantra, either silently or aloud. *See also* Mantra.

Jñānānanda [*jñānānanda*]
The bliss of the highest knowledge.

***Jñānendriya*(s)** [*jñānendriya*]
The five organs of knowledge; the powers by which the individual receives information about the world. These are the sense organs: the powers of seeing, hearing, touching, tasting, and smelling.

Jñāneshwarī [*jñāneśvarī*]
A majestic commentary in verse on the *Bhagavad Gītā*, written by Jnaneshwar Maharaj when he was sixteen. It was the first original scriptural work written in Marathi, the language of the people of Maharashtra.

Jñānī [*jñānī*]
(*lit.*, one who knows) 1) An enlightened being. 2) A follower of the path of knowledge.

Kaivalya [*kaivalya*]
(*lit.*, aloneness) The final state of "aloneness," when there is the realization that all existence is one conscious energy.

Kali Yuga [*kaliyuga*]
(*lit.*, the dark age) The present age, or world cycle, described as the Iron Age, in which righteousness and truth have degenerated and yet God can be experienced by those who make even a little effort.

Karma [*karma*]
(*lit.*, action) 1) Any action — physical, verbal, or mental. 2) Destiny, which is caused by past actions, mainly those of previous lives.

***Karmendriya*(s)** [*karmendriya*]
The five organs of action; the powers that control the actions of speech, grasping, locomotion, procreation, and excretion.

Karnataka
A state in India on the southwest coast where Swami Muktananda was born.

Kashmir Shaivism
A branch of the Shaivite philosophical tradition that explains how the formless supreme Principle, Shiva, manifests as the universe.

Katha Upanishad [*kaṭhopaniṣad*]
One of the principal Upanishads, containing the story of Nachiketa, who, given a boon by the lord of death, asks for knowledge of the Absolute. *See also* Upanishads.

Khecharī mudrā [*khecarīmudrā*]
An advanced yogic exercise, which occurs spontaneously in Siddha Yoga, in which the tip of the tongue curls back into the throat and upward into the nasal pharynx. This *mudrā* permits Kundalini to rise to the *sahasrāra*, causing the

meditator to experience *samādhi* states and taste divine nectar.

Knots of the heart
See Granthi(s).

Krishna [***kṛṣṇa***]
(*lit.*, the dark one; the one who attracts irresistably) The eighth incarnation of Lord Vishnu. The spiritual teachings of Lord Krishna are contained in the *Bhagavad Gītā*, a portion of the epic *Mahābhārata*.

Kulārnava Tantra [***kulārṇavatantra***]
A Shaiva treatise about the Guru, the disciple, the mantra, and many traditional practices of worship.

Kumbhaka [***kumbhaka***]
In hatha yoga, the holding of the breath during the practice of *prāṇāyāma*. Esoterically, true *kumbhaka* occurs when the inward and outward flow of *prāna* becomes stabilized. When this happens, the mind also stabilizes, permitting the meditator to experience the Self, which lies beyond the mind.

Kunda [***kuṇḍa***]
White jasmine; a flower of exceeding fragrance and beauty.

Kundalini [***kuṇḍalinī***]
(*lit.*, coiled one) Kundalini, also known as Kundalini Shakti, is a goddess, the divine Mother of the universe. *Kundalinī* also refers to divine power or primordial energy. This extremely subtle force lies dormant, coiled at the base of the spine in the *mūlādhāra chakra* of every human being. Once awakened, Kundalini begins to purify the whole system, traveling upward through the central channel (*sushumnā nādī*) and piercing the various subtle energy centers (chakras) until She finally reaches the *sahasrāra*, the topmost center at the crown of the head. There, the individual self merges into the supreme Self in the marriage of Shiva and Shakti, and the cycle of birth and death comes to an end. *See also* Chakra, *Shaktipāt, Sushumnā nādī.*

Maharaj [***mahārāja***]
(*lit.*, great king) A title of great respect for a saint or holy person.

Maharashtra
(*lit.*, the great country) A state on the west coast of central India. Many of the great poet-saints lived in Maharashtra, and the *samādhi* shrines of Bhagawan Nityananda and Swami Muktananda are there. *See also* Ganeshpuri.

Maitri Upanishad [***maitryupaniṣad***]
One of the principal Upanishads, recounting the teachings of the sage Maitri. *See also* Upanishad(s).

Manas [***manas***]
1) The individual mind. 2) One of the four psychic instruments; that which receives information from sense organs. *See also* Four psychic instruments.

Mantra [***mantra***]
(*lit.*, sacred invocation; that which protects) The names of God; sacred words or divine sounds invested with the power to protect, purify, and transform the individual who repeats them.

Maya [***māyā***]
The term used in Vedanta for the power that veils the true nature of the Self and projects the experiences of multiplicity and separation from God. The force of maya conceals the ultimate Truth, creating the illusion that the real is unreal, the unreal is real, and the temporary is everlasting. Maya is also spoken of as an aspect of the goddess Shakti.

Mecca
The holy city of Islam. A pilgrimage to Mecca is one of the duties of every Muslim; Muslims throughout the world face Mecca when they pray.

Moksha [***mokṣa***]
The state of liberation; enlightenment; freedom.

Muktānanda Mahān
(*lit.*, great Muktananda, the supreme bliss of freedom) A chant that is sung each morning in Siddha Yoga ashrams before the *Guru Gītā.*

Mūrti [*mūrti*]
(*lit.*, embodiment; figure; image) A representation of God or a statue of a chosen deity that has been sanctified by worship.

Nāda [*nāda*]
(*lit.*, sound) Inner sounds heard during advanced stages of meditation; celestial harmonies; the spontaneous unstruck sound experienced in the *anāhata chakra.*

Namaz
The Arabic word for prayer. Devout Muslims perform *namaz* at appointed times during each day.

Nasruddin, Sheikh
A figure originating in Turkish folklore during the Middle Ages and used by spiritual teachers to illustrate the antics of the human mind.

Neti [*neti*]
A traditional method of cleansing the sinus cavity that is used by hatha yoga adepts.

Nīla bindu [*nīlabindu*]
(*lit.*, blue point) A brilliant blue light, the size of a tiny seed; the subtle abode of the inner Self, and the vehicle by which the soul travels from one world to another, either in meditation or at the time of death. Swami Muktananda writes extensively about his powerful inner visions of *nīla bindu*, which he calls the Blue Pearl, in his spiritual autobiography, *Play of Consciousness.*

Nishchaya [*niścaya*]
Determination, conviction.

Nīti Shataka [*nītiśataka*]
A collection of poems by the sage Bhartrihari on the nature of the world and the ecstasy of transcendence.

***Niyama*(s)** [*niyama*]
Observances that are considered vital to one who is pursuing the yogic life, such as cleanliness, contentment, and mental and physical discipline. *See also Ashtānga yoga.*

Om [*oṃ*]
The primordial sound from which the entire universe emanates. Also written *Aum*, it is the inner essence of all mantras.

Om Namah Shivāya
[*oṃ namaḥ śivāya*]
(*lit.*, *Om*, I bow to Shiva) This Sanskrit mantra of the Siddha Yoga lineage is known as "the great redeeming mantra" because of its power to grant both worldly fulfillment and spiritual realization. *Om* is the primordial sound; *namah* means to honor; *Shiva* denotes divine Consciousness, the Lord who dwells in every heart. *See also* Mantra.

Paramārtha [*paramārtha*]
The highest purpose or goal of life: realization of the supreme Truth.

Practice(s)
Activities that purify and strengthen the mind and body for the spiritual path. Siddha Yoga practices include chanting, meditation, mantra repetition, hatha yoga, selfless service, and contemplation. *See also* Sadhana.

Prāna [*prāṇa*]
The vital life-sustaining force of both the body and the universe. To carry out its work, *prāna* pervades the body in five forms: *prāna*, inhalation, the primary support of the heart; *apāna*, exhalation, the power that works downward to expel waste matter; *samāna*, the power that distributes the nourishment from food to all parts of the body; *vyāna*, the power of movement within the *nādīs*, the nerve channels of the subtle body; and *udāna*, the power that carries energy upward, giving strength and radiance to the body.

Pranām [***praṇāma***]
To bow; to greet with respect.

Prāṇāya Svāhā [***prāṇāya svāhā***]
The opening words of a mantra with which a spiritual seeker may make an offering to his own vital energy; often used to offer the food one eats to one's *prāna*.

Prānāyāma [***prāṇāyāma***]
The yogic science through which the *prāna*, the vital force, is stabilized; one of the limbs of *ashtānga yoga*. *Prānāyāma* may be practiced through specific breathing exercises, since there is a link between *prāna* and the breath. *See also Ashtānga yoga.*

Prasad [***prasāda***]
A blessed or divine gift; often refers to food that has first been offered to God and later distributed.

Pratyāhāra [***pratyāhāra***]
Withdrawal of the senses from their sense objects, restraining the mind's outward-flowing tendency; one of the steps of *ashtānga yoga. See also Ashtānga yoga.*

Premānanda [***premānanda***]
The bliss of divine love.

Pūjā [***pūjā***]
1) The performance of worship. 2) An altar with images of the Guru or deity and objects used in worship.

Punya, punya karma [***puṇyakarma***]
The merit that comes from auspicious, virtuous, pure, holy, or sacred actions.

Purana(s) [***puraṇa***]
(*lit.*, ancient) The eighteen sacred books by the sage Vyasa containing stories, legends, and hymns about the creation of the universe, the incarnations of God, the teachings of various deities, and the spiritual legacies of ancient sages and kings.

Puri
Deep-fried Indian flatbread.

Rajas/rajoguna [***rajas/rajoguṇa***]
See Guna(s).

Rama/Ram [***rāma***]
The seventh incarnation of Lord Vishnu. Lord Rama is seen as the embodiment of dharma; the story of his life is told in the epic *Rāmāyana*.

Rāmāyana [***rāmāyaṇa***]
A recounting of the life and exploits of Lord Rama attributed to the sage Valmiki; one of the great epic poems of India.

Rasa [***rasa***]
1) Flavor, taste. 2) A subtle energy of richness, sweetness, and delight.

Rig Veda [***ṛgveda***]
The oldest of the four Vedas, the *Rig Veda* is composed of more than a thousand hymns. This Veda is intended for the priest whose function it is to recite the hymns inviting the gods to the fire rituals. *See also* Veda(s).

Rudram [***rudram***]
A chant from the *Krishna Yajur Veda* in which Lord Shiva is offered repeated salutations in his many manifestations; the first of these to be honored is Rudra. *See also* Veda(s).

Sadguru [***sadguru***]
(*lit.*, true Guru) A spiritual Master or teacher who has the capacity to initiate seekers and to guide them to the state of Self-realization.

Sadgurunāth mahārāj kī jay!
A Hindi phrase that means "I hail the Master who has revealed the Truth to me!" An exalted, joyful expression of gratitude to the Guru for all that has been received, often repeated at the beginning or end of an action.

Sādhaka [***sādhaka***]
A seeker on the spiritual path.

Sadhana [***sādhanā***]
1) A spiritual discipline or path. 2) Practices, both physical and mental, on the spiritual path.

Sādhya **[*sādhya*]**
The goal; that which is to be accomplished, fulfilled, or attained.

Sahasrāra **[*sahasrāra*]**
The thousand-petaled spiritual center at the crown of the head, where one experiences the highest states of consciousness.

Sākshī bhāva **[*sākṣībhāva*]**
(*lit.*, identification with the Witness) Witness-consciousness; remaining an uninvolved witness of events. *See also* Witness.

Sāma Veda **[*sāmaveda*]**
One of the four Vedas; a collection of liturgical hymns sung to melodies of great beauty. *See also* Veda(s).

Samādhi **[*samādhi*]**
The state of meditative union with the Absolute; the final stage of *ashtānga yoga*. *See also Ashtānga yoga*.

Samādhi **shrine**
Final resting place of a great yogi's body. Such shrines are places of worship, permeated with the saint's spiritual power.

Samadrishti **[*samadṛṣṭi*]**
(*lit.*, equal vision) Viewing everything as equal; experiencing the divine Consciousness that underlies all.

Sāmānya **[*sāmānya*]**
General; common; ordinary.

Samarpana **[*samarpaṇa*]**
Surrender; delivering or handing over completely.

Samatā **[*samatā*]**
Equality; fairness; identity with; impartiality.

Samsāra **[*saṃsāra*]**
The world of birth, mutability, and death.

Saptah **[*saptāha*]**
(*lit.*, seven) A term introduced by Swami Muktananda to refer to the continuous chanting of the name of God, which was often held in the ashram for seven days at a time.

Saraswati **[*sarasvatī*]**
(*lit.*, the flowing one) The goddess of speech, learning, and the arts, who is worshiped by students, teachers, scholars, artists, and musicians.

Satsang **[*satsaṅga*]**
(*lit.*, the company of the Truth) The company of saints and devotees; a gathering of devotees for the purpose of chanting, meditating, and imbibing scriptural teachings.

Sattva/sattva guna **[*sattva/sattvaguṇa*]**
See Guna(s).

Self, the
Divine Consciousness residing in the individual; *ātman*, in Sanskrit. *See also* Consciousness; *Sākshī bhāva*; Witness.

Seva **[*sevā*]**
(*lit.*, service) Selfless service; work offered to God or to the spiritual Master, performed with love and without concern for its benefits.

Shakti **[*śakti*]**
The divine Mother, who is the dynamic aspect of supreme Shiva and the creative Force of the universe; also the spiritual energy, *shakti*. *See also* Kundalini.

Shaktipāt **[*śaktipāta*]**
(*lit.*, descent of power) The transmission of spiritual energy, *shakti*, from the Guru to the disciple; spiritual awakening by grace.

Shāmbhavī mudrā **[*śāmbhavīmudrā*]**
(*lit.*, state of supreme Shiva) A state of spontaneous or effortless *samādhi* in which the eyes are open and yet the gaze is deep within, breathing is suspended without any effort, and the mind delights in the inner Self without any attempt at concentration.

***Shāstra*(s)** **[*śāstra*]**
(*lit.*, scripture) A Hindu text of spiritual science and conduct.

***Shatapatha Brāhmana* [*śatapathabrāhmaṇa*]**
One of the liturgical texts from the Indian tradition, describing the significance and performance of the rituals and sacrifices that implement the mantras of the Vedas.

Shiva [*śiva*]
1) A name for the one supreme Reality. 2) One of the Hindu trinity of gods, representing God as the destroyer, often seen by yogis as the destroyer of the barriers to identity with the supreme Self. In his personal form, Shiva is portrayed as a yogi wearing a tiger skin and holding a trident.

***Shiva Samhitā* [*śivasaṃhitā*]**
A Sanskrit text on yoga in which Ishwara, the Lord, describes the correspondence of the universe to the human body, explaining how the practices of hatha yoga (*āsana, prāṇāyāma*, and *mudrā*) and mantra yoga may be used to awaken the inner spiritual power. *See also* Kundalini.

***Shloka* [*śloka*]**
A verse.

***Shravana* [*śravaṇa*]**
(*lit.*, hearing) To hear the words or teachings of great beings or scriptures; in Vedanta, the first step in the process of imbibing knowledge.

Shree Muktananda Ashram [*śrīmuktānandāśrama*]
The Siddha Yoga ashram in South Fallsburg, New York, established in 1979 as the international headquarters of SYDA Foundation, the nonprofit organization that administers Siddha Yoga courses and publications. *See also* Ashram; *Gurukula*.

***Shri* [*śrī*]**
(*lit.*, auspiciousness) A term of great respect.

***Shruti* [*śruti*]**
(*lit.*, heard) Scripture that was divinely revealed.

***Shuddha* [*śuddha*]**
Pure; purity; perfect in itself.

***Shvetāshvatara Upanishad* [*śvetāśvataropaniṣad*]**
One of the major Upanishads in which the sage Shvetashvatara speaks of Brahman in its manifest aspect. *See also* Upanishad(s).

Siddha [*siddha*]
A perfected yogi; one who is in the state of unity-consciousness; one whose experience of the supreme Self is uninterrupted and whose identification with the ego has been dissolved.

Siddha Yoga [*siddhayoga*]
The spiritual path to union of the individual and the Divine that begins with *shaktipāt*, the initiation given by the grace of a Siddha Guru. Siddha Yoga is the name Swami Muktananda gave to this path, which he first brought to the West in 1970; Swami Chidvilasananda is its living Master. *See also Shaktipāt*.

Siddha Yoga Meditation center
A place where people gather to practice Siddha Yoga Meditation. There are over 450 Siddha Yoga centers around the world.

***Siddhi*(s) [*siddhi*]**
Supernatural powers attained through yogic practices.

***Smriti* [*smṛti*]**
(*lit.*, remembered) Writings based on that which is remembered, not revealed; scriptural commentary.

***So'ham* [*so'ham*]**
(*lit.*, That am I) The natural vibration of the Self, which occurs spontaneously with each incoming and outgoing breath. By becoming aware of *So'ham*, a seeker experiences the identity between the individual self and the supreme Self.

***Sushumnā nādī* [*suṣumnānāḍī*]**
The central and most important of all the seventy-two million subtle nerve channels in the human body, the *sushumnā* extends from the *mūlādhāra chakra* at the base of the spine to the *sahasrāra* at the

top of the head, and contains all the other major chakras. *See also* Chakra.

Sūtra(s) [*sūtra*]
Aphorism; a condensed and cryptic statement that usually can be understood only through commentary. In India, the major points of an entire philosophical system may be expressed in a series of *sūtras.*

Svayambhū [*svayambhū*]
Self-born; issuing from one's own innermost being.

Swādhyāya [*svādhyāya*]
The study of the Self; the regular disciplined practice of chanting and the recitation of spiritual texts.

Swami [*svāmī*]
A term of respectful address for a *sannyasin,* a monk.

Taittirīya Upanishad [*taittirīyopaniṣad*]
Connected to the *Yajur Veda* whose mantras celebrate the bliss and the omnipresence of Brahman, the highest Reality.

Tamas/tamoguna [*tamas/tamoguṇa*]
See Guna(s).

Tapas/tapasya [*tapas/tapasya*]
(*lit.,* heat) 1) Austerities. 2) The experience of heat that occurs during the process of practicing yoga. The heat is generated by friction between the senses and renunciation. It is said that this heat, called "the fire of yoga," burns up all the impurities that lie between the seeker and the experience of the Truth.

Turīya [*turīya*]
(*lit.,* fourth) The fourth or transcendental state, beyond the waking, dream, and deep-sleep states, in which the true nature of Reality is directly perceived; the state of *samādhi* or deep meditation. *See also Samādhi.*

Upanishad(s) [*upaniṣad*]
(*lit.,* sitting near steadfastly) The inspired teachings of the ancient sages of India. These scriptures, exceeding a hundred texts, constitute the final and highest knowledge of the Vedas. With immense variety of form and style, all of these texts give the same essential teaching: that the individual soul and God (Brahman) are one.

Vairāgya [*vairāgya*]
Dispassion; the power of renunciation by which a yogi is able to pursue the true rather than the false, the eternal rather than the ephemeral.

Vak [*vāk,* from the root *vāc*]
The goddess of speech; the divine Mother who becomes all words.

Veda(s) [*veda*]
(*lit.,* knowledge) Among the most ancient, revered, and sacred of the world's scriptures, the four Vedas are regarded as divinely revealed (*shruti*) and eternal wisdom. They are the *Rig Veda, Yajur Veda, Sāma Veda, and Atharva Veda.*

Vedanta [*vedānta*]
(*lit.,* end of the Vedas) One of the six orthodox schools of Indian philosophy; usually identified as Advaita Vedanta, or absolute nondualism. *See also* Upanishad(s); *Viveka Chūdāmani.*

Vīṇā [*vīṇā*]
A stringed musical instrument sacred to Shri Saraswati, the goddess of the arts and learning.

Vishnu [*viṣṇu*]
1) The all-pervasive supreme Reality. 2) One of the Hindu trinity of gods, representing God as the sustainer of the universe; the deity of the Vaishnavas. In his personal form, he is portrayed as four-armed, holding a conch, a discus, a lotus, and a mace. He is dark blue in color. Vishnu incarnates in each *yuga* (cycle or world period) to protect and save the world when the knowledge of dharma

(truth and righteousness) is lost. Rama and Krishna are the best known of his incarnations.

***Vishnu Sahasranām* [*viṣṇusahasranāma*]**
(*lit.*, the thousand names of Vishnu) A hymn honoring Lord Vishnu, which is chanted in Siddha Yoga ashrams.

***Viveka Chūdāmani* [*vivekacūḍāmaṇi*]**
(*lit.*, the crest jewel of discrimination) A commentary by the eighth-century sage Shankaracharya on Advaita Vedanta, expounding the teaching that the Absolute alone is real.

Void, the Great
The state of the formless Absolute; known as *mahāshūnya.*

Witness, the
The transcendental Consciousness that lies at the root of the mind and from which the mind can be observed. *See also* Self; Consciousness.

***Yajña* [*yajña*]**
A sacrificial fire ritual in which mantras are recited while different woods, fruits, grains, oils, yogurt, and *ghee* (clarified butter) are poured into the fire as an offering to the Lord. Also, any work or spiritual practice that is offered as worship to God.

***Yajur Veda* [*yajurveda*]**
One of the four Vedas, whose hymns specify sacrificial rites and the rules for their correct performance. There are two branches of the *Yajur Veda*: *krishna* (dark) and *shukla* (white). *See also* Veda(s).

***Yama*(s) [*yama*]**
Restraints that are considered vital to one who is pursuing the yogic life, such as abstention from violence, falsehood, theft, and acquisitiveness. *See also Ashtānga yoga.*

Yoga [*yoga*]
(*lit.*, union) 1) The state of oneness with the Self, with God. 2) Practices leading to that state.

***Yoga Sūtras* [*yogasūtra*]**
A collection of aphorisms, written by the sage Patanjali in the fourth century, which expound different methods for the attainment of the state of yoga, or union, in which the movement of the mind ceases and the Witness of the mind rests in its own bliss.

***Yoga Vāsishtha* [*yogavāsiṣṭha*]**
A popular Sanskrit text on Advaita Vedanta, probably written in the twelfth century, and ascribed to the sage Vasishtha. In it, Vasishtha answers Lord Rama's philosophical questions on life, death, and human suffering by teaching that the world is as you see it and that illusion ceases when the mind is stilled.

***Yogānanda* [*yogānanda*]**
The bliss of the state of yoga, union with one's innermost being.

Yogi [*yogī*]
1) One who practices yoga. 2) One who has attained perfection through yogic practices.

Index

Action(s), awareness and, 30; beneficial, xiii, xvi, karma and, 71-72; knowledge and, 26; organs of, 67; pausing and, 146; perception and, 67-68; purification and, xii, 20, 29; *rajas* and, 9, 11-14; ritual, 130; sadhana and, 18; *sattva* and, 15; self-control and, xii-xiii, 17, 22-23; silence and, 165; sweetness of, 42; *tamas* and, 11; will of God and, xiii; *see also* Discipline

Agni hotri, 136; *see also Yajña*

Aitareya Brāhmana, 142-43

Aloneness, 21-22

Amir Khusrau, 74-75

Anxiety, 189-90

Apāna, 120; *see also* Breath; *Prāna*

Ārati, 102

Arjuna, 6; self-doubt and, 19

Āsana, 18; *see also* Postures, yogic

Ashram. *See* Gurudev Siddha Peeth; *Gurukula*; Shree Muktananda Ashram

Ashram Dharma (Muktananda), 173

Ashtānga yoga, 20, 165; *see also* Yoga, discipline of

Ashtavakra Samhitā, 164

Atharva Veda, 129

Ātma samyama, 17

Ātma vichāra, 68-69, 165; *see also* Self-inquiry

Ātma vishvāsa, 2

Attachment, 11, 72-73

Attention, xvi; eating and, 111-12, 123; to God, 188-89; hearing and, 83, 91; inward-directed, 5-6; speech and, 154

Attitude, obstacles and, 200; one-pointedness and, 24; spiritual practice and, 5, 53

Auditory system, 102, 105

Austerity, xi, 28, 32-34, 37; good thoughts as, 196; silence as, 164

Avarice, freedom from, 18, 23

Awakening, inner, xv, 93, 182; *see also* Consciousness; Initiation; *Shaktipāt*

Awareness, actions and, 30, 77-78; desires and, 22-23; discipline and, ix, 45-50, 65, 122; of hunger/food, 122, 123, 132-33; mantra and, 146; meditation and, 24-25, 76-77; understanding and, 70, 202

Ayurveda, 112, 131

Baba Muktananda. *See* Muktananda, Swami

Bade Baba. *See* Nityananda, Bhagawan

Balance, xiii

Belief, 2, 3
Bells, 103
Bhagavad Gītā, 6; bliss of yoga and, 17, 19, 37-38; on digestive fire, 119-20; dispassion and, 24; Guru-disciple relationship and, 6-8; on practice of yoga, 79-80; sense pleasures and, 13
Bhaktā, 28; *see also* Devotion; Love
Bhartrihari, 153
Bhāv, 26; *see also* Devotion
Bhūmi Sūkta, 129
Birth, 84; bliss and, 1, 84; purpose of, 4; sadhana and, 37; Self and, 3
Blame, 30
Blessings, 35, 184; food and, 118-19; Saraswati and, 142; of the Siddhas, 41; sweetness and, 42; understanding and, 64
Bliss, supreme, xix, xxi, 1-2, 8; desirelessness and, 24; happiness and, 9, 15; mind and, 28; Self and, 4; *So 'ham* breath and, 21; spiritual effort and, 7, 19-37; yoga and, 8, 23-24, 38
Blue Pearl, 169
Body, human, birth and, 84; cleanliness of, 29, 110; devotion and, 26-27; discipline and, ix, 47, 56-57, 78, 88, 89, 110; improper eating and, 108-9, 110, 112-13, 115-16, 127, 128; impurity and, 10, 32-33, 110; light of the Self and, 4; mantra repetition and, 30, 116; meditation and, xv, 111; sensory overload and, 101, 110-11; *shakti* and, 33; silence and, 171-72
Brahman, 1, 24; as food, 118, 121
Brahmin priests, 145-46
Brain. *See* Mind
Breath, 148, 156; body functioning and, 111, 119, 120; God and, 105; listening and, 91; mantra and, 91; music and, 103; *prāna/apāna* (ingoing/-outgoing), 119, 120; silence and, 21; *So 'ham* and, 21; yogic, 18
Brihadāranyaka Upanishad, 143

Chāndogya Upanishad, 26, 134, 135
Chanting, with devotion, 25-26; as purification, 90-91, 104; silence of, 151, 175; *swādhyāya* and, 34-35, 157-58; vibrations of, 86, 91-92, 103; word and, 143-44
Charity, 137
Chitprakāsha, 18; *see also* Consciousness
Choice, x, 137; *see also* Discrimination
Clairaudience, 105
Cleanliness, 28, 29; remembrance and, 33
Compassion, 15
Concentration, yogic, 18, 25, 27, 28; meditation and, 25, 29-30; speech and, 146-47; *see also* One-pointedness
Conch, 103
Confidence, 2; hearing and, 98-99
Consciousness, 18, 56, 60; bliss and, 15; existence and, 4, 203; food as, 118, 120; light of, 18; meditation and, 24-25, 27, 60, 168; mind and, 195; perception and, xi, xii, 64, 69; purification and, xii, 18, 31; seeing/sight and, 70, 79; silence and, 175
Contemplation, 56, 193-94; contentment and, 31-32; of eating, 119; of hearing, 89; meditation and, 25; speech and, 146-47; teachings of yoga and, 20, 99; voice of God and, 149-50
Contentment, 28, 30-32
Conviction, 3; dispassion and, 24; Self and, 93; self-control and, 89-90
Cosmic mind, 145
Crest Jewel of Discrimination (Shankaracharya). *See Viveka Chūdāmani*
Cymbals, 103

Darkness, 9
Darshan, inner eye and, 75; longing and, 74-75
Death, 1, 36, 44; food and, 109; light of the Self and, 4; preparation for, 52; universal consciousness and, 44

Deity, meditation and, 25; offering to, 136; pausing before image of, 58-59; of silence, 176; of speech, 142, 146
Delusion, xii; discipline and, 36, 93, 94; of Janghu, 65-66, 72; *tamoguna* and, 10, 11
Desire(s), absence of, 19, 20, 22-23; contentment and, 31; for love, 138; mind and, 194, 199; seeing and, 53-54, 64; silence and, 165
Destiny, 4
Detachment, 164, 169-70; steadiness and, 168
Determination, spiritual, 3
Devotion, 26, 58-59; mantra repetition and, 29; spiritual practice and, 25, 37
Dhāranā, 18; *see also* Concentration; Contemplation
Dharma, 23, 80, 181; listening and, 86; mind and, 26; yoga and, 6
Dhu al-Nun, 55
Dhyāna, 18; *see also* Meditation
Digestion, 108-9, 114; drinking water and, 121; God and, 119, 121, 127; improper food combinations and, 110-11; *kundalinī* and, 117; meditation and, 111-12, 119; mood and, 119; overeating and, 128-29; prasad and, 136
Disciple, Amir Khusrau, 75; Arjuna, 6, 19-20; discipline and, 45-46, 77, 90-91, 97; grace and, 56; hunger for God and, 123; initiation of, xv, 110; yoga and, 6, 17, 18-19; *see also* Guru
Discipline, yoga of, ix, 5-6, 18-19, 36-37, 44-50, 88, 97-98, 125-26, 141-42; attention and, 49-50, 91, 103, 105, 111-12, 119, 188-89; eating and, 107, 110, 111-13, 115, 116, 119-26, 127-28, 130-38; God and, ix, xiii, 22, 35-36, 43, 88, 122, 123, 124; hearing/listening and, 89-90, 95-96, 105; humility and, 35-36; meditation and, 7-8, 28, 111-12, 119; path of, 39, 44, 46, 49-50, 95-96; pausing and, 58, 58-59, 147-48; perseverance and, 15; prayer(s) for, 42; purification and, 18, 25, 29-30, 33, 90-91; resistance to, 44-45; seeing and, 51-78; senses and, 15, 22-23, 49-50, 51-78, 89-92, 126; silence and, 163-64, 165-66, 168-76; speaking and, 142-60; *see also Niyamas*; Yoga
Discrimination, listening and, 86; speaking and, 145, 146-47, 153
Disease. *See* Illness
Dispassion, 7; sattvic happiness and, 14; yoga and, 23-24; *see also Vairāgya*
Distraction, 21
Divinity, discipline and, 45-50, 60; meditation and, 60; perception and, 60, 73; purification and, xii, 21, 73; senses and, 101; *So 'ham* mantra and, 21; sounds and, 28, 90-91, 104, 105-6; speech and, 142, 144, 146; *see also* God; Self
Doubts, 19, 36
Dreams, 65, 72

Earth, 41-42, 129
Eating, 126; awakening of taste and, 14; Ayurvedic guidelines for, 131; death and, 109; discipline in, 97, 107, 110, 111-13, 116, 119-26, 127-28, 130-38; drinking water while, 121; *gunas* and, 9-10; improper food combinations and, 110-11; joy and, 132; *kundalinī* and, 117; mantra and, 116, 121; meditation and, 29, 111-12, 119; prayer/worship and, 120-21, 122, 123, 124, 126-27, 128, 136-37; purposeful, 120-21, 126-27, 132-36; restraint and, 44, 110, 126-27, 128, 137; ritual and, 130-31, 135; seeing and, 56; silence and, 121; sin and, 108, 117; stomach/digestion and, 108-9, 111-12, 120; yogic fasting from, 110, 116; *see also* Food; Taste
Ecstasy, xv; understanding and, 38, 133; unity and, 73
Ego, mantra repetition and, 30; psychic instruments and, 21; surren-

der and, 35-36
Ekāgra manas, 24; *see also* One-pointedness
Ekānna (type of fasting), 116; *see also* Eating; Fasting
Eknath Maharaj, 61
Emerson, Ralph Waldo, 54
Emotion(s), xii
Endurance, 33
Energy, devotion and, 26-27; discipline and, 98, 100; of eyes/sight, 54, 57-58, 61; of God, 88; improper food combinations and, 110-11; of impurities, 57-58; of mind, xi; of speech, 147, 173; stomach and, 109, 117; wasting of, 88-89, 100; of yoga, 33; *see also* Grace; *Kundalinī*; Power; *Shaktipāt*
Enthusiasm, 50
Equality-consciousness, 191; mind and, 194
Equipoise, 91; eating and, 113, 135
Exhaustion, 33; senses and, 126; wasted energy and, 88-89; yoga of discipline and, 49
Existence, consciousness and, 4, 56; earth elements and, 73; *gunas* and, 9-10; of Self, 2, 5
Expectation(s), 44; discipline and, 46-50; sattvic happiness and, 14
Experience, blessings and, 41; confidence and, 2; discipline and, 28, 50, 65; of God, 60, 61, 109; gratitude and, 85; of mantra, 86, 91-92; of meditation, 28, 29-30, 60, 93, 155, 197; of nature, 91-92, 95, 103, 104, 129-30; of satsang, 92-93; of the Self, 5, 8; of *shaktipāt*, xv; of supreme bliss, 8, 15, 28; of Witness-consciousness, 70-71, 73-74
Eyes, power of, 52-53, 54, 70-71; Bhagawan Nityananda and, 79; focus and, 61, 77, 78; freedom from defects and, 64-65; meditation and, 56, 65; purpose of, 69-78, 93, 94; soul and, 63; Witness-consciousness and, 70-71, 75-77; *see also* Seeing, discipline in

Faith, 3, 203
Fasting, 110, 115
Fear, confidence and, 2; death and, 44; discipline and, 44, 97; improper eating and, 113; perception and, xii; of punishment, 44; surrender and, 36
Fire, cymbals and, 103; digestive, 120, 121, 127; offerings and, 136; spirit and, 42; of yoga, 32; *see also Yajña*
Food, 107-9, 117-18, 126; addiction and, 113, 137; discipline and, 111, 119-26; eyesight and, 56-57; God and, 118, 119, 126; hoarding of, 114, 118; meditation and, 111-12; mind and, 133-34; as prasad, 57, 136; purity of, 134, 135; respect for, 57, 113, 118; restraint and, 44, 137; ritual and, 130, 135
Forgiveness, 45, 99
Francis of Assisi, Saint, 155
Freedom, discipline and, 39, 46
From the Finite to the Infinite (Muktananda), 185

God, aloneness and, 22; devotion and, 26-27; discipline and, 38, 43, 50, 119, 141-42; food/eating and, 118, 120, 122, 123, 126; listening and, 87-88, 100, 103; longing and, 74, 77, 137-38; meditation and, xv, 25, 27, 181; name of, 93, 94, 98, 100, 115, 159; perception and, 59-60, 61; purposeful actions and, 126; seeing, 60, 61, 184-85, 188-89; service and, 41, 94; stomach/hunger and, 119, 123; surrender to, 35-36, 74; word and, 104, 105, 143, 150
Good company, 92-93, 160
Grace, 26, 35, 142; desires and, 23; food and, 131; of the Guru, 20, 56, 90; mantra and, 90; prayer and, 43; sadhana and, 37; self-effort and, 28, 37, 202; of the Siddhas, 41; stomach and, 109; words and, 149
Gratitude, 85, 135; chanting and, 104;

eating and, 120-21, 134; farming and, 130; prayer and, 43; seva and, 99
Gravity, 80-81
Gunas, 1; *rajas*, 11-14; *sattva*, 14-15; *tamas*, 9-10; types of happiness and, 9-16
Guru, disciple and, 6, 19-20, 74-75, 97; divinity and, 60; grace and, xv, 56, 90; initiation and, xv-xvi, 110; invocation of, 59; mantra and, 90; *see also* Disciple; Grace; Master; Siddha
Gurudev Siddha Peeth, 82; silence and, 151, 170, 174-75; *see also Gurukula*
Guru Gītā, 34; blessings of, 35; recitation of, 104
Gurukula, 34, 56, 109; discipline and, 49-50; good company and, 92-93; silence in, 170; study in the, 159; *see also* Ashram

Happiness, 9-10, 18, 31, 53; discipline and, 23, 49; *rajoguna* and, 11-14; *sattva guna* and, 13-14; spontaneous, 80; *tamoguna* and, 9-10; tranquility and, 18; Witness-consciousness and, 72
Hatha yoga, 18, 96, 165, 166
Health, 115, 127, 128
Hearing, attention and, 91-92, 95, 103; discipline in, 98-106; effect on heart and, 89, 98-99, 102; music and, 102, 105; name of God, 98, 100, 105; power of, 72, 105-6; prayer for purity of, 82-83; purification of, 90-91, 102, 105; purpose of, 93, 94, 105; wasted energy and, 89; *see also* Listening; Sense(s); *Swādhyāya*
Heart, 31, 42; discipline and, 39, 46, 137-38; eating and, 110, 113, 135; God and, 135, 137-38, 182; mantra repetition and, 30; master of one's, 80; senses and, 81-82, 89; sincerity of, 29, 74; speech and, 147, 157; spiritual practice and, 3, 39, 137-38, 157; of the universe, 41-42
Humility, 2, 172; food and, 118-19; surrender and, 36
Hunger, 108, 120; for God, 122, 123, 138; maintenance of, 127

I Have Become Alive (Muktananda), 43, 88, 96
Ignorance, 45; grace and, 90-91; of offering, 135
Illness, 44; charity and, 136; improper eating and, 112, 127, 128; wasted energy and, 89
Illusion, 15, 66-67; seeing/outlook and, 66-67, 183; sense pleasures and, 63; *see also* Maya
Immortality, 5; speech and, 143
Impulse(s), 21; mantra repetition and, 160; speech and, 154; stomach and, 109
Impurity, 9; fire of yoga and, 32; mind and, 194, 195; perception and, 52, 53, 57-58
Indulgence, 13, 33
Initiation, xv, 110; *see also* Grace; *Shaktipāt*
Inner eye, 71, 75; *see also* Witness-consciousness
Inner state. *See* State of mind
Inspiration, 5, 18, 38; eight limbs of yoga and, 18; mantra repetition and, 29; speech and, 143
Intellect, 2, 21, 30, 37
Intensive, xiii, xix, 92-93
Invocation, of Guru, 59; of Saraswati, 142
Iron Age, 9

Janghu, 65-66, 72
Japa, 29-30; *see also* Mantra; Repetition
Jñānānanda, 28
Jñānendriyas, 67
Jnaneshwar Maharaj, 6-7, 15, 38; on bliss, 132; on focus, 190-99; on food, 120; on nonduality, 23; on offering, 136; on pure vision, 73; on rajasic happiness, 11; on tamasic happiness, 11; on yogic effort,

18-19, 20, 37
Jñānī, 28
Judgment. *See* Discrimination; Self-control

Kabir, x, 56, 88, 93, 160, 168-69
Kaivalya, 22; *see also* Aloneness
Kali Yuga, 9, 48
Karma, 71-72, 136, 153
Karmendriyas, 67
Karnataka, 189
Katha Upanishad, 2, 5
Khecharī mudrā, 172
Knowledge, meditation and, 93; memory and, 134; spiritual practice and, 37, 91; Witness-consciousness and, 72
Krishna, Lord, 6, 37, 38, 191; *see also Bhagavad Gītā*; Jnaneshwar Maharaj
Kulārnarva Tantra, 116
Kumbhaka, 148; *see also* Breath; *Prāna*
Kundalinī, xv, 93; *see also Shaktipāt*

Lakshmi, Dhanya, 126
Lalleshwari, 91
Laziness (*ālasya*), improper eating and, 110; lifespan and, 112
Liberation, 38, 46, 50; silence and, 163
Light, 9, 22, 38; of Consciousness, 18, 56, 60; of the eyes, 71, 73; fire of yoga and, 33; food as, 121; meditation and, xv, 60, 168, 197; mind and, 18; of the Self, 4, 33, 70
Light on the Path (Muktananda), 28
Limitations, discipline and, 39, 46; seeing and, 52-53
Listening, 86; discipline in, 82-83, 89, 92-93, 98-106; music and, 102, 106; to name of God, 98, 100, 105; to nature, 91-92, 95, 103-4; purification and, 105; satsang and, 93; temple *ārati* and, 102
Longing, 2, 7, 123, 179; of Arjuna, 19; for darshan, 74; discipline and, 39, 46, 50, 122, 137-38
Love, 67-68, 203; *bhaktā* and, 28; discipline and, 23, 38, 50, 137; forgiveness and, 45, 99; service and, 94; unconditional, 80

Maitri Upanishad, 187
Mantra, deity of, 142, 146; eating and, 116, 121, 134; hearing/listening and, 100, 105; pausing and, 59, 148; purification and, 29, 30; repetition of, 29-30, 58, 59, 90-91, 160, 198; silence of, 151; *So 'ham*, 21; *swādhyāya* and, 34-35; Vedic, 146; vibrations of, 86, 91-92; waking and, 59; word and, 143-44; *yajña* and, 145; *see also* Purification; Repetition
Master, Siddha. *See* Siddha
Maya, 15
Meaningfulness, 39
Mecca, 53
Meditation, 71, 148; digestion and, 111-12, 119; discipline and, xiii, 7-8, 17, 28, 56, 60, 166, 181; experience of, xiii-xv, 29-30, 93; hearing and, 98, 105; mind and, 24-25, 27, 31, 186, 197; object(s) of, 25; ritual and, 130; seeing in, 60, 65, 76-77, 137-38; Siddha Yoga and, xvi, 93; silence and, 166-68; Witness-consciousness and, 71; *see also* Intensive; Mind, one-pointedness of
Merit, 4, 109; discipline and, 153; excessive speech and, 152; silence as, 164
Mind, 27, 31; desires and, 195; discipline and, 47, 185, 186, 189, 196, 202; eating and, 110, 113, 126, 133-34; energy/power of, xi, 18, 24, 72, 194; hearing and, 89, 104-5; immersion of, in God, 77; mantra/scriptural recitation and, 34-35, 198; one-pointedness of, 24, 25-26; psychic instruments of, 21; purification of, 18, 20-21, 24, 29, 34-35, 105, 187; *sattva* and, 14; self-control and, 15, 17-18, 24, 27; sensory information and, xii, 101; silence and, 174-75; solitude and, 21; stomach and, 109; supreme bliss and, 8, 30; tranquility and, 17-18; *see also* Medi-

tation; State of mind; Perception
Mindlessness, 28
Mirabai, 87, 92
Moksha, 163; *see also* Liberation
Mood, eating and, 119, 126
Muktananda, Swami, xvi; compassion of, 110; on desire, 137-38; discipline and, 43, 65, 88, 96; on eating/hunger, 114, 127, 131; fasting and, 116; and his elephant, 82; on listening, 98, 99; on longing, 123; on mindlessness, 28; on reciting holy texts, 104-5; on sight, 56, 63; on solitude, 21; on speaking, 151, 173; on supreme bliss, 1-2, 13; on *swādhyāya*, 157; on thinking, 24
Mukteshwari (Muktananda), 52, 67; on food, 126; on purpose of seeing, 69-70; on Witness-consciousness, 70
Muller, Johannes, xi
Mūrti, 59
Music, God and, 103; listening and, 91-92, 102-3; meditation and, 105; reverberations of, 98
Musical instruments, 102-3

Nāda, 28
Narada, 134
Narsi Mehta, 74, 87
Nasruddin, Sheikh, 152-53
Nervous system, improper eating and, 110
Nīla bindu, 169; *see also* Blue Pearl
Nīti Shataka, 153
Nityananda, Bhagawan, xvi, 25; eyes of, 79; grace of, 56; temple *ārati* and, 102
Nivritti, 73, 191
Niyama (regularity), 18, 27, 28, 88, 119; of austerity, 32-34; of cleanliness, 28-29; of contentment, 30-32; discipline and, 96; of surrender, 35-36; of *swādhyāya*, 34-35; *see also* Spiritual practice
Nonduality, 23-24
Obstacles, overcoming, 33, 82; attitude and, 200; restraint and, 44; surrender and, 36; *see also* Discipline; Sadhana; Yoga
Offering, 135-36; charity and, 136-37; reverence and, 58-59
Om, 175; *see also* Mantra
Om Namah Shivāya, 58, 91; listening and, 91-92; thought and, 198; *see also* Mantra
One-pointedness, 24; devotion and, 25; sadhana and, 80
Opposites, pairs of, 14
Outlook (*drishti*), 53; *see also* Attitude

Paramārtha, 188
Patanjali, 18, 165; on practice, 25; *see also Yoga Sūtras*
Patience, 172
Perception, 38; appearances and, 64, 66, 71-72; confidence and, 2; eyesight and, 51-52, 53, 56; of God, 59-60; organs of, 67; purification of, 18, 73, 90-91; self-inquiry and, 68-69; Witness-consciousness and, 72; *see also* Hearing; Sense(s); Vision
Perseverance, 15
Play of Consciousness (Muktananda), 99; on respect, 137
Poet saints, 93, 115; *see also* individual saint by name
Postures, yogic, 18, 165ww
Power, behind the universe, 80; body and, 88; of the eyes, 52-53, 54, 70-71; of hearing, 100, 103, 105; Witness-consciousness and, 71-72; of words/speech, 83, 142, 144
Praise, 2, 93, 94
Prāna, digestive fire and, 120; food as, 119, 121; *see also* Breath
Prānāyāma, 18, 28; *see also* Breath
Prasad, 57, 136
Pratyāhāra, 18, 165; *see also* Sense(s), withdrawal of
Prayer, 42, 43, 53, 156, 194; for darshan, 87-88; for discipline, 42, 48; food and, 120; reverence and, 58-59, 157; seeing divinity and, 60; silence of, 151; speech and, 144, 155-56;

Witness-consciousness and, 74
Premānanda, 28
Projection, 66-67; inner state and, 67-68
Protection, from degradation, 84; from desire, 64, 196; discipline and, 48-49; mantra and, 91; *shakti* and, 203; surrender and, 36
Pūjā, 120, 130; *see also* Worship
Punya karma, 109; *see also* Merit
Purification, of actions, 20, 29; chanting and, 90-91; contemplation and, 25, 99; discipline and, 18, 33-34, 90-91, 110; eating and, 110; fasting as, 110; hearing/listening and, 102-3; mantra repetition/*swādhyāya* and, 29-30, 34-35, 90-91; meditation and, 93, 187; of mind, 18, 20-21, 24, 25, 29-30, 99, 103, 187; music and, 102-3; of senses, 18, 20, 90-91; silence and, 155; of speech, 20, 29, 155-56; of thoughts, 20, 29-30; *see also* Yoga, discipline of
Purity, 142; of food, 134, 135; inspiration and, 18; mind and, 194, 201; of speech, 150; of will, 84
Purpose, confidence and, 2; discipline and, 48-49, 50, 138, 166; of food, 108; of sadhana, 184; of seeing/sight, 69-70, 71; self-inquiry and, 68-69; service and, 41; of silence, 166; speech and, 152; union and, 70; yoga and, 5, 50; *see also* Action(s)

Rahim, 59
Rajas, 9; happiness and, 11-14, 15; *see also Gunas*
Ram Tirth, 75
Ramanuja, 75
Rāmāyana, 108
Reason, 7
Recitation, 28, 34-35; of holy texts, 104-5, 144, 157-58; *samādhi* and, 105; *see also Swādhyāya*
Regularity, of practice. *See Niyama*
Reincarnation, 84; discipline and, 96
Religion, 34, 52, 84; discipline and, 97
Remembrance, of Baba Muktananda, 43; of cleanliness, 33; eating and, 121; of God, 74, 190; of grace, 37; seeing with discipline and, 59, 77-78; of Self, 135
Repetition, of mantra, 29-30, 160, 198; chanting and, 90-91; equipoise and, 91; impure seeing and, 58; *see also* Mantra
Respect, discipline and, 23, 38, 57; for elders, 10, 86; for food, 57, 113, 118, 123, 128, 137; listening and, 105; for power of speech, 149
Restraint, 18; eating and, 44, 110, 126-27, 128, 137; sattvic happiness and, 15; yogic discipline and, 19, 20, 27; *see also* Discipline
Reverence, for food, 118, 119, 126-27, 128, 137; listening and, 91-92; pausing and, 58-59, 147-48; recitation and, 105
Rig Veda, on hearing, 82-83; on meditation, 181; power of speech and, 144; on sweetness, 41-42
Ritual, food and, 130-31, 135; sacrifice, 135-36
Rudram, 42
Rumi, 123

Sacrifice, 135-36
Sadhana, 36-37; action and, 18, 30; courage and, 81; culmination of, 70; eating and, 119, 120, 122, 123, 124, 125-26, 134; full focus and, 80, 98, 103, 146, 188; Guru-disciple relationship and, 6, 19-20; humility and, 36; laziness (*ālasya*) and, 110; mantra and, 146; pace of, 37, 47; silence and, 174-75, 176; speech and, 144-60; worship and, 126-27; yoga of, 18, 19-37, 125-26; *see also* Discipline, yoga of; Spiritual practice
Sa‘di, Sheikh, 53
Sahasrāra, 60
Sākshī bhāva, 70; *see also* Witness-consciousness
Samādhi, 18, 19, 98; recitation of holy

texts and, 105; *see also* Union
Samarpana, 35-36; *see also* God, surrender to
Samartha Ramdas, 188-89
Sāma Veda, 103-4
Samsāra, 63, 189; *see also* Illusion
Sanatkumar, 134
Saptahs, 90-91
Saraswati, 142, 146; *see also* Speech, goddess of
Satsang, 92-93, 95; with Baba, 104
Sattva, 9, 14-15; *see also* *Gunas*
Seclusion, 21
Seeing/sight, communicative power of, 54-56; desire and, 52, 53-56, 75-76; discipline in, 51, 56-61, 65-78; freedom from defects and, 64-65; inner state and, 67-68; objects of perception and, 52-53, 56-57, 64, 67-68, 76-77; purification of, 65; self-inquiry and, 68-69; wasted energy and, 89, 188-89; Witness-consciousness and, 70-71, 76-77; worshipful, 58-60, 61, 75-76, 184-85; *see also* Sense(s)
Self, 2, 4, 5, 8; bliss of, 8; confidence in, 2, 93; fire of yoga and, 33; meditation and, 30; mind and, 27; power of the senses and, 70; purpose and, 4; seeing/sight and, 69-70; silence and, 164, 168; solitude and, 21; speech and, 143, 144; tranquility and, 18; *see also* Consciousness; Light
Self-control, 89-90; desires and, 22-23; eating and, 126; pausing and, 148; speech and, 155-56; yoga and, 17, 27, 49; *see also* Discipline
Self-effort, desires and, 23; grace and, 28, 202; meditation and, 17, 25, 28, 31; pace of, 37; yoga and, 18, 19-37; *see also* Discipline, yoga of; *Niyamas*; Sadhana; Spiritual practice; Yoga
Self-inquiry, 68-69; culmination of, 70; silence and, 165
Sense(s), choice and, 137; controlling the, 15, 22-23, 33, 63, 65, 78, 89-90, 100-1, 109-10; desires and, 22-23, 56-57, 75-77; discipline and, 48-49, 51-52, 56-62, 65-78, 89-90, 126, 141-42; eyesight and, 52-53, 54, 56, 61, 63, 64, 75-78; happiness and, 9-10, 9-16; hearing/listening, 79, 83, 88, 89-92, 100; perception and, x, xi, xii, 56, 65-78, 81; purification of, xii, 33, 90-91; purpose of, 5, 70-71, 81, 93; taste and, ix, 14, 109, 120-21, 126; withdrawal/redirection of, 18, 81-82, 165; Witness-consciousness and, 70-71, 77; *see also* Desire(s); Hearing; Seeing; Smelling; Taste; Touching
Separation, 123, 184
Serenity, chanting and, 34; closing the eyes and, 56; discipline and, 125
Service, selfless, 3; discipline and, 47, 166; purpose of, 41, 94
Seva, 47, 99, 166; *see also* Service, selfless
Shakti, 33, 147, 182, 203
Shaktipāt, xv; Baba Muktananda and, xvi; *see also* Grace, Initiation
Shāmbhavī mudrā, 79
Shāstras (sacred texts), 32
Shatapatha Brāhmana, 145
Shiva, Lord, 4
Shiva Samhitā, 4
Shloka (verse), 80
Shravana samādhi, 105; *see also* Recitation, of sacred texts
Shree Muktananda Ashram, xiii; conduct in, 43, 109, 170; Guru photos/images in, 59; *see also* Gurudev Siddha Peeth; *Gurukula*
Shrutis, 134-35
Shvetāshvatara Upanishad, 70
Siddha Master(s), blessings of, 41; dreams about, 65; initiation and, xv-xvi; lineage of, xv-xvi; silence and, 176; song(s) of, 75; words of, 103; *see also* Guru
Siddha Yoga, xvi, 132; discipline and, 43; grace and, 37; mantra and, 90; meditation and, 85; offering and, 137; satsang and, 92-93

Siddhi, 105
Silence, 21, 150, 161; chanting and, 34; discipline and, 39, 46, 163-64, 165-66, 168-77; eating and, 121; merit and, 153; speech and, 144, 149, 150; virtue of, 154-55
Sleep, food and, 114; understanding and, 38; waking from, 59; Witness-consciousness and, 72; *see also* State, of mind
Smelling, wasted energy and, 89; *see also* Sense(s)
Smritis, 135
So 'ham mantra, 21
Solitude, 19, 20, 56
Soul, courage and, 81; discipline and, 47; hearing and, 83; mantra repetition and, 30; seeing and, 57, 63; *swādhyāya* and, 35; sweetness of, 42
Sound(s), 28, 90-91, 102-3; breath and, 103; purification and, 105; of sacred texts, 105; unstruck, 105, 155; *see also* Hearing; Listening; Mantra; Music
Speech, discipline and, 47, 142-60; goddess of, 142, 146; purification of, 20, 29; silence and, 173; sound of God and, 106; sweetness of, 42; Vedic mantras and, 146; wasted energy and, 89
Spirit, 4; of God, 42; Guru-disciple relationship and, 6; of sacrifice, 136; supreme bliss and, 15
Spiritual practice, 182; action and, 17, 18, 26, 28-36, 182; attitude and, 5, 47-50; devotion and, 25; eating and, 117, 119, 120, 122, 123, 124, 125-26, 134; goal of, 19, 182; humility and, 36; laziness (*ālasya*) and, 110; mantra and, 146; one-pointedness and, 25, 26, 28, 80, 188; purification and, 18, 34-35, 65; regularity of, 18, 27, 28-36, 47, 49-50, 119; sattvic happiness and, 15; silence and, 174-75; solitude and, 21; speaking and, 144-60; tranquillity and, 17-18; *see also* Discipline; *Niyamas*; Yoga
State of mind, balance (*samata*) and, 191; desires and, 136-37; meditation and, 168; projection and, 67-68; psychic instruments and, 21; recitation of sacred texts and, 105; Self-knowledge and, 28; *shakti* and, 203; sleep and, 38, 72; understanding and, 64; waking, 21, 71, 72; Witness-consciousness and, 21, 70-71, 72; *see also* Consciousness; Mind
Stillness, 31, 91
Stomach, 108-9, 113-14; fullness and, 122; God and, 119; improper food combinations and, 110-11; *kundalinī* and, 117; meditation and, 112
Subconscious, 21; mantra repetition and, 30
Suffering, 13; discipline and, 46, 49
Sun, 95
Sundardas, 83, 90, 108, 145, 147
Surdas, 88
Surrender, 28, 35-36, 74, 185
Sushumnā nādī, 155
Svayambhū (spontaneous happiness), 80; *see also* Happiness
Swādhyāya, 34-35, 157; silence of, 151; *see also* Chanting; Mantra, repetition of; Recitation

Taittirīya Upanishad, 1, 117-18
Tamas, 9, 10, 15; *see also Gunas*
Tapas, 32; *see also* Austerity
Taste, 126; awakening of, 14; Ayurveda and, 112-13; discipline of, ix, 109-10, 141; of nectar, 104; stomach and, 109; *see also* Eating; Food; Sense(s)
Thought(s), 72, 194; eating/stomach and, 108-9, 113, 126; grace and, 202; mantra repetition and, 29, 58, 198; pausing and, 148, 197; protection of, 196; purification of, 20, 29, 102; restraint and, 44; seeing and, 58, 78; solitude and, 21; speech and, 145; sweetness of, 42; universe and, 84
Tongue, relaxation of, 172
Touching, purpose of, 93, 94; wasted

energy and, 89; *see also* Sense(s)
Tranquillity, 3, 24; sattvic happiness and, 14; self-control and, 17, 24; silence and, 166
Transformation, 35, 37; grace and, 43; of sight, 56
Trust, 2
Truth, bliss and, 9; paradox and, 81
Tukaram Maharaj, 8; on name of God, 159; on outlook, 53; on stomach, 119; on tranquillity, 24
Tulsidas, 148

Understanding, 38, 183, 202; food and, 118, 119, 126; highest, 70; of sadhana, 99; seeing and, 64, 65; speaking and, 149; Witness-consciousness and, 72
Union, ecstasy and, 73; yogic action and, 18
Universe, *ārati* music and, 103; grace of the Siddhas and, 41; heart of, xix; seeing and, 64; speech and, 145; supreme bliss and, 8, 15, 38; sweetness and, 41-42; thoughts and, 84; Witness-consciousness and, 70, 73
Upanishads, 51, 81, 134

Vairāgya, 24; *see also* Dispassion
Vak, 142, 144
Valmiki, 108
Vedas, 129, 142
Virtue, 154-55
Vishnu Sahasranām, 104
Vision, inner, cleansed perception and, 73, 78; confidence and, 2; longing and, 74, 137-38; meditation and, 60, 65, 76-77; Self and, 5
Viveka Chūdāmani, 52, 64, 155, 176
Void, Great, 38, 73

Waking state, 21; Witness-consciousness and, 71; *see also* State of mind
Wealth, 115
Welcoming, 41
Will, austerity and, 33; birth and, 84; grudges and, 98-99; meditation and, 187; purity of, 74; silence and, 172
Wisdom, 6; eye of, 71; pure vision and, 73; *see also* Witness-consciousness
Witness-consciousness, 21; eyesight and, 70-71; meditation and, 24-25; *see also* State of mind
Word(s), discipline in listening and, 87; grace and, 149; holiness of, 142-43; mind and, 145; power of, 83, 142; of Siddhas, 103
Worship, devotion and, 26-27; eating as, 126-27, 136-37; farming and, 129-130; pausing and, 58-59; of *prānas* (breaths), 120; ritual and, 130; sweetness and, 41-42; Witness-consciousness and, 74

Yajña, 68, 130; mantra and, 145; offering and, 36
Yajur Veda, 42, 194
Yama, 18, 28; *see also* Restraint
Yoga, ix, 163; confidence and, 2-3; definition of, 5; eating/eliminating and, 110, 112-13, 122, 123, 124, 126-27; eight limbs of, 18; fire of, 32; Guru-disciple and, 6, 19-20; happiness and, 9-10, 18, 31, 49; mantra and, 146; *niyamas* and, 28-36; one-pointedness and, 25, 28; path of, 20, 33, 36, 37, 44-50, 125-26; regularity and, 18, 27, 28, 49-50, 96; self-doubt and, 19, 36; silence and, 174-75; supreme bliss and, 8, 18-19, 23-24, 28; *see also* Discipline; Spiritual practice; Purification; Sadhana
Yogānanda, 28
Yoga Sūtras, 18, 25, 165; *niyamas* of, 28-36
Yoga Vāsishtha, on desirelessness, 24
Yogi(s), 20; austerity and, 33, 37; desires and, 22; eating/food and, 117, 122; seeing/eyesight and, 63; solitude and, 22; transformation and, 35

Further Reading

Swami Muktananda

Play of Consciousness
Bhagawan Nityananda of Ganeshpuri
From the Finite to the Infinite
Where Are You Going?
I Have Become Alive
Mukteshwari
The Perfect Relationship
Selected Essays
Reflections of the Self
Secret of the Siddhas
Light on the Path
I Am That
Ashram Dharma
Kundalini
Mystery of the Mind
Does Death Really Exist?
Lalleshwari
Meditate
What Is an Intensive?

Swami Chidvilasananda

Kindle My Heart
Inner Treasures
My Lord Loves a Pure Heart
Ashes at My Guru's Feet

You may learn more about the teachings and practices of Siddha Yoga Meditation by contacting:

SYDA Foundation
371 Brickman Rd.
South Fallsburg, NY 12779-0600, USA

Tel: (914) 434-2000

or

Gurudev Siddha Peeth
P.O. Ganeshpuri
PIN 401 206
District Thana
Maharashtra, India

For further information about books in print by Swami Muktananda and Swami Chidvilasananda, and editions in translation, please contact:

Siddha Yoga Meditation Bookstore
371 Brickman Rd.
South Fallsburg, NY 12779-0600, USA

Tel: (914) 434-0124